GENOCIDE IN GAZA
ISRAEL'S LONG WAR ON PALESTINE

About the Author

Emeritus Professor of International Relations at the University of Oxford, and a Fellow of St Antony's College, Avi Shlaim is a globally renowned historian of the modern Middle East. He held a British Academy Research Readership between 1995-1997; a British Academy Research Professorship between 2003-2006; he was elected Fellow of the British Academy in 2006; and he was awarded a British Academy Medal for lifetime achievement in 2017.

An Arab Jew, he was born in Baghdad in 1945; grew up in Israel; served in the Israel Defence Forces; and received his university education at Cambridge and the London School of Economics. He is based at the Middle East Centre at St Antony's College, where his main research interest continues to be the Arab-Israeli conflict, mostly recently the genocide in Gaza. He became widely known as one of the "New Historians," a small group of Israeli scholars who put forward critical interpretations of the history of Zionism and Israel, from the late 1980s onwards.

His books include *Collusion Across the Jordan: King Abdullah, the Zionist Movement, and the Partition of Palestine* (Winner of the 1988 Political Studies Association's Mackenzie Prize); *War and Peace in the Middle East: A Concise History* (1995); *The Iron Wall: Israel and the Arab World* (2000, updated edition 2014); *Lion of Jordan: King Hussein's Life in War and Peace* (2007); *Israel and Palestine: Reappraisals, Revisions, Refutations* (2009); and *Three Worlds: Memoirs of an Arab-Jew* (2023).

Shlaim is a believer in the subversive function of history, in using archival sources to challenge the received wisdom and to dispel national myths. He believes that "The historian's most fundamental task is not to chronicle but to evaluate… to subject the claims of all the protagonists to rigorous scrutiny and reject all those claims, however deeply cherished, that do not stand up."

Professor Shlaim is a frequent contributor to the print media and commentator on radio and television on Middle Eastern affairs. He has lived in the United Kingdom since 1966; he holds dual British and Israeli nationality; and he lives in Oxford.

GENOCIDE IN GAZA
ISRAEL'S LONG WAR ON PALESTINE

AVI SHLAIM

THE IRISH PAGES PRESS
CLÓ AN MHÍL BHUÍ
2024

Genocide in Gaza: Israel's Long War on Palestine
is first published in hardback on 31 October 2024,
on the occasion of Avi Shlaim's 79th birthday.

The Irish Pages Press
129 Ormeau Road
Belfast BT7 1SH
Ireland

www.irishpages.org

Copyright © Avi Shlaim & The Irish Pages Press

All rights reserved. No part of this book may be reproduced,
stored in a retrieval system, or transmitted in any form,
or by any means, electronic, mechanical, photocopying or otherwise,
without prior written permission from The Irish Pages Press.

Typeset in 14/18 pt Monotype Perpetua.
Designed and composed by RV, Belfast. Printed by Bell & Bain, Glasgow.

A CIP catalogue record for this book
is available from The British Library.

Dust-jacket photograph: Palestinian News & Information Agency (Wafa)
in contract with APAimages (adapted).

ISBN: 978-1-7390902-2-7

Also by Avi Shlaim

Collusion Across the Jordan: King Abdullah, the Zionist Movement, and the Partition of Palestine (1988)

The Politics of Partition: King Abdullah, the Zionists, and Palestine, 1921–1951 (1990)

War and Peace in the Middle East: A Concise History (1995)

The Iron Wall: Israel and the Arab World (2000)

Lion of Jordan: The Life of King Hussein in War and Peace (2007)

Israel and Palestine: Reappraisals, Revisions, Refutations (2009)

Three Worlds: Memoirs of an Arab Jew (2023)

*To my wife Gwyn Daniel and our daughter Tamar Shlaim,
partners in the struggle.*

CONTENTS

Foreword: On the War on Palestine
   Francesca Albanese   13

Britain and the Nakba:
   A History of Betrayal (2023)   21

The Diplomacy of the Israeli-Palestinian Conflict,
   1967-2023 (Report for the ICJ) (2023)   37

Benjamin Netanyahu's War Against
   Palestinian Statehood (2024)   117

Operation Cast Lead, 2008-2009 (2009)   147

Sabotaging a Ceasefire (2019)   159

Israel, Hamas and the Conflict in Gaza:
   An Overview (Report to the ICC) (2019)   167

Israel's War on Gaza (2024)   215

All That Remains (2024)   245

Israel's Road to Genocide
   (2024, Jamie Stern-Weiner & Avi Shlaim)   265

Green Light to Genocide:
   Joe Biden and Israel's War in Gaza (2024)   309

The Two-State Solution:	
Illusion and Reality (2021)	341
Epilogue	365
Coda by Blinne Ní Ghrálaigh, KC: The Case	
Before The International Court Of Justice	385
Endnotes	407
Acknowledgements	431

FOREWORD
Francesca Albanese

Contributing a Foreword for Professor Avi Shlaim's new book is an honor and would ordinarily be cause for enthusiasm, especially for someone like me, for whom Avi Shlaim's scholarship has elucidated so much in understanding the complex history of Palestine. His works have unearthed the layers of ignorance that obscure our comprehension amid the tsunami of false and conflicting narratives that flood the landscape of this so-called "Israeli-Palestinian conflict". These are not, however, ordinary times, not even in the pained history of Palestine. As I take on this responsibility, there is nothing joyous about chronicling the horrors of genocide, as Professor Shlaim has done across this urgent and timely collection of essays and scholarship that demands our reflection and our collective action. By extension, there is little that induces celebration in endorsing such an effort, rather it is with reverent sorrow that I urge all to absorb this necessary work.

Having reluctantly become chronicler of an unfolding genocide in my own domain, I feel a deep affinity with Avi Shlaim in his trajectory of coming to the conclusion that not only has Israel committed acts of genocide, but that such epilogue was a tragedy foretold.

As a lawyer appointed to the role of UN Special Rapporteur on the Occupied Palestinian Territories, my primary responsibility since May 2022 has been to monitor and document violations of international law in the occupied Palestinian territory. While scholars like Professors Ilan Pappe, Martin Shaw and Raz Segall were already sounding the alarm for the risk of genocide prior to 7 October, I have seen the situation for Palestinians taking a catastrophic turn after that date, under our collective watch. Recently, we marked one year since the onset of what appears to be the breaking point, opening arguably the darkest chapter in the history of Israel and Palestine, with impacts felt profoundly by both Palestinians and Israelis. What may have been a sustained crescendo of persistent violations has unequivocally erupted into acts that can only be described as genocidal, namely aiming to destroy the Palestinians as a group "as such".

This analysis, on which Avi Shlaim and I agree, is considered "contested" and it is of course challenged by Israeli officials and its pundits, who concede, at most, that Israel may have committed "excesses" which are not uncommon in war. What drives this downplaying of the conclusion that Israel has committed genocide is a mix of misunderstanding, selective morality or simply bad faith.

The common perception of what constitutes genocide is clearly shaped by the massive horror of the Holocaust, and probably the features of the Rwandan genocide, where the industrial-sized scale and brutality of the extermination have been definitive in our collective understanding of the crime. But genocide is not defined by personal opinions or particular histories. You can have genocide without mass killing or extermination. What matters, under the law, is that specific criminal acts are committed with the intent to destroy a group, in whole or in part, as such. This is what the Genocide Convention, adopted on the ashes of the Holocaust, establishes; and alongside it, the primary and prevailing aim to prevent genocide. Properly understood, genocide is a process, not an act, and it takes place in stages. Those stages have been manifestly evident in Palestine, and have still gone unchecked, unpunished.

For Palestinians living under Israeli rule, the struggle has always been marked by oppression brought about by martial law, brutal practices of occupation, colonisation, annexation and apartheid, but the events following 7 October have cataclysmically intensified these challenges. I unequivocally condemned the Hamas-led attacks that targeted Israeli civilians, resulting in tragic losses of life. Yet, what has followed in Gaza is a wholesale destruction that, even as I write this Foreword, with conservatively more than 42,000 Palestinians already killed, including 17,000 children butchered often in full sight and broadcast to the world – has elicited little more than indifference from many Western powers and media outlets. Rather, they have continued unperturbed in their pontification on Israel's right to defend itself; the sweeping and astonishing implication of which is that self-defense offers a licence to kill, maim, starve, torment, displace, torture, rape, and annihilate.

In light of what I had documented since October 2023, by March 2024 I concluded that there were reasonable grounds to believe Israel had committed acts of genocide against the Palestinian people, based on the nature and scale of the atrocities. Hundreds of statements from Israeli officials, enacted by soldiers who had turned into willful executioners, confirmed an intent to destroy the Palestinian people as a group, while their distortion of the most foundational principles of international humanitarian law was being used to camouflage the link between Israel's conduct and intent. Since March, my certainty as to the perpetration of genocide has only grown, despite a prevailing narrative that seeks to diminish the atrocities in Gaza. It is colonial amnesia that has allowed us to forget the countless lives lost in various regions worldwide at the hands of settler-colonial regimes from Latin America to Africa to Australia. But it is the memory and struggle of the descendants of those same peoples, who in their own demands for justice, have assured for all of us that this broader context can and must bring clarity to the present moment.

Today, we face a dire reality where the destruction of Gaza has led to terms like "domicide", "urbicide", and "cultural genocide" being used by experts as they try to find words to convey the utter devastation inflicted upon the Palestinian people. The numbers are staggering: tens of thousands have been killed, maimed, including an inordinate number of children and the erasure of whole family lines, in what can only be seen as an attempt to annihilate a population. Moreover, the ongoing displacement, destruction of essential infrastructure, and increasing violence against Palestinians only compound the tragedy. Moreover, these events are far from confined to the Gaza Strip; since October 7, we have witnessed an alarming escalation of violence in the West Bank, with an extraordinary number of casualties not seen since the second intifada, and the mass incarceration of thousands amidst horrific abuse within the prison system. These actions, understood within the context Avi Shlaim lays bare for us, confirm the genocidal culmination of a long-standing colonial process aimed at the erasure of the Palestinian people. Indeed, for over 76 years, this oppressive endeavour has sought to dismantle their right to self-determination across all dimensions – demographically, territorially, culturally, economically and politically.

The international community stands atop a precipice. The ongoing impunity afforded to Israel has emboldened its heinous actions and is now shredding the principles of international law. The International Court of Justice Advisory Opinion, which explicitly declared Israel's actions unlawful and aimed at annexation, offers a pivotal moment for change. It is a clarion call which all States must heed. The requirement to fundamentally shift how they engage with both Israel and the Palestinian people, and the need to cease any engagement with Israel that recognises its occupation as legal or its presence as normal, is a not just a moral duty or a compassionate act in this dire moment, it is a non-derogable duty to which States are legally abound.

For every one of us, the time to act is now. The very existence of the Palestinian people themselves is in peril, and it is pure folly to imagine any of these actions will make the Israelis safer and more secure in a world where they have committed, hopefully, the last genocide of contemporary history. Moreover, if the international community fails to hold Israel accountable in the wake of this unrelenting violence, it will have consciously broken the very foundation of international law as developed over the past century. As the ICC prosecutor has warned, selective application of the law could result in its complete collapse. And as we watch the first live-streamed settler-colonial genocide, we must make sure that justice is delivered; as only justice, in its broadest meaning, can heal the wounds that political expedience has allowed to fester for decades. As I wrote in concluding my last report, *Genocide as Colonial Erasure*, "the devastation of so many lives is an outrage to humanity and all that international law stands for".

While this book by Avi Shlaim sheds light on the ongoing atrocities that mark our collective history, it also serves as a poignant reminder of the pressing responsibility we all share. We must confront the reality of genocide, ensuring that the voices of the oppressed are not just heard but actioned, and that the lessons of the past guide our path toward the creation of a world in which justice and accountability prevail.

Francesca Albanese is the United Nations Special Rapporteur on the Occupied Palestinian Territories.

— 2023 —

BRITAIN AND THE NAKBA: A HISTORY OF BETRAYAL

An unbroken thread of duplicity, mendacity and chicanery connects British foreign policy from Balfour to the Nakba to the present day.

Britain created the conditions that made the Palestinian Nakba possible.

In 1948, the Palestinians experienced a collective catastrophe of monumental proportions: some 530 villages were destroyed; more than 62,000 homes were demolished; about 13,000 Palestinians were killed; and 750,000 Palestinians, two-thirds of the Arab population of the country were driven out of their homes and became refugees.

This was the climax of the Zionist ethnic cleansing of Palestine.

In its essence, Zionism had always been a settler-colonial movement. Its ultimate aim was to build an independent Jewish state in Palestine on as much of the land as possible and with as few Arabs within its borders as possible. Zionist spokesmen constantly reiterated that they meant no harm to the Arab inhabitants of the country, that they wanted to develop the country for the benefit of both communities.

But this was largely rhetoric, *kalam fadi* in Arabic, empty talk.

The Zionist movement was propelled by the logic of settler colonialism. Settler colonialism is a mode of domination characterised by what historian Patrick Wolfe has termed "a logic of elimination". Settler colonial regimes seek to extinguish the native people, or at least to extinguish their political autonomy. The elimination of the native people is a precondition for expropriating the land and its natural resources.

Noam Chomsky, the eminent Jewish-American intellectual, observed that "settler colonialism is the most extreme and sadistic form of imperialism". The hallmark of settler colonialism is ruthlessness and the disregard for law, justice and morality.

The Zionist movement was nothing if not ruthless. It did not plan to cooperate with the native Arab population for the common good. On the contrary, it planned to supplant them. The only way the Zionist project could be realised and maintained was by expelling a large number of Arabs from their homes and taking over their land.

In Zionist jargon, such evictions and expulsions were deceptively referenced and concealed with a softer term – "transfer".

— PATH TO STATEHOOD —

Zionist settler colonialism was connected by an umbilical cord to Britain, the pre-eminent European colonial power of the day. Without the support of Britain, the Zionist movement could not have achieved the degree of success that it did in its quest for statehood.

Britain made it possible for its junior partner to embark on the systematic takeover of the country. Yet, the path to statehood was far from smooth. From its inception in the late 19th century, the Zionist movement encountered a major obstacle along its path: the land of its dreams was already inhabited by another people. Britain enabled the Zionists to overcome this obstacle.

On 2 November 1917, Britain issued the notorious Balfour Declaration. Named after Foreign Secretary Arthur Balfour, it promised British support for the establishment of "a national home for the Jewish people in Palestine".

The purpose of the declaration was to enlist the help of world Jewry in the war effort against Germany and the Ottoman Empire. A caveat was added that "nothing shall be done which may prejudice the civil and religious rights of existing non-Jewish communities in Palestine". While the promise was fully fulfilled, the caveat was dropped and forgotten.

In 1917, the area later called Palestine was still under Ottoman rule. The Arabs constituted 90 percent of the population of the country, with the Jews constituting 10 percent and owning only two percent of the land. The Balfour Declaration was a classic colonial document because it accorded national rights to a small minority but merely "civil and religious rights" to the majority.

To add insult to injury, it referred to the Arabs, forming the vast majority of the population, as "the non-Jewish communities in Palestine". Arab resistance to British rule was inevitable from the start.

There is an Arabic saying that something that starts crooked, remains crooked. In this case, at any rate, it is difficult to see how the British administration of Palestine could be straightened without incurring the wrath of its Zionist beneficiaries.

On 11 August 1919, Balfour wrote in an oft-quoted memorandum: "Zionism, be it right or wrong, good or bad, is rooted in age-long traditions, in present needs, in future hopes, of far profounder import than the desires and prejudices of the 700,000 Arabs who now inhabit that ancient land."

In other words, the Arabs did not count while their rights, including their natural right to national self-determination, were dismissed as no more than "desires and prejudices".

In the same memorandum, Balfour also stated that "so far as Palestine is concerned, the Powers have made no statement of fact which is not admittedly wrong, and no declaration of policy which, at least in the letter, they have not always intended to violate". There could hardly be a more arresting admission of British duplicity.

— "SACRED TRUST OF CIVILISATION" —

In July 1922, the League of Nations gave Britain the mandate over Palestine. The task of the mandatory power was to prepare the local population for self-government and to hand over power when they became capable of governing themselves.

The mandates were described in the Covenant of the League as "a sacred trust of civilisation". Their declared purpose was to develop the territory for the benefit of its native people, and to turn the former

Arab provinces of the defeated Ottoman Empire into modern nation-states. In reality, they were little more than a cover for neo-colonialism.

Strong Zionist lobbying induced Britain to insist on the incorporation of the Balfour Declaration into the Palestine Mandate. It is often said that this transformed a loose British promise into a binding legal obligation. This is not so for two main reasons.

First, the mandate contravened Article 22 of the Covenant, which required the people of the area concerned to be consulted in the choice of the mandatory power. Balfour refused to consult the Arabs because he knew too well that, if given a say, they would vehemently reject British rule.

Second, Britain could not assume the mandate, because in 1922 it had no sovereignty over Palestine. The sovereign until 1924 was Turkey, the successor to the Ottoman Empire. This point has been made forcefully by the American jurist John Quigley in an unpublished article entitled "Britain's Failure to Gain Legal Standing for the Balfour Declaration". In the abstract, he summarises the argument in the following way:

> The document that Britain composed for its governance of Palestine (Mandate for Palestine) called for the implementation of the Jewish national home mentioned in the Balfour

Declaration. However, Britain's governance of Palestine, purportedly under the mandate scheme of the League of Nations, never gained a lawful foundation. The League of Nations had no power under the League Covenant to attribute legal significance to the Mandate for Palestine, or to give Britain a right to govern.

Britain failed to gain sovereignty, which was a prerequisite for governing Palestine or for holding a mandate. Britain gave varying explanations at different times in an effort to show that it did hold sovereignty. The United Nations did not question Britain's legal standing in Palestine but accepted the legitimacy of the mandate for Palestine as a basis for dividing the country. The issue of territorial rights in historic Palestine remains unresolved to the present time.

In Quigley's opinion, Britain never moved past the status of belligerent occupant. He develops this argument, with a great deal of compelling evidence, in his 2022 book *Britain and its Mandate Over Palestine: Legal Chicanery on a World Stage*. Chicanery is not too strong a word to describe the manner in which Britain manipulated the League of Nations to give it power over Palestine, or the way in which it misused this

27

power to turn Palestine from an Arab-majority state into a Jewish-majority state.

— OBLIGATION TO PROTECT ARAB RIGHTS —

The importance of including the commitment to a Jewish national home cannot be overestimated. It is what fundamentally differentiated the Palestine Mandate from all the other mandates for the Middle Eastern provinces of the Ottoman Empire.

The British mandate for Iraq, the French mandate for Syria, and the French mandate for Lebanon were all about preparing the local population for self-government. The Palestine mandate was about enabling foreigners, Jews from anywhere in the world, but especially from Europe, to join their co-religionists in Palestine and to turn the country into a Jewish-controlled national entity.

The mandate included an explicit obligation to protect the civil and religious rights of the Arabs – "the non-Jewish communities in Palestine". Britain utterly failed to protect these rights. The first British high commissioner for Palestine, Sir Herbert Samuel, was both a Jew and an ardent Zionist.

During his tenure, Britain introduced a series of ordinances that allowed for unrestricted Jewish immigration to Palestine, and Jewish purchase of lands, which Palestinians had farmed for generations.

The Arabs demanded restrictions on Jewish immigration and land acquisitions. They also demanded a democratically elected national assembly, which would reflect the demographic balance. Britain resisted all these demands and held back from introducing democratic institutions. The basic guideline for mandatory policy was to withhold elections until the Jews became the majority.

In 1936, an Arab revolt broke out against British rule in Palestine. It was a national revolt that lasted until 1939. The British army was deployed to crush it. The army acted with the utmost brutality and often in violation of the laws of war. Its methods included torture, the use of human shields, detention without trial, draconian emergency regulations, summary executions, collective punishment, house demolitions, the burning of villages and aerial bombardment.

Much of this violence was directed not just against the rebels, but against villagers who were suspected of aiding and abetting them. British counter-insurgency gravely weakened Palestinian society: around 5,000 Palestinians were killed, 15,000 injured, and 5,500 imprisoned.

— FINAL BRITISH BETRAYAL —

Rashid Khalidi, the eminent Palestinian historian, has argued, convincingly in my opinion, that Palestine was not lost in the late 1940s, as is commonly believed, but in the late 1930s. The main reason he gives for this point of view is the devastating damage that Britain inflicted on Palestinian society and its paramilitary forces during the Arab Revolt. This argument is advanced in Khalidi's chapter in a book co-edited by Eugene Rogan and me, *The War for Palestine: Rewriting the History of 1948*.

The final British betrayal of the Palestinians occurred as the struggle for Palestine entered its most crucial phase following the end of the Second World War. By this time, Britain had fallen out with its Zionist protégés and the extremists among them conducted a campaign of terror designed to drive British forces out of the country. The most notorious episode in this violent campaign was the attack, in July 1946, by the Irgun, the National Military Organisation, on the King David Hotel in Jerusalem which housed the British administrative headquarters.

Following this attack and other attacks, the embattled British government decided unilaterally to relinquish the mandate. On 29 November 1947, the United Nations passed a resolution to partition Mandate Palestine into two states, one Jewish, the other Arab.

The Jews accepted partition and the Arabs rejected it. Consequently, Britain refused to implement the UN partition plan on the grounds that it did not enjoy the support of both parties.

There was another reason, however: hostility to the Palestinian national cause. The Palestinian national movement was led by Hajj Amin al-Husseini, the grand mufti of Jerusalem, who had fallen out with the British and fled the country during the Arab Revolt.

In British eyes, a Palestinian state was synonymous with a mufti state. Hostility towards the Palestinian leadership and Palestinian statehood was therefore a constant and defining factor in British foreign policy from 1947 to 1949.

The mandate ended at midnight on 14 May 1948. Britain's way out of the quandary was to encourage its client, King Abdullah of Jordan, to invade Palestine upon the expiry of the mandate, and to conquer the West Bank that the UN had allocated to the Arab state. By this time, the wily king had reached a tacit agreement with the Jewish Agency to divide up Palestine between themselves, at the expense of the Palestinians.

The tacit agreement was that the Jews would establish a Jewish state in their part of Palestine, while Abdullah would gain control over the Arab part, and that they would make peace after the dust had settled.

— FAKE NEUTRALITY —

During the civil war that broke out in Palestine in the run-up to 14 May, Britain stood on the sidelines, thereby abdicating its responsibility to maintain law and order. Its fake neutrality inevitably helped the stronger Zionist side. During the last months of the mandate, the Zionist paramilitary forces went on the offensive and intensified the ethnic cleansing of the country.

The first big wave of Palestinian refugees happened on Britain's watch. Britain effectively abandoned the native Palestinians to the tender mercies of Zionist settler colonialists. In short, Britain actively created the conditions for its own selfish imperialist ends, in which the Palestinian catastrophe – "the Nakba" – could unfold. An unbroken thread of duplicity, mendacity, chicanery and skulduggery connects British foreign policy from the beginning of its mandate to the Nakba.

The way in which the mandate ended was the worst blot on Britain's entire record as the great power in charge of Palestine. It showed how little Britain cared about the people it was supposed to protect and prepare for self-government.

When the going got tough, the mandatory power simply cut and ran. There was no orderly transfer of power to a local body. The "sacred trust of civilisation"

[continues after "Portfolio of Maps"]

PORTFOLIO OF MAPS

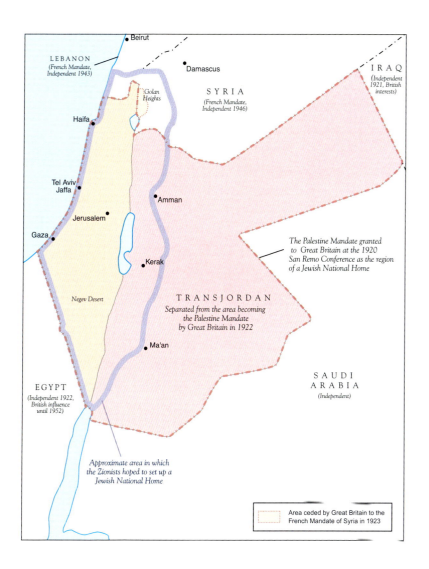

The 1920 Palestine Mandate and related boundaries. Transjordan, subsequently to 1921-1922, was administered essentially as a separate British protectorate.

I

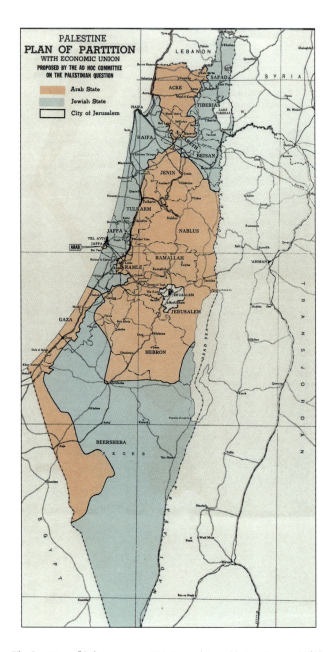

The Partition of Palestine as per UN General Assembly Resolution 181(II), 29 November 1947. In the subsequent fighting, Israel would capture much of the area granted by the Resolution to the Palestinian Arab state, including its entire Northern enclave. (Source: United Nations)

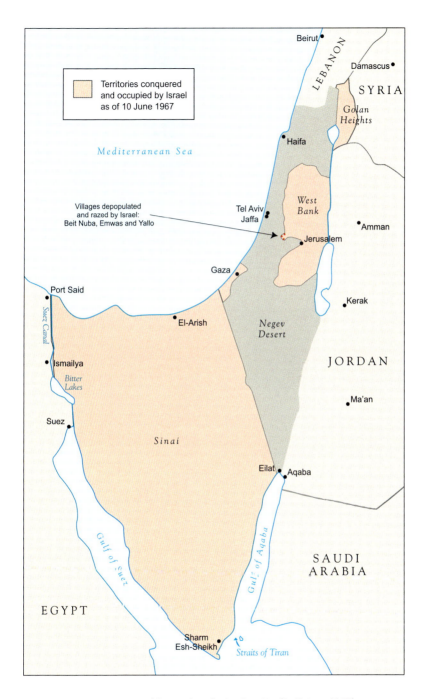

Territories captured by Israel in the Six-Day War (5-10 June 1967).

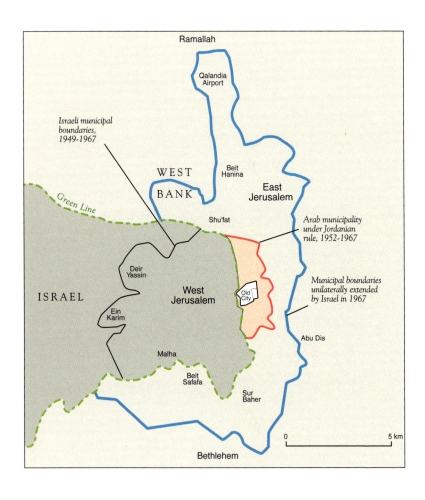

Jerusalem and its immediate environs before and after the Six-Day War (5-10 June 1967).

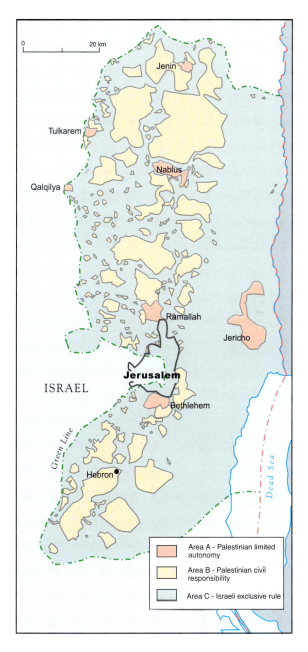

Areas A, B, and C as envisaged by the Oslo II Agreement (1995). East Jerusalem, effectively annexed by Israel in 1980, is shown between the dotted green line and the solid brown line, while the entirety of the Jerusalem area is shown within the solid brown line.

Gaza, showing names of cities and entry points. (Source: Wikimedia)

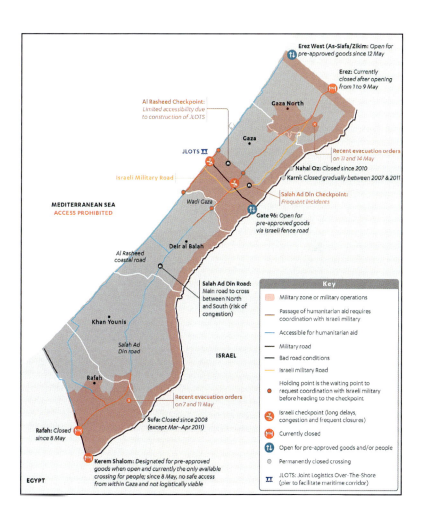

Gaza, showing humanitarian access constraints – May 2024. (Source: ICAI)

This image from September 2023 at the UN is associated with Netanyahu's "day after" plans for the Gaza Strip. The image is notable for literally wiping the rest of Palestine (the entirety of the West Bank including East Jerusalem) off the map. (Source: screenshot)

had been finally, irreversibly and unforgivably brutalised and betrayed.

Lord Balfour's dream turned into a Palestinian nightmare. In the collective consciousness of the Palestinians, the Nakba is not an isolated event but a continuous historical process. Today, over 5.9 million refugees are registered with UNRWA, the United Nations agency for Palestine refugees.

Hanan Ashrawi coined the term "ongoing Nakba" to denote the continuous Palestinian experience of violence and dispossession at the hands of Zionist settler colonialism. In a speech at a UN conference in 2001, she referred to the Palestinian people as "a nation in captivity held hostage to an ongoing Nakba, as the most intricate and pervasive expression of persistent colonialism, apartheid, racism, and victimisation."

— CONTRADICTION IN BRITISH POLICY —

It is melancholy to have to add that no British government has ever apologised for the part that Britain played in the emasculation of Historic Palestine. The last five Conservative prime ministers, starting with David Cameron, have all been staunch supporters of Israel.

In 2017, on the centenary of the Balfour Declaration, then Prime Minister Theresa May stated that it was "one of the most important letters in history. It demonstrates Britain's vital role in creating a homeland for the Jewish people. And it is an anniversary we will be marking with pride." There was no mention of the Palestinian victims of this important letter.

Boris Johnson, in his 2014 book *The Churchill Factor*, described the Balfour Declaration as "bizarre", "a tragically incoherent document" and "an exquisite piece of FO fudgerama". But in 2015, on a trip to Israel as mayor of London, Johnson hailed the Balfour Declaration as "a great thing".

In October 2017, in his capacity as foreign secretary, Johnson introduced a debate in the House of Commons on the Balfour Declaration. He repeated Britain's pride in the part it played in creating a Jewish state in Palestine. Despite a large majority for recognising Palestine as a state, he declined to do so, saying the time was not right.

This exposed a basic contradiction in the heart of British policy: advocating a two-state solution but recognising only one.

It was left to Johnson's successor, Liz Truss, to demonstrate the depth of Tory politicians' indifference to Palestinian sensitivities and the length to which they would go to ingratiate themselves with Israel and its uncritical supporters in this country. During her campaign for election as Conservative Party leader, she floated the idea of moving the British embassy from Tel Aviv to Jerusalem.

Luckily, during her 49-day premiership, Truss was not able to follow up on this asinine idea.

Current British foreign policy is unapologetic about the Nakba and unashamedly pro-Zionist. A policy paper issued by the government on 21 March 2023 was entitled "2030 Roadmap for UK-Israel Bilateral Relations". This paper covers trade and cooperation in a large number of spheres.

But it also includes a British pledge to oppose the referral of the Israel-Palestine conflict to the International Court of Justice, to oppose the global, grassroots, non-violent Boycott, Divestment, Sanctions (BDS) movement for ending the Israeli occupation, and to work towards reducing the scrutiny of Israel at the UN.

In short, the policy paper gives Israel the full spectrum of immunity for its illegal actions and indeed crimes against the Palestinian people. As such, it is a faithful reflection of the pro-Zionist bias in British foreign policy over the last 100 years.

This piece was originally published on Middle East Eye, *on 10 May 2023.*

— 2023 —

THE DIPLOMACY OF THE ISRAELI-PALESTINIAN CONFLICT, 1967-2023

(Report for the ICJ)

This report offers context for the legal questions posed to the International Court of Justice by the request of the UN General Assembly for an Advisory Opinion relating to legal consequences arising from discriminatory policies and practices of Israel in the occupied Palestinian territories. It reviews some of the international attempts to resolve the Israeli-Palestinian conflict from the June 1967 War to the present and analyses the reasons for their failure. Three major themes emerge from the survey of the diplomatic history of this 56-year period. First is the gradual moderation of the Palestine Liberation Organisation's programme, culminating in the 1993 Oslo Accord in which it gave up its claim to 78% of Mandate Palestine. The second is Israel's illegal activities, increasing diplomatic intransigence, and creeping annexation of the occupied Palestinian territories. The third is the failure of the international community to propose and pursue a resolution of the conflict that would address Palestinian rights and needs, above all the right to national self-determination.

In origins and in essence the Arab-Israeli conflict is a clash between two national movements, Jewish nationalism (or Zionism) and Palestinian nationalism. There were two peoples and one land, hence the conflict. There are two main dimensions to Arab-Israeli relations, the inter-communal and the inter-state: the inter-communal is the conflict between Jews and Arabs in Palestine; the inter-state conflict is between the State of Israel and the neighbouring Arab states. The latter intervened in the inter-communal conflict on the side of the Palestinians during the Arab Revolt in the late 1930s. President Anwar Sadat of Egypt led the trend towards Arab disengagement from the conflict by signing a peace treaty with Israel in 1979. Jordan signed a peace treaty with Israel in 1994. Four Arab states signed the Abraham Accords with Israel in 2020. All Arab states remain involved in this conflict, in varying degrees, to this day. But the clash between Israeli and Palestinian nationalism remains the heart and the core of this conflict. It is this aspect that makes it one of the most prolonged, bitter, and intractable conflicts of modern times.

I
— THE AFTERMATH OF —
— THE SIX-DAY WAR —

The June 1967 War, popularly known as the Six-Day War, was a major turning-point in the history of the Middle East. Israel claimed that it was a defensive war, a war of "no choice". Before the war, Egypt's President Gamal Abdul Nasser removed the UN Emergency Force in Sinai and closed the Straits of Tiran to Israeli shipping. These were certainly provocative acts. But the fact remains that Israel fired the first shot and that a diplomatic route out of the crisis was available, but Israel chose not to take it. In the course of the war Israel conquered the Golan Heights from Syria, the West Bank (including East Jerusalem) from Jordan, and the Sinai Peninsula and Gaza Strip from Egypt, thereby trebling its territory. After the June 1967 war, Israel was in control of 100% of mandatory Palestine.

As a result of the war, the situation in the Middle East changed fundamentally: the Arab states now had a direct stake in the conflict with Israel while Israel, for the first time in its history, had something concrete to offer the Arab states in return for peace, and it could do so without compromising its security. A majority in the cabinet were willing to trade land for peace with Egypt and Syria subject to provisions to safeguard Israeli security. No such flexibility, however, was evident in relation to the West Bank. A wave of secular nationalism converged with an upsurge of religious messianism to preclude any compromise on the eastern front. The great majority in the country and the cabinet wanted to hold on to the West Bank either for security reasons or for ideological reasons, viewing it as an integral part of *"Eretz Israel"* or the Land of Israel.

With regard to the West Bank, Israel had two diplomatic options on the morrow of victory: a Jordanian option and a Palestinian option. Israel and Jordan had always been "the best of enemies". King Hussein continued the policy of moderation and accommodation with Israel which his grandfather, Abdullah I, had put in place. And like his grandfather, King Hussein had a common interest with Israel in suppressing Palestinian nationalism.

In 1964 the Palestine Liberation Organisation (PLO) had been formed by a resolution of the Arab League. Its mission, as its name indicated, was to liberate Palestine. While directed against Israel, the radical factions within the PLO aspired to replace the Hashemite Kingdom of Jordan with the Republic of Palestine. It was a complex triangle involving Israel, Jordan, and the PLO. The situation was akin to a room with three men but only two chairs. Israel firmly occupied one chair and the PLO had no realistic chance of dislodging it. Replacing the Hashemite monarchy in Amman was a distant but more realistic prospect. Hence the mistrust between the Hashemite rulers of Jordan and the PLO.

Back in 1963, King Hussein had initiated secret talks with Israeli officials. This remarkable dialogue across the battle-lines broke down on the eve of the Six Day War. Mistrust of Israel led Hussein to sign a defence pact with President Nasser and to commit his army to the war with Israel. After only three days of fighting, he lost half his kingdom, including the Old City of Jerusalem, the jewel in the Hashemite crown.

Immediately after the end of the war, on 2 July 1967, Hussein renewed his secret contacts with the Israelis. He offered them total peace for total withdrawal. But the mood in Israel had hardened against compromise in the aftermath of victory. The Israeli cabinet offered Hussein the Allon Plan, named after deputy Prime Minister Igal Allon. Under the Allon Plan,

Jordan stood to recover roughly 70% of the West Bank but Israel would have kept the Jordan Valley, most of the Judean desert along the Dead Sea, and a substantial area around Greater Jerusalem. Hussein rejected the offer out of hand. The secret talks resumed but the political deadlock persisted.[1]

In addition to the Jordanian option, Israel had a Palestinian option. For a brief period after the war, when it became clear that a deal with King Hussein on Israel's terms was not in the cards, Israel's policy-makers considered a Palestinian alternative. A group of West Bank notables, led by the lawyer Aziz Shehadeh, approached Israeli officials to say that they did not want to return to Hashemite rule and that their preference was to reach an agreement with Israel on an autonomous Palestinian state on the West Bank and the Gaza Strip. At the request of the Israelis, Shehadeh produced a written plan for a Palestinian state that would sign a peace agreement with Israel. He received no response.[2]

The debate between the proponents of the Jordanian option and the Palestinian option turned out to be largely academic because Israel was not prepared to withdraw from all the West Bank. There were significant divisons of opinion within the National Unity Government that had been formed on the eve of the war. Menachem Begin, the leader of the right-wing Gahal (later Likud) party, advocated the immediate annexation of the whole of the West Bank. Defence Minister Moshe Dayan led the hawkish wing of the Labour Party. On 7 June 1967, standing by the Wailing Wall, Dayan declared, "The IDF liberated Jerusalem this morning. We reunited divided Jerusalem, the bisected capital of Israel. We have returned to our holiest places, we have returned in order not to part from them ever again."[3] The dovish wing of the Labour Party was represented by Foreign Minister Abba Eban who was willing to restore most of the West Bank, but not the Old City of Jerusalem, to Jordan in return for peace. No one had a clear idea on what to do with the million Arabs who lived on the West Bank. As then Prime Minister Levi Eshkol never tired of reminding his colleagues: "You like the dowry, but you don't like the bride!"

To perpetuate the territorial status quo, Eshkol and his cabinet started to create facts on the ground in the form of Jewish settlements in the occupied territories. To conceal this reality, they adopted a diplomacy of deception.[4] While publicly proclaiming that Israel wanted peace, they took concrete measures to render the occupation permanent. To reduce the number of Arabs in their extended domain, they decided to prevent the quarter of a million Palestinian refugees, some of them second time refugees, from returning to their homes on the West Bank. Israel had blocked the return of 750,000 Palestinian refugees after the 1948 war. After the June 1967 war, it repeated the pattern of not allowing civilians to return to their homes. Moshe Dayan was dubbed "the emperor of the occupied territories". He orchestrated the policy of demographic engineering, and entrenching the occupation. This policy was in line with the original Zionist project of building a Jewish state over as much of the land of Palestine as possible with as few Arabs as possible within its borders.

An Arab summit conference was held in Khartoum, the Sudanese capital, between 29 August and 1 September 1967. It was the first meeting of the Arab leaders since their defeat in the June War. The conference ended with the adoption of the famous three noes of Khartoum: "no recognition, no negotiation, and no peace" with Israel. On the face of it these declarations showed no sign of readiness for compromise. In fact, the conference was a victory for the Arab moderates who argued for trying to obtain the withdrawal of Israel's forces by political rather than military means. Arab spokesmen interpreted the Khartoum declarations to mean no formal peace *treaty*, but not a rejection of a state of peace; no *direct* negotiations, but not a refusal to talk through third parties; and no *de jure* recognition of Israel, but *de facto* acceptance of its existence as a state. President Nasser and King Hussein set the tone at the summit and made it clear subsequently that they were prepared to go much further than ever before toward a settlement with Israel.[5]

The Khartoum summit marked a real change in the Arab approach to Israel, a change from confrontation to negotiation. At Khartoum, Nasser advised King Hussein to explore the possibility of a peaceful settlement with Israel. Israel's intelligence services obtained the verbatim text of the Khartoum deliberations and apprised the cabinet of the sea change they heralded in the Arab attitude. Major General Aharon Yariv, the director of military intelligence, informed the Knesset Foreign Affairs and Security Committee that the summit decided to go for a political, not military solution. But Israel's leaders feared the new manifestation of Arab moderation: it posed a threat to their expansionist plans. They therefore chose to portray the conclusions of the summit as the climax of Arab intransigence in order to justify the toughening of their own posture. Foreign Minister Abba Eban advised that since the world press was inclined to characterize the Khartoum resolutions as moderate, the government of Israel had to expose them as extreme. The new line Isreal adopted was that the Khartoum summit closed every door and every window that might lead to a peace settlement. Abba Eban famously quipped: "The Arabs never miss an opportunity to miss an opportunity for peace."

The most significant international pronouncement on the Arab-Israeli dispute after the Six-Day War was UN Security Council Resolution 242 of 22 November 1967. The preamble to the resolution emphasized the inadmissibility of the acquisition of territory by force and the need to work for a just and lasting peace. Basically, the resolution proposed a package deal, the trading of land for peace between Israel and its neighbours.

As Professor Rashid Khalidi explains in his report, Resolution 242 caused deep anger among Palestinians because it ignored their political rights and merely referred to them as a "refugee problem". By ignoring the right to national self-determination of the Palestinian people, Resolution 242 reinforced the view, widely held in the Global South, that the UN was not a genuinely international body, but the instrument of the Global North, and especially of the five permanent members of the Security Council.

Resolution 242 was accepted by Egypt and Jordan but not by Syria. Israel's position was ambiguous but widely regarded as amounting to a rejection. Israel declared that before it would withdraw from any part of the territories, there must be direct negotiations leading to a contractual peace agreement that incorporated secure and recognized boundaries. The problem was that Israel refused to spell out what it meant by "secure and recognised boundaries" then and it still refuses to do so today. Israel insisted that the peace agreements must be in place before beginning any withdrawal from the territories. But by pursuing its expansionist policy, it undermined the prospect of a negotiated agreement.

Resolution 242 has been the basis of most international plans for peace in the region since 1967. History shows that at the inter-state level this formula is sound. In 1979, Israel agreed to return to the international border, to give back to Egypt every inch of the Sinai Peninsula, and it received in return a peace treaty which is still standing today. In 1994, Israel signed a peace treaty with the Hashemite Kingdom of Jordan and returned some land it had occupied along their common border in the south. This was a bilateral treaty between the two states which left Israel in occupation of the rest of the West Bank of the Jordan River. This treaty, too, survived all the turmoil in the region and is still effective today. Had Israel wanted a peace agreement with Syria, it would most probably have been within its reach through negotiations. But there was a price tag: complete Israeli withdrawal from the Golan Heights and a return to the international border. The problem was that on the northern front, as on the eastern front, Israel preferred land to peace. This was due to the strategic importance of the Golan

Heights as well as the fertile agricultural land and water resources it contained.

II
— SETTLEMENTS IN THE —
— OCCUPIED TERRITORIES —

As mentioned, soon after the ending of hostilities, Israel started building civilian settlements in the newly occupied Arab territories. The new spaces were not called occupied territories but officially named as the Administered Territories. This clearly implied that the administration of these territories would be temporary, pending a final political settlement. However, pressure on the government to authorise the establishment of civilian settlements on these territories began to build up from below, from both secular nationalists and religious extremists.

The government asked the Legal Counsel of the Foreign Ministry for an opinion on whether civilian settlements in the administered territories were permitted under international law. The Counsel was Theodor Meron, a 37 years-old Holocaust survivor who went to win many honours for services to criminal justice and international humanitarian law. On 18 September 1967, Meron submitted a memorandum to Prime Minister Levi Eshkol. "My conclusion", he wrote, "is that civilian settlement in the administered territories contravenes the explicit provisions of the Fourth Geneva Convention." The memo was top secret but it was later discovered and published by the American-Israeli author Gershon Gorenberg.[6]

Meron accepted that there were conflicting claims regarding the status of the West Bank, but he warned that the international community would not accept settlement in any of the territories. He noted that during the Six-Day War a military order had instructed that Israel's military courts should apply the Geneva Conventions in the West Bank. The Fourth Geneva Convention says that "An Occupying Power should not deport or transfer parts of its own civilian population into territory it occupies." The memo went on to stress that "The prohibition therefore is categorical and not conditional upon the motives for the transfer or its objectives. Its purpose is to prevent settlement in occupied territory of citizens of the occupying state." If it was decided to go ahead with Jewish settlement in the administered territories, it seemed to Meron vital that settlement be carried out by military and not civilian entities. It was also important in his opinion that such settlement was "in the framework of camps and is, on the face of it, of a temporary rather than permanent nature."

The legal opinion was clear-cut: establishing civilian settlements on occupied territory would violate the

Fourth Geneva Convention. The government nevertheless chose to ignore the advice of its Legal Counsel and to go ahead with the building of settlements in all the occupied territories.

What began as private enterprise quickly turned into a government-sponsored project. The government used the map of the Allon Plan as a guide to authorising settlements. In other words, it only authorised the building of civilian settlements in areas it intended to keep permanently. Some religious-Zionist zealots from the settler movement Gush Emunim defied the government and proceeded without authority to establish small settlements in locations of religious significance. Rather than face them down, the government usually reached a compromise that enabled them to stay.

III
— THE DIPLOMACY OF ATTRITION —

The UN Secretary-General appointed Dr Gunnar Jarring, a Swedish diplomat, as a mediator with the task of promoting an Arab-Israeli settlement on the basis of Resolution 242. Having rejected 242, Syria declined to participate in his mission. The other Arab states had high expectations of his mission, whereas Israel had none at all. Israel had no trust in the impartiality of the UN or in its capacity to mediate. The deeper reason, however, was that Jarring's task was to implement Resolution 242 and this meant trading land for peace at a time when Israel was becoming increasingly wedded to the territorial status quo. The Israeli tactic was to give Jarring proposals and documents to which he was to obtain Arab reactions. The aim was to keep his mission alive and prevent the matter from going back to the UN, where Israel thought it would be blamed for the failure.

On 8 February 1971, to try to jump-start the process, Jarring addressed Egypt and Israel with identical memoranda outlining his own proposals for resolving the dispute between them. Of Egypt he requested an undertaking to enter into a peace agreement with Israel; of Israel, to withdraw to the former Egypt-Palestine international border. Egypt gave Jarring all the undertakings he asked for. The reply marked a breakthrough: it was the first time that an Egyptian government declared publicly its readiness to sign a peace treaty with Israel. But by this time the Israeli position had hardened against territorial compromise. Moshe Dayan's mantra had taken hold: "Better Sharm el-Sheikh without peace than peace without Sharm el-Sheikh." The Israeli reply to Jarring, reflecting this attitude, was a categorical refusal to restore the previous boundary. It ended with a short but highly significant sentence: "Israel will not withdraw to the pre–5 June 1967 lines." The reply sealed the fate of Jarring's mission. All other international efforts to promote a settlement of the conflict similarly came to naught in the face of Israel's inflexibility.

When Golda Meir succeeded Levi Eshkol as Prime Minister in 1969, Israel's diplomatic posture hardened further. As she writes in her autobiography, "Intransigent" was her middle name.[7] Mrs Meir did not want to go down in Israel's history as a leader who retreated from territory. But she also reflected the political consensus which held that the post-1967 status quo was greatly to Israel's advantage and that Israel's military supremacy ensured that it could be perpetuated indefinitely. More than all other Israeli leaders, however, she had a propensity for self-righteousness. "All the wars against us", she once said, "have nothing to do with us." Mrs Meir's overriding foreign policy aim was to preserve the post-war territorial status quo and to refuse to make any concessions for the sake of peace. In March 1969, a month after she succeeded Eshkol as Prime Minister, President Nasser launched the War of Attrition against Israel. Failure to bring about Israeli withdrawal from the occupied territories by diplomatic means led the Egyptian leader to resort to military means.

War in Egypt was justified by the slogan "That which was taken by force can only be recovered by force". Nasser's immediate goal was to prevent the conversion of the Suez Canal into a de facto border while his ultimate aim was to force Israel to withdraw to the pre-war border. The strategy consisted of artillery bombardment of Israel's positions on the canal front, occasional air attacks, and hit-and-run commando raids. The War of Attrition was ended by a ceasefire in August 1970. Unlike the June 1967 war, it ended in a draw rather than a clear-cut Israeli victory. Like all the Arab-Israeli wars since 1967, the War of Attrition was fought by Israel not to safeguard its security but in order to protect its territorial conquests.

Anwar Sadat, who succeeded Nasser as President in September 1970, reverted to the diplomatic track. In February 1971, Sadat presented his proposal for an interim settlement based on a partial Israeli withdrawal to the Sinai Passes and the reopening of the Suez Canal to international shipping. Mrs Meir's reply was a polite rejection.

In March 1972, Jordan's King Hussein unveiled his federal plan for a United Arab Kingdom. The federation was to consist of two regions: the region of Jordan, comprising the East Bank, and the region of Palestine, comprising the West Bank and the Gaza Strip. Each region was to have its own government and its separate judicial system. Mrs Meir's rejection of this plan was swift and categorical.

As stated, Mrs Meir firmly held the opinion that the territorial status quo was stable and it could be sustained easily and at low cost. After the War of Attrition, she conducted what can be best described as the diplomacy of attrition. Her policy, in a nutshell, was to let Sadat sweat it out, with his range of options constantly narrowing, until he had no choice but to sue for peace on Israel's terms. Mrs Meir succeeded in persuading Dr Henry Kissinger, the American Secretary of State, of the realism of her chosen course of action.

IV
— THE OCTOBER 1973 WAR —

In the end, the diplomacy of attrition backfired with disastrous consequences. Its aim was to compel the Arabs to accept the post-1967 territorial status quo. But to President Sadat of Egypt and President Hafiz al-Assad of Syria the status quo was humiliating and intolerable. On 6 October 1973, the Day of Atonement, the holiest day in the Jewish Calendar, Egypt and Syria launched a surprise attack on Israel. The aim of the offensive was to capture some of the territory they had lost in 1967, to force the US and Soviet Union to intervene, and to initiate a diplomatic process that would force Israel to withdraw from further parts of occupied Arab lands.

Israel and the United States were taken by complete surprise. The entire rationale for their previous policy was shattered overnight. In the initial phase of the war Israel suffered significant setbacks on both the Egyptian and the Syrian fronts but, with the help of a massive American airlift of arms, it launched a successful counter-offensive. In the aftermath of the war, Kissinger had to move fast to construct a new foreign policy that had an Arab as well as an Israeli dimension. He embarked on his step-by-step diplomacy which resulted in Israeli-Egyptian and Israeli-Syrian military disengagement agreements. Kissinger did not broker a military disengagement agreement on the eastern front because Jordan had not participated in the October War. But there was a deeper reason: any negotiations were bound to bring forth Jordanian as well as Palestinian claims to sovereignty over the West Bank. Kissinger knew that any concessions on the West Bank would trigger the collapse of Golda Meir's coalition government. He therefore chose to keep the Palestinian issue on the back burner.

Although the Palestine Liberation Organisation had not participated in the October War, its political standing improved as a result of the war. It also took a major step to moderate its political programme. The Palestinian National Charter called for an armed struggle to liberate the whole of mandatory Palestine. The Palestinian National Council (PNC), the parliament of the worldwide Palestinian community, which convened in Cairo in June 1974, shifted the emphasis from the armed struggle to a political solution by means of a phased programme. As a first stage, it approved the establishment of "a patriotic, independent fighting people's regime in any part of the Palestinian territory which will be liberated."[8] This was an ambiguous formula, but it conveyed a willingness to consider the possibility of a Palestinian state alongside Israel rather than in place of it.

On the Israeli side, however, the PNC resolution was interpreted as the result of a change of tactics rather than a genuine change of aims. Frequent references were made to the PLO's "theory of stages" to make the point that a Palestinian state in part of Palestine would only serve as a base for continuing the armed struggle to liberate the whole of Palestine. Itzhak Rabin, who replaced Golda Meir as Prime Minister after the October War, adhered to the orthodox line of refusing to recognize or to negotiate with the PLO. His aim was to keep the Palestinian question "in the refrigerator". He took the view that Israel must refuse to talk to what he considered a terrorist organization that was committed to its destruction. Nor was he prepared to consider a Palestinian state alongside Israel; this, he said, "would be the beginning of the end of the State of Israel". For all practical purposes, his position was essentially the same as that of Golda Meir. He remained firm and inflexible: Israel would never recognize the PLO, enter into any negotiations with the PLO, or agree to the establishment of a Palestinian state.

The Arab position towards the PLO did change in the aftermath of the war. Previously, the position had been that Jordan should represent itself and the Palestinians in diplomatic negotiations with Israel. At the end of October 1974, an Arab League summit meeting was held in Rabat, Morocco. King Hussein suffered a major diplomatic defeat because the summit endorsed the claim of the PLO to be "the sole legitimate representative of the Palestinian people". The summit also reaffirmed the right of the Palestinian people to set up an independent national authority, led by the PLO, on any part of Palestine that was liberated. The implication of these resolutions was that the territories captured in 1967 should not revert to Jordan but go to the Palestinians to establish an independent state. A month later Yasser Arafat, the chairman of the PLO, was invited to address the UN General Assembly, which proceeded to pass Resolution 3236 (XXIX) affirming the right of the Palestinian people to, among other things, national self-determination and national independence and sovereignty.

Rabin's principal departure from the foreign policy of his predecessor was the Interim Agreement with Egypt, signed on 1 September 1975. The agreement was also known as "Sinai II" because it followed on from the 1974 separation-of-forces agreement that Kissinger had brokered. The agreement provided for Israeli withdrawal in Sinai to the eastern ends of the Mitla and Gidi Passes, creation of a UN-monitored buffer zone in the evacuated area, and Israeli withdrawal from the oil fields at Abu Rudeis and Ras Sudar. It also stipulated the opening of the Suez Canal to Israeli non-military cargo ships, and the establishment of American early-warning stations in the area of the passes. The basic terms of the agreement were not dissimilar to those offered by President Sadat in his interim settlement proposal of February 1971.

Sinai II contained one novel feature: direct American involvement and underwriting. Israel always preferred to negotiate with the pre-eminent western power of the day rather than with the Arabs. On this occasion, Rabin made it clear to Henry Kissinger that the cabinet would not ratify the Sinai II agreement unless it was accompanied by an American-Israeli agreement. This "memorandum of agreement" detailed US commitments to Israel following from the interim agreement. The memorandum pledged American support "on an on-going and long-term basis to Israel's military equipment and other defense requirements, to its energy requirements and to its economic needs." More specifically, it promised a positive response to Israel's request for F-16 fighter planes and Pershing missiles with conventional warheads. In a separate "memorandum of agreement", which was kept secret, the United States confirmed that it would not negotiate with or recognize the PLO or initiate any moves in the Middle East without prior consultation with Israel.

V
— THE CAMP DAVID ACCORDS —

Whereas Henry Kissinger's focus was on bringing about Egypt's disengagement from the Arab-Israeli conflict, President Jimmy Carter's aim was a comprehensive resolution of the conflict. Carter did not shy away from addressing the core of the conflict – the Palestinian problem. He was the first American president to speak about the need for establishing "a Palestinian homeland". His initial idea was to convene an international conference with the Soviet Union and all the parties to the conflict. An Israeli veto of the Soviet Union led him to switch to a trilateral summit between himself,

President Sadat, and Prime Minister Menachem Begin at the presidential retreat in Camp David, Maryland.

Menachem Begin was the leader of the Likud, a right-wing nationalistic party that came to power in 1977, ending three decades of Labour Party hegemony. The Labour Party was a pragmatic centre-left party which advocated territorial compromise with Jordan over the West Bank. The Likud was an ideological party dedicated to what it called "the Whole Land of Israel". It believed that the borders of the State of Israel should correspond to the borders of the Land of Israel. For the Likud the West Bank and the Gaza Strip were an integral part of the Land of Israel. By claiming that the Jewish people have an exclusive right to sovereignty over their ancestral homeland, Likud rejected any rival claims from either Jordan or the Palestinians. To underline their rejection of rival claims over the West Bank, Likud leaders usually referred to it by its Biblical names – Judea and Samaria.

The initial positions of the principals at Camp David were poles apart. Sadat's position was that a Palestinian state should be established in the West Bank and the Gaza Strip. Begin's position was that "the Palestinian Arabs residing in Judea, Samaria and the Gaza District should enjoy self-rule." Under American pressure, Begin did produce a Palestinian autonomy plan but Begin's autonomy applied only to people and not to the land they inhabited. In other words, he was prepared to keep Israel's claim to sovereignty over the West Bank and the Gaza Strip in abeyance while negotiations were in progress but not to give it up. He ruled out in advance any notion of an independent, sovereign Palestinian state. The PLO dismissed Begin's plan as autonomy to collect their own garbage and to swat their own mosquitos.

Thirteen days of assiduous negotiations led to the conclusion, on 17 September 1978, of the Camp David Accords. The eventual outcome of these talks, the "Framework for Peace in the Middle East", had two parts: (1) a process for achieving Palestinian self-government in the West Bank and Gaza, and (2) a framework for the conclusion of a peace treaty between Israel and Egypt. The subsequent negotiations on Palestinian autonomy were protracted but unsuccessful. The main obstacle to an agreement was Israel's refusal to give up its claim to sovereignty over the West Bank and the Gaza Strip and its rigidly narrow parameters for Palestinian autonomy.

The talks between Israel and Egypt led to the signature of a peace treaty, on 26 March 1979, at the White House. It was the first peace agreement between Israel and an Arab state. Israel agreed to withdraw from the whole of the Sinai Peninsula, and Egypt promised to establish normal diplomatic relations between the two countries and open the Suez Canal to Israeli ships. UN forces were to be stationed in the area to supervise the demilitarisation of Sinai and to ensure the freedom of navigation. All these provisions were duly carried out over three years, in accordance with a detailed timetable. In most Arab countries, however, the peace with Israel was seen as an act of betrayal and Egypt was expelled from the Arab League. The PLO also denounced the accords.

Carter's hope for a national home for the Palestinian people did not materialise. Begin got what he wanted: a peace agreement with Egypt that stood on its own. Moreover, he believed that giving back Sinai would enable his country to consolidate its control over the West Bank, over Judea and Samaria, as he preferred to call it. Begin strongly objected to the term "occupied territories". For him Judea and Samaria were "liberated territories". This sense of entitlement goes a long way to explain Begin's refusal to revert to the pre-war status quo on the West Bank. For him the peace treaty with Egypt was not a step on the road to an overall settlement but the final destination.

The Camp David summit was not simply a missed opportunity to begin the groundwork for a two-state solution to the Israeli-Palestinian conflict. It seriously diminished the possibility of progress towards Palestinian statehood in the long run. As Seth Anziska argues in

Preventing Palestine, the breakthrough peace agreement between Egypt and Israel created a roadblock to peace between Israel and the Palestinians.[9] In Israel the Camp David Accords are universally acclaimed while the Oslo Accords (discussed below) are controversial. Anziska shows the strong connections between the two sets of accords and the extent to which Oslo drew on the Camp David autonomy plan. Palestinian autonomy became the template for future would-be peacemakers. But there was never any realistic possibility that mere autonomy would satisfy the national aspirations of the Palestinians.

VI
— THE LONDON AGREEMENT —

The next major attempt to resolve the Arab-Israeli conflict was undertaken by King Hussein of Jordan in 1987. His Israeli interlocutor was Shimon Peres who served as Foreign Minister in a national unity government headed by Itzhak Shamir, Menachem Begin's successor as leader of the Likud and Prime Minister. Following the inconclusive result of the 1984 elections, Labour and Likud formed a coalition government with Peres and Shamir rotating as Prime Minister and Foreign Minister after the first two years. The two principal parties of the coalition cancelled each other's foreign policy. Labour believed in territorial compromise over the West Bank and its preferred partner was the Jordanian monarchy, not the PLO. Shamir believed that the whole of the West Bank belonged to Israel and this ruled out partnership for partition with either Hashemites or Palestinians. He was a proponent of the doctrine of permanent conflict and the unilateralist par excellence. To the extent that he engaged in diplomatic activity at all, it was only to gain time, to increase the number of Jewish settlers, and to entrench Israel's occupation of the West Bank.

King Hussein's basic idea was to convene an international conference in order to provide cover for subsequent bilateral negotiations between Jordan and Israel. Shamir, however, was adamantly opposed to the whole idea of an international conference, even a purely ceremonial one. The Americans, too, remained cool to the idea of convening an international conference because they did not want the Soviet Union to be involved in Middle Eastern diplomacy. Hussein met Peres in London, on 17 April 1987, at the home of the King's Jewish friend, Lord Mischon. At the end of a long day of negotiations and drafting, they initialled a document that came to be known as the London Agreement. It contained three parts.

The first part proposed that the UN Secretary-General should invite the five permanent members of the Security Council and the parties to the Arab-Israeli conflict to negotiate a peaceful settlement based on Security Council Resolutions 242 and 338. (Resolution 338, passed during the 1973 October War, called on the parties to cease fire and proceed immediately to implement Resolution 242). The second part of the London Agreement proposed that the conference should invite the parties to form bilateral committees to negotiate on issues of mutual interest. The third part noted the agreement that the Palestinian issue would be discussed by a joint Jordanian-Palestinian delegation, which would not include members of the PLO.

Shamir was irreconcilably opposed to the London Agreement and used his authority as Prime Minister to thwart it. Although the London Agreement dealt only with procedure and did not commit Israel to anything of substance, he feared that it would open the door to a territorial compromise on the West Bank which was favoured by the Labour Party. King Hussein suspected that Shamir would oppose the London Agreement and he said so to Shimon Peres. Peres replied that in that case he would break up the national unity government and make the London Agreement the centrepiece of Labour's manifesto at the subsequent election. But when it came to a head, Peres lacked the courage of his convictions. He fixed his colours firmly to the fence.

Shamir himself, by his own account, grew weary of the incessant manoeuvres to find a peaceful solution to the Arab-Israeli dispute. "The presenting and rejecting of peace plans", he wrote in his autobiography, "went on throughout the duration of my Prime Ministership; not a year passed without some official proposal being made by the United States, or Israel, or even Mubarak, each one bringing in its wake new internal crises, expectations and disappointments – though I had become more or less immune to the latter."[10] These plans rarely contained new elements, Shamir complained; what they amounted to was "peace in exchange for territory; recognition in exchange for territory; never 'just' peace."

VII
— THE FIRST INTIFADA —

Shamir was committed to maintaining the status quo in the occupied territories, and it was maintained, at least on the surface. Settlement activity was strongly encouraged by Likud-led governments to reinforce their claim to sovereignty over the whole of the West Bank. Below the surface, Palestinian frustration and despondency were increasing all the time. A feeling of hopelessness took hold as the Palestinians watched more and more of their land being swallowed up by Israeli settlements. Economic conditions remained miserable, while Israel's military government was becoming more intrusive and heavy-handed. The spark that ignited the Palestinian uprising, or intifada, was a traffic accident on 9 December 1987, in which an Israeli truck driver killed four residents of Jabaliya, the largest of the eight refugee camps in the Gaza Strip. The Palestinian response took the form of protests, civil disobedience, the throwing of stones and Molotov cocktails. From Gaza the disturbances spread to the West Bank. Within days the occupied territories were engulfed in a wave of popular street demonstrations and commercial strikes on an unprecedented scale.

The outbreak of the intifada was completely spontaneous. There was no preparation or planning by the local Palestinian elite or the PLO, but the PLO was quick to jump on the bandwagon of popular discontent against Israeli rule and to play a leadership role alongside a newly formed body, the Unified National Command. In origin the intifada was not a nationalist revolt. It had its roots in poverty, in the miserable living conditions of the refugee camps, in hatred of the occupation, and, above all, in the humiliation that the Palestinians had to endure over the preceding twenty years. But it developed into a statement of major political import. The aims of the intifada were not stated at the outset; they emerged in the course of the struggle. The ultimate aim was self-determination and the establishment of an independent Palestinian state. In this respect the intifada may be seen as the Palestinian war of independence.

The IDF resorted to draconian measures to suppress the intifada but to no avail. Events in the occupied territories received intense media coverage. The world saw pictures of Israeli troops firing on stone-throwing demonstrators, or beating those they caught, among them women and children. Israel's image suffered serious damage as a result of this media coverage. During the 1988 session of the General Assembly, several resolutions were passed condemning Israel and calling on it to abide by the Geneva Convention for the protection of civilians in times of war.

King Hussein viewed with mounting concern the events unfolding on the West Bank of the Jordan River. He was worried that the intifada would spread from the West Bank to the east bank of the river and destabilise his regime. To forestall this possibility, he made a decision of historic significance. On 31 July 1988, he announced that Jordan was cutting its legal and administrative ties with the West Bank. (Jordan had continued to pay the salary of about a third of the civil servants on the West Bank during the preceding two decades of Israeli occupation.) Many East Bankers felt they got nothing but ingratitude for their efforts to help the Palestinians and that the time had come to cut their losses. The King himself felt that Jordan was fighting a losing battle in defending positions that had already fallen to the PLO. After two decades of trying to blur the distinction between the East Bank and the West Bank, he concluded that the time had come to assert that the East Bank was not Palestine and that it was up to the Palestinians to decide what they wanted to do with the West Bank and to deal with the Israelis directly over its future. Israel now found itself alone in the arena with the PLO.

VIII
— THE PNC RESOLUTIONS —
— AND THE —
— MADRID PEACE CONFERENCE —

The PLO rose up to the challenge. Yasser Arafat, the chairman of the PLO, took the lead in moderating its political programme. At the meeting of the PNC, in Algiers in mid-November 1988, Arafat won a majority for the historic decision to recognise Israel's right to exist, to accept all the relevant UN resolutions going back to 29 November 1947, and to adopt the principle of a two-state solution. The claim to the whole of Palestine, enshrined in the Palestinian National Charter, was finally laid to rest and a declaration of independence was issued for a mini state in the West Bank and Gaza with East Jerusalem as its capital. This revolution in Palestinian political thinking coincided with the rise to power in Israel of a hard-line Likud government headed by Itzhak Shamir. Just as the Palestinians were moving towards territorial compromise, Israel was moving away from it. Its rejection of the PNC declaration was absolute and unconditional. In Israeli eyes the PLO was a terrorist organisation and talking to it was therefore out of the question.

Yasser Arafat supported Iraq's invasion of Kuwait in August 1990; this did not help the Palestinian cause, to use an understatement. In one of his smarter moves, Saddam Hussein said Iraq would withdraw from Kuwait if Israel withdrew from all occupied Arab territories. Having threatened "the mother of all battles" if the US intervened, he now proposed what amounted to the mother of all linkages. The US insisted on sequential rather than simultaneous withdrawal: first Iraq would have to withdraw its forces from Kuwait, only then would the US address the Israeli occupation. The Gulf war ejected Iraq out of Kuwait. In the aftermath of the war, towards the end of October 1991, the Americans and the Soviets convened an international peace conference in Madrid to which they invited a large number of delegations, including a non-PLO Palestinian delegation.[11] Although the PLO itself was not invited, the official Palestinian delegation coordinated its moves with the PLO office in Tunis.

This was the first time the Palestinians represented themselves at a major international conference. A joint Jordanian-Palestinian delegation with non-PLO Palestinian members provided an umbrella for Palestinian participation. The Palestinians from the West Bank and Gaza were there on a footing of equality with the Israelis: the heads of the Jordanian and Palestinian delegations were allowed as much time as the head of the Israeli delegation for their opening speech to the plenary. In his opening speech, Itzhak Shamir came close to rejecting the whole basis of the conference – UN resolutions 242 and 338 and the principle of land for peace.

The Palestinians adopted the olive branch strategy. Dr Haidar Abdel-Shafi, an elderly physician from Gaza who headed the Palestinian delegation, was the epitome of moderation, of Palestinian nationalism with a human face. The contrast between his speech and Mr Shamir's speech could have hardly been more striking in tone, spirit or substance. It was, by any standards, a remarkable speech and its impact was only heightened by the quiet, dignified quality of the delivery.[12] Dr Abdel-Shafi reminded the audience that it was time for the Palestinians to narrate their own story. While touching on the past, his speech was not backward-looking but forward-looking. He sought neither an admission of guilt nor vengeance for past iniquities but rather a just peace.

Dr Abdel-Shafi's basic message was that the Palestinians were genuinely committed to peaceful co-existence, that the Israeli occupation had to end, that the Palestinians had a right to self-determination, and that they were determined to pursue this right relentlessly until they achieved statehood. The intifada, he suggested, had already begun to embody the Palestinian state and to build its institutions and infrastructure. But while staking a claim to Palestinian statehood, Dr Abdel-Shafi qualified it in two significant ways. First, he accepted the need for a transitional stage, provided interim arrangements were not transformed into permanent status. Secondly, he envisaged a confederation between an ultimately independent Palestine and Jordan.

Dr Abdel-Shafi's speech in Madrid was both the most eloquent and the most moderate presentation of the Palestinian case ever made by an official Palestinian spokesman since the beginning of the conflict at the end of the nineteenth century. The PLO, for all its growing moderation, had never been able to articulate such a clear-cut peace overture to Israel because of its internal divisions and the constraints of inter-Arab politics. No PLO official had ever been able to declare so unambiguously that a Palestinian state would be ready for a confederation with Jordan. The whole tenor of the speech was more conciliatory and constructive than even the most moderate statements of the PLO. In the words of Afif Safieh, a senior PLO official, the entire stance of the Palestinian delegation at Madrid was "unreasonably reasonable".[13]

Two tracks for further negotiations were established at the end of the Madrid conference: an Israeli-Arab track and an Israeli-Palestinian track. The official negotiations between the two sets of delegations took place under American auspices in Washington DC. So long as the Likud remained in power, however, no progress could be achieved on either track. The centrepiece of Likud's ideology was "the Whole Land of Israel" or Greater Israel, and on this there could be no compromise. The aim was to achieve a Jewish majority on the West Bank and to prevent the birth of a Palestinian state. In an interview with the *Ma'ariv* daily newspaper, after losing the election of 23 June 1992, Shamir admitted that his tactic in the peace talks was stonewalling. "I would have carried on autonomy talks for ten years", he said, "and meanwhile we would have reached half a million people in Judea and Samaria." "Moderation", Shamir explained, "should relate to the tactics but not to the goal... the integrity of the Land of Israel."[14]

In the final sentence of his book, *Summing Up: An Autobiography*, Shamir wrote: "If history remembers me at all, in any way, I hope it will be as a man who loved the Land of Israel and watched over it in every way he could, all his life."[15]

IX
— THE OSLO ACCORD —

The Labour Party's victory in the 1992 election did not bring about an abrupt change of policy. Itzhak Rabin, the leader of the party, was not a dove. The traditional foreign policies of the rival parties led by the two Itzhaks displayed some striking similarities. Both Labour and the Likud preferred to treat the Arab-Israeli conflict as an interstate conflict. Both parties denied that the Palestinians had a right to national self-determination. Both always refused to negotiate with the PLO, and this refusal was absolute rather than conditional. Both were also unconditionally opposed to the establishment of an independent Palestinian state. Although Labour was open to territorial compromise in the West Bank, it envisioned returning that territory to Jordan. Suspicion of the Arabs and a deep sense of personal responsibility for Israel's security were the twin hallmarks of Rabin's worldview.

For Rabin the Arabs represented first and foremost a military threat, and he consequently tended to view all developments in the region from the narrow perspective of Israel's security needs. What changed was not the priorities of the Labour government, but a dramatic drop in the price for peace offered by the PLO, with which Israel had been negotiating indirectly since the Madrid conference. Yasser Arafat, who was still out in the cold because of his support for Iraq's invasion of Kuwait, was threatened by the growing prestige of the Palestinian leaders from the West Bank and Gaza. He therefore urged them to be uncompromising in the official talks in Washington DC while opening a secret channel to the Israeli government in Oslo. The PLO delegation in Oslo had no map experts and no lawyers. In the secret talks in the Norwegian capital, it made one concession after another to the Israelis. The result was the Oslo Accord, signed in the White House, on 13 September 1993, with President Bill Clinton acting as Master of Ceremonies.

The official name of the accord was "The Declaration of Principles on Interim Self-Government Arrangements". It applied only to Gaza and to the West Bank city of Jericho. The signing of the accord was preceded by an exchange of letters of recognition. Mutual rejection was replaced by mutual recognition. However, while the PLO recognised Israel's right to live in peace and security, Israel only recognised the PLO as the representative of the Palestinian people and as a partner in bilateral negotiations. There was no recognition of any Palestinian national rights. It was only agreed that a Palestinian Authority (PA) would be established and assume governing responsibilities in the Gaza Strip and part of the West Bank over a five-year period.

The accord was silent on all the key issues in the conflict: Jerusalem, the right of return of the 1948 Palestinian refugees, the status of the Israeli settlements on occupied Palestinian territory, and the borders of the Palestinian entity. All these issues were left to negotiations in the fourth year of the transition period. There was no mention, let alone a promise, of an independent Palestinian state at the end of the road. All the so-called "final status" issues were left for future negotiations and these were bound to reflect the power relations between the parties. The most fatal flaw in the accord was that it did not require Israel to have a freeze on settlement expansion during the transition period. The PLO leadership thought that in return for giving up their claim to 78% of mandatory Palestine they would eventually get an independent state over the remaining 22% with a capital city in East Jerusalem. But it was not to be.

The Interim Agreement on the West Bank and Gaza Strip ("Oslo II"), signed in Washington on 28 September 1995, represented some progress in extending Palestinian self-government. It provided for elections to a Palestinian council, the transfer of legislative authority to this council, the withdrawal of Israeli forces from the Palestinian centers of population, and the division of the West Bank into three areas – A, B, and C. Area A consisted of Palestinian towns and urban areas; Area B consisted of Palestinian villages and less densely populated parts; and Area C consisted of the lands confiscated by Israel for the Jewish settlements. Area A was placed under exclusive Palestinian control and in Area B the Palestinians exercised civilian authority. Area C, which encompasses 60% of the West Bank, was placed under exclusive Israeli control.

Benjamin Netanyahu, the leader of the opposition at the time, denounced Oslo II as a surrender to terrorists and a national humiliation, and he vowed to bring down the government. He gave an inflammatory speech from the grandstand of a mass rally in Jerusalem in which demonstrators displayed an effigy of Rabin in SS uniform. And he continued to play an active part in a campaign of incitement against the democratically elected Labour government. The campaign hit its lethal climax when Itzhak Rabin was assassinated by a Jewish fanatic on 4 November 1995. Unlike most political assassinations, this one achieved its primary aim – derailing the peace process.

X
— THE BREAKDOWN OF THE —
— OSLO PEACE PROCESS —

Shimon Peres succeeded Itzhak Rabin as party leader and Prime Minister. During his short-lived premiership he made some serious mistakes, most notably the green light he gave to the Shin Bet, Israel's internal security agency, to assassinate Yahya Ayash, a Hamas bomb maker.[16] This ended a tacit ceasefire with Hamas and resulted in a series of horrific suicide bombs that seriously damaged the credibility of the government.

Peres's second major mistake was the invasion of Lebanon in April 1996. "Operation Grapes of Wrath" was meant to bring security to Galilee by bombing the Hizbullah guerrilla bases in southern Lebanon. But Israel's massive use of air and ground forces was ill-conceived and ill-fated. An Israeli shell that killed 102 refugees sheltering in the UN base in Qana provoked an international outcry and forced Peres to retreat. The operation ended in a military, political, and moral failure. From a seemingly unassailable 20-point lead, Peres kept losing ground to Netanyahu: Jewish terror helped Labour; Palestinian terror helped the Likud.

Netanyahu defeated Peres by a margin of less than 1% in the election of May 1996 and immediately set about destroying the foundations for the peace that his Labour predecessors had begun to build. Netanyahu spent his three years in power in a successful attempt to freeze, subvert, and undermine the Oslo accords. He kept talking about reciprocity while acting unilaterally in demolishing Arab houses, opening a tunnel in the old city of Jerusalem, imposing curfews, confiscating more and more Arab land. Under intense American pressure, Netanyahu signed the Wye River Memorandum in October 1998, promising to turn over another 11 per cent of the West Bank to the Palestinian Authority. But he reneged on this agreement. Ironically, it was not the Labour opposition that brought down his government but his own nationalist and religious coalition partners who considered that he had gone soft on the Palestinians and that he had compromised the integrity of the historic homeland.

Netanyahu's rise to power marked a break with the pragmatism that characterised Labour's approach to the Arab world and the reassertion of a nationalistic ideological hard line. In 1993, three years before Netanyahu became Prime Minister and just before he was elected leader of the Likud, he published a book under the title *A Place Among the Nations: Israel and the World*. The central theme of the book is the right of the Jewish people to the whole Land of Israel. History was rewritten in order to demonstrate that it was not the Jews who usurped the land from the Arabs, but the Arabs who usurped it from the Jews. Netanyahu's image of the Arabs was comprehensively negative and it did not permit the possibility of diversity or change. Much of his venom was reserved for the Palestinians. For him the Palestinian problem was not a genuine problem but an artificially manufactured one. Compromise with the PLO was completely out of the question because its goal was the destruction of the State of Israel, and this goal allegedly defined its very essence.[17]

Once in power, Netanyahu continued to deny that the Palestinians had any right to national self-determination. He treated the Palestinian Authority not as an equal partner on the road to peace but as a defective instrument of Israeli security. The expansion of Jewish settlements on the West Bank proceeded apace, in flagrant violation of the spirit, if not the letter, of Oslo. The so-called peace process became a charade: all process and no peace. In fact, it was worse than a charade for it gave the Likud just the cover it needed to pursue the aggressive Zionist colonial project on the West Bank.

On Netanyahu's watch the Oslo peace process broke down. Why did it break down? There are two radically different answers to this question. Netanyahu maintains that the Oslo accords were doomed to failure from the start because they were incompatible with Israeli security and with the historic right of the Jewish people to the Whole Land of Israel. The other view is that, following the return of the Likud to power, Israel reneged on its side of the bargain. More specifically, the Oslo accords were killed by the relentless expansion of Jewish settlements in the occupied territories. Settlement expansion involved seizing more and more Palestinian land. Land-grabbing happened also under previous Labour governments but was significantly increased under the Likud.

XI
— CAMP DAVID II —

The Labour Party, under the leadership of Ehud Barak, won the elections of 17 May 1999 with a clear mandate to return to the Oslo path. Like Rabin, Barak was a soldier who later in life turned to peace-making. While donning civilian clothes, Barak remained essentially a soldier. Barak is what in Hebrew is known as a *bitkhonist* – a security-ist. As Prime Minister, no less than when he was army chief of staff, he had three priorities: security, security, and security. All developments in the region, including the peace process, were viewed by Barak from the narrow perspective of Israel's security needs and these needs were significantly inflated.

Barak saw relations with the Palestinians as a zero-sum game. It is only a slight exaggeration to say that Barak approached diplomacy as if it were the extension of war by other means. His *modus operandi* was not peace by compromise but peace by ultimatum. Barak famously described Israel as "a villa in the jungle". Leaving aside the racist undercurrent, this clearly indicated the importance he attached to maintaining the separation between Israel and its neighbours.

From his first day in office, Barak pursued a policy of "Syria first", of working for a breakthrough on the Syrian track. Syria was a major military power whereas the Palestinians were not. As a military threat to Israel they were, as Barak pointed out, completely negligible. By removing Syria from the conflict, Barak hoped to change the whole strategic landscape in the region and to leave the Palestinians even more weak and isolated and therefore more likely to accept whatever terms Israel eventually chose to offer them for the final settlement. The main reason for the failure of the Israeli-Syrian negotiations was Barak's refusal to accept total Israeli withdrawal to the lines of

4 June 1967 on the Golan Heights. It was only after the talks with Syria failed that Barak turned, belatedly and reluctantly, to the Palestinian track. He did not do well on this track either.

On Barak's watch Israel accelerated the pace of settlement on the West Bank. True, some settlement activity had gone on under all three previous Prime Ministers. But under Barak the building of settlements proceeded at a frenetic pace and in blatant disregard for the spirit of Oslo. More houses were constructed, more Arab land was confiscated, more access roads were built to isolated Jewish settlements. For the Palestinian population these settlements were not just a symbol of the hated occupation but a source of daily friction and a constant reminder of the danger to the territorial contiguity of their future state. Barak seemed intent on repackaging rather than ending the occupation and on tightening Israel's control over the Palestinian territories.

Barak asked Bill Clinton to convene a summit with himself and Yasser Arafat. He thought that at a trilateral summit, he and the American President would be able to force Arafat to accept a settlement on Israel's terms. Bill Clinton obliged by convening a summit at Camp David in Maryland in July 2000. Arafat warned Clinton that the positions of the two sides were too far apart and that if the summit failed, it would make things not better but worse. Clinton persuaded Arafat to go anyway by promising that if the summit failed, there would be no finger pointing.

At the summit Barak refused to meet face-to-face with Arafat to negotiate. Through his aides he sent successive offers, the last of which was for a demilitarised Palestinian state on the Gaza Strip and 90% of the West Bank. This offer did not meet two of Arafat's key demands: Palestinian sovereignty over the Muslim holy places in the Old City of Jerusalem and the right of return of the Palestinian refugees. There was a chance that Arafat would have given up one demand if the other was satisfied; there was no chance he would give up on both. The summit failed basically because the Israeli offer was not good enough. Yet, no sooner had the conference failed, when both Barak and Clinton pointed the finger of blame at Arafat.

On his return home, Barak propagated the myth of the "generous offer" and the notion that there was no Palestinian partner for peace. The historical record showed that there was a serious Palestinian partner for peace but not on Barak's terms. This was most clearly demonstrated by the PLO's endorsement of the Oslo Accord. Nevertheless, virtually the whole Israeli nation, left, right, and centre, accepted Barak's explanation for the failure of the Camp David summit. The claim that there was no Palestinian partner for peace had far-reaching electoral consequences. It seriously damaged the peace camp in general and the Labour Party in particular. For if there was no Palestinian partner for peace, why vote for a party that advocated negotiations and compromise? It made more sense to vote for a tough, uncompromising leader.

XII
— THE CHAMPION OF —
— VIOLENT SOLUTIONS —

Ariel Sharon, the new leader of the Likud, fitted the bill. He was the champion of violent solutions. On 28 September 2000, he staged a much-publicised visit to al-Haram al-Sharif, the Noble Sanctuary, in the Old City of Jerusalem which the Jews call the Temple Mount. Flanked by a thousand security men and in deliberate disregard for the sensitivity of the Muslim worshippers, Sharon walked into the sanctuary with what he claimed was a message of peace. The day after his visit, following Friday prayers, large-scale riots broke out around the Old City. Palestinians on the Temple Mount threw rocks over the Western Wall at Jewish worshippers and Israeli policemen fired rubber-coated steel bullets, killing four Palestinian youths. In the days that followed, demonstrations erupted all over the West

Bank and Gaza. This was the beginning of the second intifada which lasted until 2005 and claimed the lives of 1,100 Israelis and 4,907 Palestinians.

The return to violence helped the Likud to win the elections of 6 February 2001. During the 2001 election campaign, Sharon declared that the Oslo accords were null and void. Rejecting the notion that Oslo had been "the peace of the brave", he dubbed it "the peace of the grave". He drew up a list of "red lines" that he vowed not to cross: no dismantling of settlements, no withdrawal from the Jordan Valley, no concessions on Jerusalem. The dominant narrative during Sharon's premiership was the "war on terror". Here he was in his element, making the fight against militant Palestinian groups such as Hamas and Islamic Jihad the top priority of his government.

After 9/11, the al-Qaeda attack on the twin towers, Sharon was the first world leader to jump on the bandwagon of the "Global War on Terror". His message to the neoconservatives in George W. Bush's administration was that they were on the same side: the Americans were fighting terror worldwide while he was fighting terror in his back yard. The Palestinian Authority, the embryonic government of the state-in-the-making, was according to him a terrorist entity. He therefore proposed to deal with it as one should deal with terrorists – with an iron fist. No peace negotiations took place between 2001 and 2006 and it was highly revealing that Sharon regarded this as something to be proud of. Because he disliked compromise, he also rejected all international peace plans aimed at a two-state solution.

The most important plan came from the Arab side. At its summit meeting in Beirut, on 28 March 2002, the Arab League unanimously adopted a Saudi plan that became known as the Arab Peace Initiative (API). This API offered Israel peace and normalization with all 22 members of the Arab League in return for agreeing to an independent Palestinian state on the West Bank and Gaza with a capital city in East Jerusalem. Sharon ignored the initiative and the following day he declared war on the Palestinians.

The defining moment of Sharon's premiership occurred on 29 March 2002. It was the first day of "Operation Defensive Shield", launched in retaliation against a Hamas suicide attack in Netanya which killed 29 Israelis and wounded close to 150. The IDF was ordered to reoccupy the big Palestinian cities on the West Bank which the Oslo II agreement had placed under the control of the Palestinian Authority. In many ways the operation was a replay of Sharon's 1982 war in Lebanon: it was directed against the Palestinian people; it stemmed from the same unjustified equation of all Palestinians with terrorists; it was based on the same denial of Palestinian national rights; it employed the same strategy of brutal and overwhelming military force; and it displayed the same disregard for public opinion, international law and UN resolutions. Sharon's real agenda was to put the clock back; to sweep away the remnants of Oslo; to cripple the Palestinian Authority; to inflict pain and misery on the Palestinians; to replace Yasser Arafat with a pliant, collaborationist leadership; and to extinguish all hope for a free Palestine. Sharon continued his "war on terror" until the end of his life.

XIII
— THE BARRIER IN THE WEST BANK —
— AND DISENGAGEMENT FROM GAZA —

Sharon was an ardent nationalist and a territorial expansionist who hoped to realise in his own lifetime the dream of Greater Israel. His ultimate aim was to redraw unilaterally Israel's borders, incorporating large swaths of occupied territory. Stage I was to build on the West Bank the so-called security barrier which the Palestinians call the apartheid wall. The wall is three times as long as the pre-1967 border and its primary purpose is actually land-grabbing. At some points the barrier deviates from the Green line to penetrate as much as 14 miles into the West Bank, a huge distance considering that the width of the West Bank ranges from 12.5 to 35 miles. Occasionally, the Israeli Supreme Court would rule in favour of Palestinian plaintiffs and order the re-routing of a section of the wall for which there was no obvious security reason but in most cases the IDF ignored the rulings.

Stage II in Sharon's grand strategy consisted of the unilateral disengagement from Gaza in August 2005. This involved the uprooting of 8,000 Jews and the dismantling of 22 settlements. Withdrawal from Gaza was presented to the world as a contribution to the Quartet's Roadmap (discussed below), but it was not. It was not a prelude to a peace deal with the Palestinian Authority but a prelude to further expansion on the West Bank. It was a unilateral Israeli move undertaken in what was seen as an Israeli national interest. The withdrawal from Gaza was part of the determined right-wing Zionist effort to prevent any progress towards an independent Palestinian state and to consolidate Israel's grip over the West Bank. In the year after the withdrawal, another 12,000 Israelis settled on the West Bank, further reducing the scope for an independent and territorially contiguous Palestinian state.

"The Roadmap for Peace" had been launched by the Quartet – America, Russia, the UN, and European

Union – on 30 April 2003, just over a month after the invasion of Iraq. Before the invasion, Tony Blair and George W. Bush had promised that after disarming Iraq, they would address the situation in Israel-Palestine. The roadmap was the long-awaited plan for resolving the Israeli-Palestinian conflict. It envisaged three phases leading to an independent Palestinian state alongside Israel by the end of 2005. The Palestinian leaders embraced the Roadmap with great alacrity. The Israeli attitude towards the roadmap was very different. Likud's ideology of a Greater Israel was simply incompatible with a genuine two-state solution. The expansion of settlements on the West Bank, the construction of the wall, and the destruction of the infrastructure of the Palestinian Authority were the three key elements in Likud's strategy for undermining the two-state solution. Sharon had fourteen reservations and he had the temerity to tell the Americans that he would present the roadmap to his government for consideration only if all fourteen amendments were included in the text. The Americans yielded. What the government eventually approved was not the Quartet's excellent roadmap but Sharon's emasculated version of it.[18] Another major international initiative to resolve the conflict was dead on arrival.

XIV
— EHUD OLMERT'S PEACE PLAN —

Disagreements on foreign policy within his own party drove Sharon to quit the Likud in November 2005 and form a new centrist party, Kadima, which means Forward in Hebrew. In January 2006, Sharon went into a coma from which he never recovered. He was succeeded as party leader and Prime Minister by his deputy, Ehud Olmert. Like Sharon, Olmert was a lifelong supporter of Greater Israel. Another element of continuity was the privileging of military force over diplomacy to achieve political objectives. Olmert only departed from Sharon's position by declaring publicly that the wall being built on the West Bank was not just a security measure but the marker of Israel's final border.

A police investigation of a series of corruption scandals led Olmert to announce, on 28 September 2008, his intention to resign – though he stayed on as a caretaker Prime Minister until May 2009. Olmert's main claim to be a peacemaker rested on an offer he made to Mahmoud Abbas, who was elected President of the State of Palestine and the Palestinian National Authority following Yasser Arafat's death in 2004. The meeting took place at Olmert's residence on 16 September 2008 – twelve days before he announced his resignation. After leaving office, Olmert made the offer public, claiming he had been willing to place the entire Old City under an international regime, divide Jerusalem, give the Palestinians 93.5 per cent of the West Bank with one-to-one swaps for the areas to be retained by Israel, and absorb 5,000 refugees inside the Green Line over a period of five years.

This was certainly a far-reaching proposal which addressed all the key permanent status issues. On Jerusalem and borders Olmert went well beyond what Ehud Barak had been prepared to offer. Yet Olmert's version of events in the last moments of 2008 is not entirely accurate. By his own account, Olmert demanded that Abbas meet him the very next day, together with map experts, in order to arrive at a final formula for the border between Palestine and Israel. Abbas asked to take the map with him to show to his experts. Olmert declined, fearing the map would be used not for closure but as the starting point in future negotiations. Abbas was not prepared to be rushed by the "caretaker" Prime Minister on a matter of such supreme importance and no meeting took place the following day. Olmert claimed that he never heard from Abbas again and that the most generous offer in Israel's history remained without a Palestinian answer. But Olmert and Abbas did negotiate subsequently, on more than one occasion. Far from ignoring the offer, the Palestinians requested clarifications which they did not receive. Palestinian doubts about Olmert's credibility were compounded by his deep unpopularity at home and his imminent political demise. He was a "lame-duck" Prime Minister and his constitutional authority to sign the agreement he proposed was wide open to challenge.

Even without the added complications of internal Israeli rivalries, Olmert's peace initiative faced an uncertain future. On a number of critical issues the two sides remained far apart. The Palestinians were not told whether Olmert's percentages for the West Bank included or excluded the Jewish neighbourhoods of Jerusalem. Nor was there agreement on the West Bank settlements to be removed: Olmert, for example, insisted on keeping Ariel which extended nearly halfway across the West Bank and this was not acceptable to the Palestinians. Olmert stipulated that IDF forces remain in the future Palestinian state and this too was not acceptable to the Palestinians. Olmert offered to allow 5,000 refugees to return to Israel; Abbas wanted 150,000 to return over a period of ten years. So even if his hold on power had been much firmer, it is far from certain that Olmert could have reached an overall settlement.

XV
— PALESTINIAN ELECTIONS —
— AND HAMAS VICTORY —

Mahmoud Abbas had serious domestic problems of his own following the decision by Hamas, the Islamic Resistance Movement, to enter the political process. In January 2006, free and fair elections were held in the West Bank and the Gaza Strip and Hamas unexpectedly won a decisive victory over Fatah. Fatah was the largest faction in the PLO and it became the dominant party in the post-Oslo Palestinian Authority with a majority in the Palestinian Legislative Council or parliament. Numerous international observers confirmed that the elections had been both peaceful and orderly. Hamas won a clear majority (74 out of 132 seats) in the Palestinian Legislative Council and it proceeded to form a government. Israel refused to recognise the new government; the United States and European Union followed its example. Israel resorted to economic warfare by withholding tax revenues while its western allies suspended direct aid to the Hamas-led Palestinian Authority.

With Saudi help the warring Palestinian factions managed to reconcile their differences. On 8 February 2007, Fatah and Hamas signed an agreement in Mecca to stop the clashes between their forces in Gaza and to form a government of national unity. They agreed to a system of power-sharing, with independents taking the key posts of foreign affairs, finance, and the interior. And they declared their readiness to negotiate a long-term ceasefire with Israel.

With external encouragement, Fatah began planning to stage a coup in order to recapture power. Hamas found out and pre-empted the Fatah coup with a violent seizure of power in Gaza in June 2007. At this point the Palestinian national movement became fractured, with Fatah ruling the West Bank and Hamas ruling the Gaza Strip. Israel responded to the Hamas move by declaring the Gaza Strip a "hostile territory". It also enacted a series of social, economic, and military measures designed to isolate and undermine Hamas. Most significant of these measures was the imposition of a blockade. The purpose of the blockade was purportedly to stop the transfer of weapons and military equipment to Gaza, but it also restricted the flow of food, fuel, and medical supplies to the civilian population.

The Palestinians bear the ultimate responsibility for the fragmentation of their national movement. The differences between the pragmatic Fatah and the theocratic Hamas are not superficial. But Israel actively worked to deepen the cleavage by a policy of divide and rule. Had Israel's aim been genuine peace with the Palestinians, a strong and unified Palestinian leadership would have helped to achieve it. Israel's real aim, however, was to maintain its dominant position in the occupied territories and to this end it pursued a policy of playing off the Palestinian parties against one another. Additionally, Israel played a part in undermining Palestinian democracy which at that time was the only democracy in the Arab world with the possible exception of Lebanon. One consequence of Israel's actions was to delegitimize President Abbas, to weaken his authority, and to make him appear like a collaborator.

Three months after announcing his resignation, on 27 December 2008, Ehud Olmert presided over the launch of a war on the Gaza Strip. The name given to the war was "Operation Cast Lead". Its undeclared political objectives were to drive Hamas out of power, cow the people of Gaza into submission, and crush the Islamic resistance to the Israeli occupation. The idea was to make life for the inhabitants of Gaza so unbearable that they would revolt against their Hamas rulers. Israel was determined to destroy Hamas because it knew that its leadership, unlike that of Fatah, would stand firm in defence of the national rights of the Palestinian people and refuse to settle for an emasculated Palestinian entity on Israel's terms.

Israeli propaganda presented the Gaza war as an act of self-defence to protect its civilians against

Hamas rocket attacks but in fact the rocket attacks had effectively ended in June 2008 as a result of an Egyptian-brokered truce between Hamas and Israel. The IDF wrecked the truce by launching, on 4 November, a raid into Gaza and killing six Hamas fighters. Israel also failed to honour its obligation under the terms of the ceasefire to lift the blockade of Gaza. In December, Hamas offered to renew the truce on the basis of the original terms but Israel ignored the offer and launched an invasion.

Operation Cast Lead was not a war in the usual sense of the word but a one-sided massacre. For twenty-two days, the IDF shot, shelled, and bombed Hamas targets and at the same time rained death and destruction on the defenceless population of Gaza. In its main aim of driving Hamas out of power Operation Cast Lead was a complete failure. While the military capability of Hamas was weakened, its political standing was enhanced. Internationally, the main consequence of the Gaza War was to generate a powerful wave of popular sympathy and support for the long-suffering Palestinians. As always, Israel claimed to be the victim of Palestinian violence, but the sheer asymmetry of power between the two sides left little room for doubt as to who was the real victim. This was indeed a conflict between David and Goliath but the Biblical image was inverted – a small and defenceless Palestinian David faced a heavily armed, overbearing Israeli Goliath. While leaving the basic political problem unresolved, the war thus contributed to Israel's political isolation on the world stage. At home, however, Operation Cast Lead enjoyed the support of 90 per cent of the population who saw it as a necessary act of self-defence. This high level of popular support translated into a further shift to the right in the parliamentary election held the following month.

XVI
— BLOCKING THE PATH —
— TO A PALESTINIAN STATE —

The Likud won the elections of 10 February 2009 and proceeded to form a right-wing government. Its election manifesto retained an explicit rejection of a Palestinian state. The new government was led by Benjamin Netanyahu, who had already demonstrated his nationalist credentials in his first term in office. Netanyahu and the majority of his ministers remained firmly wedded to the agenda of Greater Israel. In the worldview of Netanyahu, and that of his even more extreme religious-nationalist coalition partners, only Jews have historic rights over "Judea and Samaria". The main thrust of their policy was the expansion of Jewish settlements on the West Bank and the accelerated Judaization of East Jerusalem. They were determined that no progress should be made on any of the key issues in the Israeli-Palestinian conflict. Jerusalem, as always, lay at the heart of the dispute. By putting Jerusalem at the forefront of their expansionist agenda, ministers knowingly and deliberately blocked progress on any of the other "permanent status" issues.

Only at the rhetorical level was there any discernible change and this was made only grudgingly in response to strong pressure from the Obama Administration in the United States, which came to power in January 2009. In a speech at Bar-Ilan University, on 14 June 2009, Netanyahu endorsed for the first time a "demilitarized Palestinian state", provided that Jerusalem remained the undivided capital of Israel and provided the Palestinians recognized Israel as the nation state of the Jewish people and gave up the right of return of the 1948 refugees. He also claimed the right to "natural growth" in the existing Jewish settlements on the West Bank while their permanent status was being negotiated.

Most observers, however, inside as well as outside the Likud, doubted that Netanyahu meant what he said. Senior Palestinian official, Saeb Erekat, said that the Bar-Ilan speech had "closed the door to permanent status negotiations" due to its declarations on Jerusalem, refugees and settlements. Most foreign leaders thought that Netanyahu's speech did not live up to what was agreed on by the international community as a starting point for achieving a just and lasting peace in the region.

By blocking the path to a Palestinian state, Netanyahu's government strained relations with the Obama administration and made a mockery of the American-sponsored peace process. In the early months of his first administration, Obama correctly identified settlement expansion as the main obstacle to a two-state solution. In his Cairo speech, on 4 June 2009, he made it clear that "The United States does not accept the legitimacy of continued Israeli settlements".[19] During his first term in office, Obama had three confrontations with Netanyahu over the demand for a complete settlement freeze, but nothing came of it.

In response to pressure from the US, the Israeli government did announce, on 25 November 2009, a partial ten-month freeze on settlement construction. But by insisting on excluding East Jerusalem altogether and going forward with the 3,000 housing units already approved for the rest of the West Bank, the government turned the settlement freeze into little more than a cosmetic gesture. The announcement had no significant effect on actual housing and infrastructure construction in and around the settlements. In September 2010 Netanyahu agreed to enter direct talks, mediated by the Obama administration. But toward the end of the month the ten-month partial freeze expired, and the government approved new construction in the West Bank and East Jerusalem.

In an effort to persuade Netanyahu to extend the ten-month partial settlement freeze by sixty days, Obama offered a long-term security agreement, a squadron of F-35 fighter jets worth $3 billion, and the use of the American veto on the UN Security Council to defeat any resolution that was not to Israel's liking. Secure in the knowledge that aid to Israel is determined not by the President but by Congressional appropriations and that Congress is overwhelmingly pro-Israeli, Netanyahu rejected Obama's offer.

XVII
— THE KERRY ROUND OF PEACE TALKS —

The Palestinians responded to Netanyahu's moves by suspending their participation in the peace talks and insisting on two conditions for returning to the conference table: a complete freeze on construction activity in the occupied territories, and the 4 June 1967 lines as the basis for negotiations.

The diplomatic deadlock persisted until July 2013, when John Kerry, who served as the US Secretary of

State during Obama's second term, persuaded the two sides to restart talks with the goal of achieving a "final status agreement" within nine months. Netanyahu categorically rejected the two basic Palestinian conditions, but he agreed to resume peace talks without any pre-conditions. In general, he considered peace talks to be an American interest, not an Israeli one. On the other hand, he did not wish to incur the opprobrium of being a peace refusnik. The Palestinians knew that the Israeli government was not serious about negotiations because it was unwilling to end the occupation or to acknowledge Palestinian national rights. They also feared that, as in the two decades after Oslo, Israel would exploit peace talks that go nowhere slowly in order to appease the international community, dig itself deeper into their land, and break it into isolated enclaves over which the Palestinian Authority would have no real power. Palestinian negotiators only agreed to join in the talks to avoid being cast as the unwilling party. In the first three months of the talks Netanyahu instructed his negotiators to adopt hard-line positions while refusing to state his ultimate objective. His ultimate endgame remained Greater Israel.

John Kerry was an energetic and assiduous peacemaker. He was also a true friend of Israel. He tried to bring about an end to occupation not to punish Israel but as a way of enabling Israel to preserve both its

Jewish and democratic character. In his first year as Secretary of State, Kerry made no less than ten trips to the region in a relentless effort to nudge the two parties closer to an agreement. Yet the peace talks he led with such conviction produced no positive results.

Kerry's sincere effort to save Israel from itself earned him nothing but ingratitude and abuse. Moshe Ya'alon, Israel's former Minister of Defence, told the mass-circulation *Yediot Aharonot* in January 2014: "Secretary of State John Kerry — who comes here determined, who operates from an incomprehensible obsession and a sense of messianism – can't teach me anything about the conflict with the Palestinians."[20] Ya'alon also dismissed Kerry's security plan for the Jordan Valley as "not worth the paper it is printed on". "All that can 'save us' is for John Kerry to win a Nobel Prize and leave us in peace", said Ya'alon.

Kerry for his part, in a major speech he gave in his last month in office, spoke with unprecedented clarity and harshness about the Israeli government and the Prime Minister whom he accused of thwarting peace in the Middle East by his settlement policy. The speech also gave public voice to the Obama administration's long-held concern that Israel was heading towards international isolation and was condemning itself to a future of low-level, perpetual warfare with the Palestinians.

XVIII
— PALESTINIAN UNITY —
— AND ISRAEL'S —
— MILITARY ESCALATIONS IN GAZA —

Diplomatic standstill was accompanied by the escalation of IDF military assaults on Gaza. In November 2012, the Israeli government ordered the extra-judicial assassination of Ahmed Jabari, the chief of Hamas's military wing in Gaza, while he was reviewing the terms of a proposal for a permanent truce from Israeli peace activist Gershon Baskin. The timing of the assassination suggests a deliberate attempt to pre-empt the threat of a diplomatic solution. At any rate, Israel broke the informal ceasefire to launch Operation Pillar of Defence in November 2012, its second major military operation against Gaza following disengagement. In eight days of intense aerial bombardment, 132 Palestinians were killed. The operation ended with a ceasefire brokered by Egypt. This specified that Israel and the Palestinian factions would stop all hostilities and that Israel would open the border crossings to allow the movement of people and the transfer of goods. During the three months that followed the ceasefire, only two mortar shells were fired from Gaza. The IDF, on the other hand, failed to end the closure, made regular incursions into Gaza, strafed Palestinian farmers working in their fields near the border, and fired at fishing boats inside Gaza's territorial waters.

Hamas for its part continued to abide by the ceasefire for another eighteen months. But in April 2014 it committed what Israel considered an unforgivable transgression: it reached a reconciliation agreement with Fatah and proceeded, on 2 June, to form a unity government with responsibility to govern the Gaza Strip as well as the West Bank. The unity government produced by the accord was in fact remarkably moderate both in its composition and in its policies. It was a government of Fatah officials, technocrats, and independents. To escape isolation and bankruptcy, Hamas handed over power to the Fatah-dominated, pro-Western Palestinian Authority in Ramallah. The unity government explicitly accepted the three conditions of the Quartet for receiving Western aid: recognition of Israel; respect for past agreements; and renunciation of violence.

Nevertheless, Netanyahu immediately denounced the new government as a vote not for peace but for terror and threatened Palestinian President Mahmoud Abbas with a boycott. For Netanyahu any sign of Palestinian unity or moderation posed a threat to the existing order. Israel therefor responded with economic warfare. It prevented the 43,000 civil servants in Gaza from moving from the Hamas payroll to that of the Ramallah government and it tightened the siege around Gaza's borders thereby nullifying the two main benefits of the merger.

Israel followed up with a military assault on Gaza on 8 July 2014 that it portrayed as an act of self-defence in response to Hamas rockets launched against its civilian population. But these rocket attacks were themselves a response to a violent crackdown against Hamas supporters on the West Bank following the abduction and murder of three Israeli teenagers on 12 June 2014. Netanyahu stated that Hamas was responsible for the abduction and that Hamas would pay the price. He could produce no evidence, however, to support the charge because there was no evidence. The murders were committed by a lone cell without the knowledge of the Hamas leadership.

Operation Protective Edge was the third Israeli attack on Gaza in six years, the fiercest in the firepower it deployed, and the most devastating in its impact. The aerial and naval bombardment of the enclave was followed by a large-scale land invasion. The toll on the Palestinian side after 50 days of intermittent fighting was over 2,200 dead, mostly civilians, including 577 children. On the Israeli side the death toll was 67 soldiers and five civilians.

Behind Israel's ever-changing stated military objectives for the war lurked undeclared geopolitical aims.

First and foremost was the desire to reverse the trend towards Palestinian reconciliation and to undermine the unity government. This was in keeping with the policy of "divide and rule" and of keeping the two branches of the Palestinian family geographically separate. Then there was the urge to punish the people of Gaza for electing Hamas and for continuing to support it in defiance of Israel's repeated warnings. The overriding aim, however, was to defeat the struggle for Palestinian independence and to maintain the colonial status quo.

The late Israeli sociologist Baruch Kimmerling coined a word to describe this policy: "politicide". Politicide is defined in a book with that title as "a process that has, as its ultimate goal, the dissolution of the Palestinians' existence as a legitimate social, political, and economic entity."[21] Applied to this context, politicide means denying the Palestinians any independent political existence in Palestine. The idea is to make the Palestinians so vulnerable, divided, and exhausted by the struggle for physical survival that they would cease to constitute a coherent political community capable of asserting its right to sovereignty on even a fraction of historic Palestine.

It was not only rocket attacks that Israel does not tolerate but also peaceful protest. On 30 March 2018, a campaign of protest was launched by Palestinian activists in the Gaza Strip along the perimeter fence with Israel. It was called "The Great March of Return". The protesters demanded the UN-sanctioned right of return of the 1948 Palestinian refugees and their descendants to their homes in present-day Israel and the lifting of the Israeli blockade of Gaza. Underlying the protest was a Palestinian shift away from violence towards non-violent forms of resistance. Israel's response to the demonstrations, however, was swift and savage and included the use of live ammunition against unarmed civilians, killing hundreds.

XIX
— THE "UNITY INTIFADA" —

In May 2021 there was another major escalation of hostilities between Israel and Palestinian armed groups in Gaza. Israeli police provoked the crisis by raiding the Al Aqsa mosque in the Muslim Quarter of the Old City of Jerusalem on 6 May, manhandling worshippers, and firing rubber-tipped bullets and stun grenades at protesters. The attack came during the holy month of Ramadan when tensions often run high. Another cause for the unrest was a march by far-right-wing Israelis through the Muslim Quarter of the Old City on Jerusalem Day, an annual event to mark the capture of the city in June 1967. Hamas demanded that Israel remove its security forces from the Al Aqsa mosque compound by 10 May. Minutes after the deadline passed, it fired more than 150 rockets into Israel from Gaza. Israel retaliated by launching airstrikes into the Gaza Strip on the same day. The Israeli government continued to restrict access to the mosque and a popular plaza where young people like to congregate; it did nothing to de-escalate the crisis. Eleven days of clashes left 227 Palestinians dead, including 64 children, and 1,000 injured, while 12 Israelis, including two children, were killed by rocket fire.

The catalyst for the flare-up of violence was recent efforts by Israel to evict Palestinian families from the Sheikh Jarrah neighbourhood in East Jerusalem. This became a rallying cry for the Palestinian protesters who saw it as ethnic cleansing. Evictions were accompanied by house demolitions. According to the UN Office for the Coordination of Humanitarian Affairs, 6,825 Palestinian owned structures were demolished because of a lack of permits over the course of the previous decade. As a result, 9,662 people, including thousands of children, were forcibly displaced. The threatened displacements in Sheikh Jarrah and other Jerusalem neighbourhoods was not an anomaly, but part of a larger pattern of Palestinian dispossession.

One noteworthy feature of this crisis was the unusually high number of Palestinian citizens of Israel who protested in solidarity with Gaza following the airstrikes. The Palestinians of the West Bank, East Jerusalem, the Gaza Strip, and Israel itself appeared united in confronting the oppressor. It was this remarkable unity that lent to this round of violence the name of "the unity intifada". Once again, the inter-communal, as opposed to the inter-state, aspect of the conflict came to the fore.

Taken together the five outbursts of violence, or mini-wars, in Gaza reflect a profoundly militaristic Israeli outlook and a colonial mindset. Israeli generals talk about their recurrent military incursions into Gaza as "mowing the lawn". By this they mean weakening Hamas, degrading its military capability, and impairing its capacity to govern. This operative metaphor implies a task that has to be performed regularly and mechanically and with no end in sight. It also alludes to indiscriminate slaughter of civilians and inflicting the kind of damage on the civilian infrastructure that takes several years to repair. Under this rubric, there is no lasting political solution: the next war is always just a matter of time.

XX
— THE ABRAHAM ACCORDS —

At the inter-state level of the Arab-Israeli conflict Israel scored notable achievements. In the second half of 2020 four Arab states (the United Arab Emirates, Bahrain, Sudan, and Morocco) signed the so-called Abraham Accords, normalising relations with Israel. None of these states have a border with Israel and none of them is officially at war with Israel. Nevertheless, the accords were hailed as a historic turning point in the Arab-Israeli conflict. There is no question that the accords represented a major diplomatic victory for Netanyahu. For decades Netanyahu has been arguing, against the conventional wisdom, that it would be possible to normalise relations with the Gulf states without the need to resolve the conflict with the Palestinians first. This is what he calls the outside-in approach: developing open diplomatic, economic, and strategic relations with the Gulf states in order to isolate and weaken the Palestinians and compel them to settle the conflict on Israel's terms.

Arguably, however, the Abraham Accords do not merit the grand epithet of "historic" because they do not touch the root cause of the Arab-Israeli conflict. The Palestinian problem is the core and it has been the central issue in Arab politics since 1945. Until very recently, there was a broad consensus in the Arab world in favour of an independent Palestinian state alongside Israel as the price of peace with the Jewish state. This consensus found its most authoritative expression in the Arab Peace Initiative, adopted unanimously by the Arab League summit conference in Beirut in March 2002. As noted earlier, the API offered Israel peace and normalisation with all 22 members of the Arab League in return for agreeing to an independent Palestinian state on the West Bank and the Gaza Strip with a capital city in East Jerusalem. Israel rejected the offer at the time and has continued to ignore it ever since.

What all four Abraham Accords have in common is that they represent peace on Israel's terms; in other words, peace for peace rather than land for peace. Israel has not had to pay any price for normalisation with the four signatories of the Abraham Accords. Palestinians in the West Bank and the Gaza Strip remain under military occupation. The Palestinian response has been uniformly hostile, denouncing the deal as a betrayal of the Palestinian struggle for liberation and even as a stab in the back.

XXI
— CONCLUSION —

The beginning of wisdom for the international community is to acknowledge that it has failed to discharge its moral and legal obligations towards the Palestinian people and to learn from its mistakes. The first major mistake was the incorporation of the Balfour Declaration in the League of Nations Mandate for Palestine. This enabled the Zionist movement to embark on the gradual takeover of the country at the expense of the Palestinians. The second major mistake was the 1947 UN partition resolution which made war between Arabs and Jews inevitable. The circumstances surrounding the establishment of the the state of Israel and the 1948 Arab-Israeli war are the subject of an ongoing controversy between traditional Zionist historians and revisionist or "new historians" of whom the present author is one. But there is no denying the fact that the establishment of Israel involved a monumental injustice to the Palestinian people.

Zionism was not simply about creating an independent Jewish state in Palestine but about extending its borders as far as possible and reducing the number of Arabs within its borders. In 1917 the Jews owned two percent of the land; in 1947 they owned seven percent of the land; the UN allocated to the Jews 55 percent of mandatory Palestine; by the end of the 1948 war the Israelis had conquered 78 percent of the territory, and by the end of the June 1967 war they had effective control of 100 percent of mandatory Palestine. Initially, Israel claimed that the occupation was temporary, pending a political settlement of the conflict. But its own diplomatic intransigence frustrated the international quest for a settlement. In the meantime, Israel kept expanding its illegal colonies on occupied Palestinian territory. It withdrew unilaterally from Gaza in 2005 but it continued to consolidate and to deepen its colonial project on the West Bank. Today there are around 670,000 Jewish settlers on the West Bank. From today's perspective it is therefore fair to say that Israel is addicted to occupation.

There is the broadest international consensus behind the idea of a two-state solution to the Israeli-Palestinian conflict. Once upon a time this was a viable option but Israel has killed it by blockading Gaza, denying access between Gaza and the West Bank, and planting civilian settlements and military bases across the length and breadth of the West Bank. It has become fashionable to say that the two-state solution is dead because of the settlements. The present author would argue that the two-state solution was never born because no Israeli government has ever offered a settlement based on the 1967 lines. Yet in some corners of the international community, the two-state solution continues to serve as a convenient slogan long after it has ceased to be a serious policy option.

The international community therefore urgently needs to develop a new understanding of the situation in Israel-Palestine. It needs a new narrative for addressing the relations between Israel and the Palestinians, one based on the real facts of this tragic situation, international law, the norms of civilized international behaviour, and common human decency. It also needs to hold Israel to account for its illegal practices, excessive use of military force, ethnic cleansing, and war crimes. The UN has passed countless resolutions critical of Israel's actions but these resolutions have had no discernible effect. The conclusion to be drawn from this record is clear: as long as there is no price to pay, Israel will continue to act with impunity.

The basic problem here is Zionist settler colonialism so the solution must involve an end to the occupation and restoring to the Palestinian people their natural right to national self-determination. To say that Israel is guilty of the international crime of Apartheid, as many major human rights organisations have done in their reports in recent years, may be accurate but not enough. The current Israeli Apartheid regime can only be properly understood in the historical context of Zionist settler-colonialism.[22]

This piece was originally published as "Annex 2" to "Legal Consequences Arising From the Policies and Practices of Israel in the Occupied Palestinian Territory, Including East Jerusalem (Request For Advisory Opinion)", Written Statement of the State of Qatar, International Court of Justice.

— 2024 —

BENJAMIN NETANYAHU'S WAR AGAINST PALESTINIAN STATEHOOD

There are two widely held beliefs about Benjamin Netanyahu, Israel's longest serving prime minister and the architect of the war on Gaza that followed the Hamas attack on southern Israel on 7 October 2023. One is that he is deliberately prolonging this war out of narrow political and legal self-preservation. In November 2019, Netanyahu was officially indicted for breach of trust, accepting bribes, and fraud. As long as he is prime minister, he does not have to stand trial. Once he ceases to be prime minister, his trial will resume and, if found guilty, he may end up in jail. In political terms, too, Netanyahu is probably a dead man walking. Once the fighting stops, the pressure will increase for a public inquiry and for the holding of a new election, an election that the public opinion polls predict would end in a catastrophic defeat for Netanyahu and his party. To save his skin and to stay out of prison, so the argument goes, he is deliberately prolonging the war and resisting all the UN and other calls for a ceasefire.

The other common belief is that Netanyahu is prolonging the Gaza war because he is in hock to Israel's ultranationalist far-right. The Likud-led coalition formed by Netanyahu in December 2022 includes two far-right, proto-fascist parties with notoriously Islamophobic as well as homophobic leaders. The minister of national security is Itamar Ben-Gvir, the leader of "Jewish Power", who was considered unfit to serve in the Israeli army on account of his extreme political views, and who was later convicted for inciting racism and supporting a terrorist group. At his home in the violent settler enclave of Kiryat Arba, near Hebron, Ben-Gvir used to hang a portrait of the American Jewish settler Baruch Goldstein, who had massacred 29 Arab worshippers in the Ibrahimi Mosque in Hebron in 1994. The minister of finance, Bezalel Smotrich, the leader of "Religious Zionism", is another settler who openly advocates the ethnic cleansing of the Palestinian territories. Both parties encourage settler violence against Arabs, advocate the formal annexation of the West Bank, and support the resettlement of Jews in the Gaza Strip after the expulsion of its Palestinian inhabitants.

Various considerations no doubt affect Netanyahu's decisions on matters of war and peace; personal interest and political calculation are probably prominent among them. It is patently obvious that Netanyahu is a selfish, mendacious, and a thoroughly cynical politician, who is prone to placing his personal advantage above the good of his country. It is also true that, with its inclusion of the Jewish Power and Religious Zionism parties, Netanyahu's coalition is the most right-wing, xenophobic, messianic, apocalyptic, and overtly racist government in Israel's history. But on the other hand, as will be argued here, these explanations for Netanyahu's Gaza policy obscure as much as they reveal. Netanyahu is not a moderate right-wing politician who has fallen among hawks. He himself is a far-right, racist Jewish supremacist; a devoted proponent of Greater Israel whose life's mission has been to prevent the establishment of an independent Palestinian state. The one consistent theme in Netanyahu's long and chequered political career has been his ideological commitment to an exclusive Jewish state in all of Mandatory Palestine from the river to the sea. In the context of this long war on Palestinian statehood, the Gaza onslaught is not an opportunistic aberration, but a logical terminus.

— FOUNDATIONS —

Benjamin Netanyahu grew up in a fiercely nationalistic Jewish home. His father, Benzion Netanyahu, was a historian of Spanish Jewry; an adviser to Ze'ev Jabotinsky, the founder of Revisionist Zionism; and the editor of the Revisionists' daily newspaper *Ha-Yarden*. Jabotinsky was the spiritual father of the Israeli right. He and his party were the main ideological opposition to the mainstream socialist Labour Zionism. The Revisionists advocated a revision of the "practical Zionism" of David Ben-Gurion and Chaim Weizmann. Whereas "practical Zionism" called for Jewish settlement of *Eretz Yisrael* (the Land of Israel), the Revisionists insisted on the Jewish right to sovereignty over the whole of Mandatory Palestine and Transjordan. They were territorial maximalists who rejected the partition of Palestine and laid claim to both sides of the Jordan River, including the east bank which is present day Jordan. The fact that no Jews lived on the east bank of the Jordan made no difference to them.

For Benzion Netanyahu "Jewish history was in large measure a history of holocausts". The core of his belief was that Jews have always been and will always be persecuted by all those around them. To his way of thinking, peace with Arabs was a dangerous illusion because Arabs could not be trusted. He was convinced that, whatever they may say, Arabs remained determined to destroy the Jewish state. From his father Benjamin inherited the notion of Us versus Them, of a preordained and inescapable conflict between Arabs and Jews, and the fear that Jewish history would come to an end unless the Jews could defend themselves. "In the Middle East", he said in 2018, "there is a simple truth: There is no place for the weak."[23] The foundational axiom of both father and son was that military power was the only solution to the Jewish predicament, and the only instrument for attaining and preserving Jewish independence in the ancestral homeland.

Jabotinsky also believed in the primacy of force. In 1923, he published an article under the title "On the Iron Wall (We and the Arabs)". If any one document deserves to be called the bible of Zionist foreign policy, this is it. Its author argued that "there is not even the slightest hope of ever obtaining" a political agreement with the Arab inhabitants of Palestine, because Zionist and Arab aspirations were fundamentally opposed: "Every indigenous people will resist alien settlers as long as they see any hope of ridding themselves of the danger of foreign settlement." From this he concluded that the Zionist goal of an independent Jewish state in Palestine could only be achieved unilaterally and by military force: behind an iron wall of Jewish military power.

For Jabotinsky, however, the iron wall was not an end in itself but a means to an end. It was intended to compel the Arabs to abandon any hope of defeating the Jews. Once this happened, Jabotinsky predicted, the Arab hardliners would be discredited and the moderates would come to the fore, open to compromise. Then and only then should the Zionists proceed to the second stage of the strategy: negotiations with the local Arabs about their status and rights in Palestine. In other words, Jewish military strength was to pave the way to an eventual political settlement with the Arab residents of Palestine. Jabotinsky did not spell out the endgame but what he appeared to envisage was limited autonomy for the Arabs, under Jewish rule, rather than full sovereignty.

Benjamin Netanyahu was elected leader of the Likud in March 1993. That year he also published a book that set out his political creed, *A Place Among the Nations: Israel and the World*. The book was inspired by the teaching of Ze'ev Jabotinsky and Benzion Netanyahu. It presented the most embattled possible version of the history of Zionism and the State of Israel. Its central theme was the right of the Jewish people to the whole Land of Israel, including Judea and Samaria – the biblical names for the West Bank. History was rewritten from a Revisionist perspective in order to demonstrate that it was not the Jews who usurped the land from the Arabs, but the Arabs who usurped the land from the Jews. Britain was portrayed as no friend of the Jews and the chapter on the British Mandate in Palestine was simply called "The Betrayal". The whole world was portrayed as hostile to the Jewish state and anti-semitism was said to lie at the root of this hostility.

Netanyahu viewed Israel's relations with the Arab world as one of permanent conflict, as a never-ending struggle between the forces of light and the forces of darkness. His image of the Arabs was consistently and comprehensively negative and it did not admit the possibility of diversity or change. His book did not contain a single positive reference to the Arabs, their history or their culture. Arab regimes were portrayed as ready practitioners of violence against the citizens of their own countries and across their borders: "Violence is ubiquitous in the political life of all the Arab countries. It is the primary method of dealing with opponents, both foreign and domestic, both Arab and non-Arab." In addition, Netanyahu claimed that "international terrorism is the quintessential Middle East export" and that "its techniques everywhere are those of the Arab regimes and organizations that invented it".[24] The Arab world was described as deeply hostile towards the West and to the western notion of democracy. Netanyahu conceded that a few Arab rulers were friendly to the United States but warned against the delusion that this reflected the real sentiments of the Arab masses. Such rulers, in his view, "frequently represent only a thin crust lying over a volatile Arab and Islamic society".[25]

Much of Netanyahu's vehemence and venom was reserved for the Palestinians. He launched a fierce assault on the notion that the Palestinian problem constituted the core and heart of the Middle East conflict. For him the Palestinian problem was not a genuine problem but an artificially manufactured one. He denied that the Palestinians had a right to national self-determination and argued that the primary cause of tension in the Middle East was inter-Arab rivalry. For Netanyahu compromise with the PLO was completely out of the question because its goal was the destruction of the State of Israel, and this goal allegedly defined its very essence. This, in his view, was what distinguished the PLO from the Arab states, even the most radical ones. While these states would clearly prefer to see Israel disappear, their national life was not dependent on Israel's destruction: "But the PLO was different. It was constitutionally tied to the idea of Israel's liquidation. Remove that idea and you have no PLO."[26]

Chapter 7 in Netanyahu's book is called "The Wall", alluding to Jabotinsky's 1923 article. In this chapter Netanyahu expanded on the military value of dominating the heights of the (Syrian) Golan and the mountains of (Palestinian) Judea and Samaria. He buttressed his arguments with maps that highlighted Israel's geostrategic vulnerability. Over and over again, he quoted a Pentagon Plan, dated 18 June 1967, in support of his argument that for Israel to protect her cities, she must retain military control over virtually all the territory west of the Jordan River. There was no mention of the many Israeli generals who took the view that control over the West Bank was not a military necessity. Netanyahu's conclusion was that the whole of western Palestine constituted one integral territorial unit: "To subdivide this land into two unstable, insecure nations, to try to defend what is indefensible, is to invite disaster. Carving Judea and Samaria out of Israel means carving up Israel."[27]

The book espoused Jewish sovereignty across Greater Israel, imposed by military force against an Arab populace it depicted as implacably and existentially hostile. It showed that Netanyahu was the Revisionist movement and Benzion's faithful son. These entrenched ideological commitments would underpin Netanyahu's consistent political project: to consolidate Jewish domination, thwart diplomacy with Palestinian leaders, and prevent a Palestinian state.

— POWER —

The iron wall was the basic Zionist strategy in the confrontation with the Arabs, under both Labour and right-wing parties, from the 1920s onwards. Itzhak Rabin, the leader of the Labour Party, was the first Israeli prime minister to move from stage one to stage two of the strategy of the iron wall. He did so by concluding the Oslo I Accord with the Palestine Liberation Organisation (PLO) on 13 September 1993, followed by a sequel two years later. In both cases he negotiated from a position of unassailable strength which enabled him to more or less dictate the terms to the other side. Under the first accord, the PLO gave up its claim to 78 percent of Mandatory Palestine in the hope of securing an independent state alongside Israel, on the Gaza Strip and the West Bank with a capital city in East Jerusalem. The accord itself did not mention, let alone promise, an independent Palestinian state at the end of the five-year transition period. Yet, given the scale of the concessions made by the PLO, eventual independence on a fifth of its patrimony was not an unreasonable expectation.

Netanyahu's book, *A Place Among the Nations*, was published six months before the Oslo I Accord was signed. The agreement did precisely what Netanyahu had been warning against: it recognized the PLO, it conceded that the Palestinian people had a legitimate right to self-government, and it began the process of partitioning western Palestine. The Oslo II accord, signed in Washington on 28 September 1995 and approved by the Knesset by a narrow majority a week later, represented another significant step on the stony road to peace. Netanyahu, then leader of the opposition, led an inflammatory campaign that did not just criticise the agreement but also delegitimised the democratically elected government that had negotiated it. In a notorious rally of the "nationalist camp" in Zion Square in Jerusalem, he whipped up the crowd to a veritable frenzy. In the crowd were fascist thugs who held up a fake picture of Rabin in an SS uniform. Netanyahu did not call them to order. On the contrary, he played a leading role in the campaign of incitement that culminated in the assassination of Rabin by a Jewish fanatic. At Rabin's funeral, Leah, his widow, refused to shake Netanyahu's outstretched hand. But she received Yasser Arafat at her home when he came to convey his condolences. Arafat's handshake, she explained, symbolised for her the hope for peace, whereas Netanyahu's handshake represented the rejection of peace with the Palestinians.

In the lead up to the elections of May 1996, following Rabin's assassination and the brief premiership of Shimon Peres, Netanyahu repeatedly denounced the Oslo accords as incompatible both with Israel's security and with the right of the Jewish people to the whole Land of Israel. The Likud won the election of May 1996 against the Labour Party by a margin of less than one percent. But on the morrow of this slenderest of electoral victories, Netanyahu declared war on the peace policy of his slain predecessor. Netanyahu came to power with the self-appointed mission of subverting the Oslo accords and preventing the establishment of a Palestinian state. He spent his first term in office, from 1996 to 1999, in a largely successful attempt to freeze, subvert, and ultimately undermine the fragile peace agreements with the Palestinians. The Oslo accords raised a fundamental question: was Israel ready to accept a Palestinian national entity alongside it? To this question Netanyahu gave an emphatically negative answer.

Throughout his five subsequent terms in office, Netanyahu remained fixated on the first part of Jabotinsky's iron wall strategy – on accumulating more and more military power – while avoiding stage two: serious negotiations with the PLO to find a political solution to the conflict. The official policy guidelines of his first government were pure ethnocentric nationalism. The chapter on education promised to cultivate Jewish values and to put the Bible, the Hebrew language, and the history of the Jewish people at the centre of the school curriculum. The foreign policy guidelines expressed firm opposition to a Palestinian state, to the Palestinian refugees' right of return, and to the dismantling of Jewish settlements in the occupied territories. The assertion of Israeli sovereignty over the whole of Jerusalem was explicit and categorical. So was the commitment to continue developing settlements as "an expression of Zionist fulfilment". The guidelines side-lined altogether Israel's obligations under the Oslo accords.

On 14 June 2009, in his second term in office, Netanyahu gave a speech at Bar-Ilan University in which he grudgingly accepted a "Demilitarized Palestinian State". This was hailed as a reversal of his opposition to an independent Palestinian state. But he only made the speech under strong American pressure, and the change of direction was more apparent than real. In the first place, Netanyahu placed conditions – demilitarisation, no Palestinian capital city in East Jerusalem, no Jewish settlement removed from the West Bank – that precluded genuine Palestinian sovereignty. At the level of rhetoric, then, Netanyahu's speech was consistent with the position taken by his director of communications and policy planning, David Bar-Illan, back in 1996. Asked whether the Netanyahu government opposed the idea of a Palestinian state, Bar-Illan replied: "Semantics don't matter. If Palestinian sovereignty is limited enough so that we feel safe, call it fried chicken."[28] In practice, meanwhile, Netanyahu remained a stalwart rejectionist on the question of Palestinian statehood. The litmus test of an authentic commitment to a two-state solution is a freeze of settlement activity in the occupied Palestinian territories while negotiations are in progress. Under Netanyahu's leadership, however, settlement expansion went ahead at full tilt, especially in and around Jerusalem.

In 2013 and 2014, Netanyahu obstructed, and ultimately derailed US-sponsored peace talks with the PLO. US Secretary of State John Kerry was a firm friend of Israel. He wanted to resolve the conflict in order to enable Israel to preserve its character as a Jewish and democratic state. In his first year in office, Kerry made no less than eleven trips to the region in search of a breakthrough. Netanyahu, however, was not a genuine partner for peace. He considered the proposed peace process as an American interest, not an Israeli one. So he entered the negotiations in bad faith and employed characteristically devious tactics to ensure their failure. In private, he told Kerry that he accepted the two basic Palestinian conditions for resuming the talks: a freeze on settlement activity; and the 1967 lines as the starting point for negotiations. But after a year of negotiating in bad faith, Netanyahu publicly went back on his private assurances, making it clear that the shuttle was an exercise in futility. Publicly humiliated and deeply disappointed, Kerry announced the end of his mission. He blamed Israeli settlement expansion for the diplomatic failure and warned that the Netanyahu government's policies were leading toward an apartheid state.

During the 2015 election campaign, Netanyahu brought his rhetoric back into line with his real stand on Palestinian statehood. He vowed that, if re-elected, no Palestinian state would emerge on his watch. His party, the Likud, had consistently rejected the idea of an independent Palestinian state. Its 1977 platform, the year it first came to power, opened with the declaration that "the right of the Jewish people to the land of Israel is eternal and indisputable and is linked with the right to security and peace; therefore, Judea and Samaria will not be handed to any foreign administration; between the Sea and the Jordan there will only be Israeli sovereignty." The "Peace & Security" chapter of the 1999 Likud Party platform could not have been more explicit. "The Government of Israel", it stated, "flatly rejects the establishment of a Palestinian Arab state west of the Jordan river." In all subsequent elections the Likud strictly adhered to this intransigent, peace-spurning, fundamentalist position.

This record cannot be reconciled with the idea that Netanyahu holds the balance between the centre-right and the far-right elements in his government. The truth of the matter is that he shares the profoundly illiberal, anti-Palestinian, and Jewish-supremacist views of his far-right coalition partners. His political brand is a noxious blend of anti-democratic, racist-supremacist, and ultranationalist populism. It was he who had introduced the Nation-State Law in July 2018, four years before he formed an alliance with the religious-Zionist parties. Israel has no written constitution, but it has Basic Laws that define the character of the state. This particular Basic Law turned Israel officially into an apartheid state by declaring that "the right to exercise national self-determination in the State of Israel is unique to the Jewish people." What this implied was that even if the Palestinian citizens of Israel became the majority, only Jews would have the right to national self-determination. This is the very definition of apartheid: two classes of citizens and no equality.

The policy guidelines of the 2022 coalition government are even more extreme than the Basic Law of 2018. They open with the stark statement that "the Jewish people have an exclusive and inalienable right to all parts of the Land of Israel." The Nation-State Law refers to the Jewish people's right to national self-determination within the pre-1967 borders; the 2022 policy guidelines assert this right over the whole Land of Israel. This amounts to a flat denial of any Palestinian right to national self-determination anywhere between the river and the sea. This denial should come as no surprise. As this chapter has shown, Netanyahu's commitment to a Greater Israel is long-standing. He has never believed in trading "land for peace" with the Palestinians. He advocates instead "peace for peace". According to this formula, Israel can make peace with the Arab states without making any concessions on the Palestinian issue. The Abraham Accords he signed in 2020 with four Arab states – the United Arab Emirates, Bahrain, Morocco, and Sudan – seemed to vindicate his approach. They certainly represented a major foreign policy triumph for Netanyahu. But they were predicated on the assumption that the Palestinian people could be side-lined indefinitely.

— GAZA —

The Hamas attack on Israel on 7 October 2023, in which 1,200 Israelis, mostly civilians, were killed and 250 taken hostage, disproved this assumption and shattered the entire policy built round it. It was the first time that Hamas fighters broke down the fence around Gaza and attacked inside Israel's own territory, targeting military bases as well as civilian settlements, including revellers at a musical festival. Members of Islamic Jihad, a small militant organisation, and unaffiliated individuals joined in the violent cross-border raid. The Gaza Strip had often been compared to an open-air prison. On this occasion the angry inmates broke out of the prison and went on a killing spree, committing horrible atrocities in the process. This was an unprecedented and catastrophic Israeli security failure. For decades the Israeli public had been taught that might is right. The Hamas attack exposed this lie but that was not the lesson that the Israeli public drew. It is no exaggeration to say that the whole of Israeli society was unhinged by the trauma of 7 October. The trauma unleashed a tsunami of hatred towards the perpetrators and loud calls for revenge. Revenge followed on a massive scale and out of all proportion to the attack. Revenge, however, is not a policy.

Domestic anger was also directed at Netanyahu, but he, as is his wont, refused to admit any personal responsibility for the egregious intelligence and security failures. Rather than admit that his own policy had been misguided, Netanyahu tried to appease the angry public by promising total victory and the total eradication of Hamas as both a political and a military organisation. This entailed a screeching U-turn. Prior to 7 October, Netanyahu's policy had been not to solve but to "manage" the conflict with the Palestinians. To this end it was necessary to separate the West Bank from Gaza, to weaken the Palestinian Authority (PA) on the West Bank, to maintain the blockade of Gaza which had been in force since Hamas assumed power there in 2007, and to allow Hamas to govern Gaza but not to pose a threat to Israel's security. The policy also entailed a preference for channelling international monetary aid to Gaza via the Qatari government instead of the PA, in order to keep the Palestinian leadership divided and render political negotiations impossible. Acquiescing in Hamas's administration of an isolated Gaza, while seeking to prevent the emergence of a unified and moderate Palestinian leadership, was a cynical ploy in support of the false argument that Israel had no partner for peace.

In March 2019 Netanyahu reportedly told his Likud colleagues: "Anyone who wants to thwart the establishment of a Palestinian state has to support bolstering Hamas and transferring money to Hamas … This is part of our strategy – to isolate the Palestinians in Gaza from the Palestinians in the West Bank." The context for this statement was an internal debate within the Likud. The Hamas-Qatar debate was not between allowing some money to be delivered to Hamas versus not allowing any. Everyone recognised that some money had to be transferred to Gaza's administration or else the population would die. The dispute was rather between two different mechanisms for transferring money to Hamas: via the Palestinian Authority or via Qatar. Netanyahu preferred Qatar because it kept Hamas and the PA separate.

By launching the murderous attack on Israel on 7 October, Hamas sent a clear signal that the status quo was intolerable, and that it would continue to lead the national resistance to the Israeli occupation. While Israel regards Hamas as a terrorist organisation, Hamas regards itself as a national liberation movement similar to the one that led the Algerian struggle for independence from France. Just as the Algerian struggle involved considerable civilian suffering at the hands of the French forces, the Hamas leaders have factored in serious Palestinian civilian suffering in the struggle for independence.

Hamas is not a secular but an Islamic resistance movement. Its attack on southern Israel was in part a response to the Israeli infringements of Muslim prerogatives in the Old City of Jerusalem. Hence the name of the operation: the Al-Aqsa Flood. The military operation also carried a message to the Kingdom of Saudi Arabia which, under strong pressure from the American administration, was preparing to join the circle of the Abraham Accords by signing a peace treaty with Israel. An Israeli peace treaty with Saudi Arabia, the wealthiest of the Gulf states, would be a serious blow to the Palestinian national movement and, as such, another feather in Netanyahu's cap.

Netanyahu's response to the Hamas attack was to unleash Operation Swords of Iron, a savage military offensive that has been raining death and destruction on the Gaza Strip ever since 7 October. The specific target of the operation was Hamas and its military wing, but it was also conceived as an attack on the entire society of the enclave. It is the civilians who have paid the heaviest price as a direct consequence of this operation. The number of Hamas combatants killed is not known. But the overall toll at the time of writing (15 June 2024) stood at 37,232 people killed and 85,037 wounded. More than 15,000 of the casualties are children. Women and children together account for around two-thirds of the dead. An additional 10,000 people are estimated to be buried under the rubble. 1.9 million out of a population of 2.3 million have been forcibly displaced, most of them several times, and some of them were bombed from the air after going to what the IDF designated as "safe areas". By obstructing humanitarian aid from reaching Gaza, Israel is in effect using starvation as a weapon of war. More than a million people, including children, are the victims of a looming, man-made famine which is a war crime, as is the forcible displacement of civilians.

The "collateral damage" exacted by Israel in this indiscriminate act of revenge for the Hamas attack was colossal. According to the latest data from the UN's

Office for the Coordination of Humanitarian Affairs and the World Health Organization, as of 9 June, more than half of Gaza's homes have been destroyed or damaged; 80% of commercial facilities; 88% of school buildings; all 12 universities; 16 out of 35 hospitals; 130 ambulances; and 267 places of worship. The unprecedented scale of the destruction has given rise to a macabre terminology: domicide for the destruction of the housing stock; econocide for the wholesale destruction of the economy; ecocide for the destruction of the agricultural land and the natural landscape; scholasticide for the destruction of the educational system; and finally, the crime of all crimes – genocide.

Netanyahu's change of policy toward Hamas – from containment to destruction – reflected the group's decisive rejection of the role he had scripted for it: Israel's enforcer in Gaza. But this tactical switch did not reflect any shift in Netanyahu's ideological commitments or overarching objectives. Before October 7, Netanyahu supported using military might to induce Palestinians to permanently acquiesce in Jewish supremacy across the whole Land of Israel. This remains his project. That is why, even as Netanyahu insists on indefinite Israeli security control of the enclave, he refuses to say how Gaza would be governed after the fighting stops. Israel's US and European allies, along with much of the Arab world, would like to see the

PA go back to Gaza and replace Hamas. Netanyahu is opposed to this plan, and this opposition is consistent with his long-standing positions. On the one hand, he reflexively champions solutions that are violent and unilateral. On the other hand, he fears that a unified Palestinian leadership would strengthen the case for a two-state solution.

In place of a viable framework for post-war governance in Gaza, Netanyahu's aim seems to be to destroy the Gaza Strip and to render it uninhabitable. In November 2023, the right-wing daily *Yisrael Hayom* revealed that the prime minister seeks to "reduce the number of Palestinian citizens in the Gaza Strip to the minimum possible". One way of reducing the number of Palestinians in Gaza is to push them over the border into Egypt's territory in northern Sinai. A leaked paper dated 13 October 2023 of the Israeli Ministry of Intelligence suggests that there is an actual plan for depopulating Gaza. Egypt has expressed the strongest opposition to this plan of demographic aggression. However, the IDF capture of the border posts between Gaza and Egypt and the herding of over a million refugees into Rafah at the hideously over-crowded southern tip of the enclave, suggest that the Israeli government has not abandoned its plan for the ethnic cleansing of the Gaza Strip.

Netanyahu's "total war" in Gaza has serious repercussions for the situation on the West Bank. For decades the pressure on the Palestinians in this area has been immense and unrelenting. Since the coming to power of Netanyahu's messianic government in December 2022, this pressure has increased at an alarming pace. During the first half of 2023, his government approved 12,855 new housing units in the illegal settlements on the West Bank. At least 547 Palestinians, including 134 children, were killed by armed settlers and by Israeli soldiers in that year. UN observers recorded 1,227 incidents of settler violence in 2023 that resulted in casualties and/or damage to property. Emboldened by the government, the hard-core ideological settlers exploit the ongoing war in Gaza to push forward their agenda of forcing Palestinians to leave their villages. According to B'Tselem, the Israeli human rights group, settlers have forced at least eighteen Palestinian communities – over 1,000 people – to flee their homes since 7 October.

Again, these developments merely accelerated the systematic colonisation and dispossession project that Netanyahu has always promoted. From his first day in office, Netanyahu was determined to push forward the struggle for "the Whole Land of Israel". This was his reason for sabotaging the Oslo accords: he thought they spelled disaster for Zionism. Under his leadership, through six terms spanning sixteen years in power, settlement expansion continued, more and more Arab land was stolen, the ethnic cleansing of East Jerusalem gained momentum, and the settlers were encouraged to behave as if they were the only lords of the land from the river to the sea. At the time of the signing of the first Oslo Accord in 1993, there were approximately 110,000 settlers in the West Bank and around 140,000 in East Jerusalem. Today there are more than 700,000.

It is also unsurprising that Netanyahu has presented the Gaza war as pitting "the sons of light" against "the sons of darkness"[29] and promised "the victory of Judeo-Christian civilization against barbarism".[30] Netanyahu already employed a Manichean moral framing in his 1993 book, while the idea of Arabs as irredeemably hostile traces back to his father. The "Judeo-Christian" refinement draws as well on the idea of a "Clash of Civilisations", popularised by Harvard Professor Samuel Huntington in the 1990s following the end of the Cold War. It posited that after the collapse of the Soviet Union international conflict was no longer between nation states but between the West and the rest. In this scheme of things Israel was regarded not as part of the Middle East but as part of the West, of the "Free World" as it used to be called. For someone in the business of denying another people their rights and of running a racist regime of horrendous structural violence, this is a clever rhetorical gambit.

The war in Gaza, however, is not a clash of cultures or religions. Nor is it a clash between two opposing sets of values. It is a clash between a brutal colonial power and its victims, between the occupier and the occupied, between the oppressor and the oppressed. It is an indiscriminate, murderous, and genocidal war waged by one of the strongest militaries in the world not just against Hamas but against the defenceless people of Gaza. If there are any barbarians in this war, it is Israel's political and military leaders, not the long-suffering people of Gaza. Netanyahu's claim of victory, meanwhile, is premature to say the least: so far it has been a moral defeat for Israel, a military failure, and a political disaster, turning Israel into an international pariah.

— A LOGICAL ENDPOINT —

Israel's protracted war on Gaza has been attributed to Netanyahu's struggle for personal survival or else his political reliance upon the far-right. The deeper truth is that Netanyahu's resort to unilateral military might, his understanding of the Palestine conflict as zero sum, his refusal to concede that the representatives of Gaza have any legitimate grievances, his resort to genocidal incitement, and his commitment to Jewish sovereignty from the river to the sea are all wholly consistent with his long-standing positions.

Blaming the Gaza onslaught on Netanyahu's current legal predicaments obscures the relentless consistency of his political project over decades, while blaming Netanyahu's dependence on his far-right collaborators ignores the extent to which their respective projects are one and the same. Such explanations also obscure the extent to which the policies and premises of the far-right, including Netanyahu, are shared across Israeli politics and throughout Israeli society. At the institutional level, it defies credibility to suppose that Netanyahu could prosecute a military offensive of such magnitude for purely personal considerations, if he did not have considerable support within the military and intelligence establishments. Politically, the Gaza onslaught was not waged by Netanyahu alone but by a national unity government that included Israel's most popular opposition leader, Benny Gantz.[31] Gantz previously ran for office by declaring that "only the strong survive" while claiming credit for having bombed parts of Gaza "back to the Stone Age" – positions Netanyahu could hardly disagree with.[32] Israeli public opinion has overwhelmingly supported the Gaza campaign, or else believed the violence should be further escalated. More generally, Netanyahu did not become Israel's longest-serving prime minister by standing apart from Israeli Jewish society but by embodying it.

It follows that Netanyahu's vicious incitement and his criminal conduct in Gaza are not personal aberrations. They reflect the steady drift of Israeli society from a semblance of freedom and democracy to utter moral depravity. This process has been going on since the Israeli victory in the June 1967 war. The occupation of the Palestinian territories has eroded the foundations of Israeli democracy, violated core Jewish values, and turned Israel into a nation of oppressors and war criminals. The Labour-led governments were responsible for initiating this process by the building of illegal settlements on Palestinian land but under the Likud it reached its most cruel, indeed genocidal climax. In truth, the origins of Israel's moral decadence go further back even than 1967. Israel has always been a settler-colonial state. The logic of settler colonialism is the elimination of the native. The ethnic cleansing of Palestine is not a discrete event that ended with the 1948 war but an ongoing process. What is new in the current war on Gaza is that Zionist settler colonialism has gone beyond ethnic cleansing to the brink of genocide.

Francesca Albanese, the UN special rapporteur on the situation of human rights in the Palestinian territories, submitted in March 2024 a report entitled "Anatomy of a Genocide". The context, facts, and analysis of Israel's conduct in the war on Gaza led her to conclude that "there are reasonable grounds to believe that the threshold indicating Israel's commission of genocide is met." "More broadly," she explained, "they also indicate that Israel's actions have been driven by a genocidal logic integral to its settler-colonial project in Palestine, signalling a tragedy foretold." Nothing better personifies the truth of this verdict than the political career of Benjamin, the son of Benzion Netanyahu.

24 June 2024

— 2009 —

OPERATION CAST LEAD, 2008-2009

The only way to make sense of Israel's senseless war in Gaza is through understanding the historical context. Establishing the state of Israel in May 1948 involved a monumental injustice to the Palestinians. British officials bitterly resented American partisanship on behalf of the infant state. On 2 June 1948, Sir John Troutbeck wrote to the foreign secretary, Ernest Bevin, that the Americans were responsible for the creation of a gangster state headed by "an utterly unscrupulous set of leaders". I used to think that this judgment was too harsh but Israel's vicious assault on the people of Gaza, and the Bush administration's complicity in this assault, have reopened the question.

I write as someone who served loyally in the Israeli army in the mid-1960s and who has never questioned the legitimacy of the state of Israel within its pre-1967 borders. What I utterly reject is the Zionist colonial project beyond the Green Line. The Israeli occupation of the West Bank and the Gaza Strip in the aftermath of the June 1967 war had very little to do with security and everything to do with territorial expansionism. The aim was to establish Greater Israel through permanent political, economic and military control over the Palestinian territories. And the result has been one of the most prolonged and brutal military occupations of modern times.

Four decades of Israeli control did incalculable damage to the economy of the Gaza Strip. With a large population of 1948 refugees crammed into a tiny strip of land, with no infrastructure or natural resources, Gaza's prospects were never bright. Gaza, however, is not simply a case of economic under-development but a uniquely cruel case of deliberate de-development. To use the Biblical phrase, Israel turned the people of Gaza into the hewers of wood and the drawers of water, into a source of cheap labour and a captive market for Israeli goods. The development of local industry was actively impeded so as to make it impossible for the Palestinians to end their subordination to Israel and to establish the economic underpinnings essential for real political independence.

Gaza is a classic case of colonial exploitation in the post-colonial era. Jewish settlements in occupied territories are immoral, illegal and an insurmountable obstacle to peace. They are at once the instrument of exploitation and the symbol of the hated occupation. In Gaza, the Jewish settlers numbered only 8,000 in 2005 compared with 1.4 million local residents. Yet the settlers controlled 25% of the territory, 40% of the arable land and the lion's share of the scarce water resources. Cheek by jowl with these foreign intruders, the majority of the local population lived in abject poverty and unimaginable misery. Eighty per cent of them still subsist on less than $2 a day. The living conditions in the strip remain an affront to civilised values, a powerful precipitant to resistance and a fertile breeding ground for political extremism.

In August 2005 a Likud government headed by Ariel Sharon staged a unilateral Israeli pullout from Gaza, withdrawing all 8,000 settlers and destroying the houses and farms they had left behind. Hamas, the Islamic resistance movement, conducted an effective campaign to drive the Israelis out of Gaza. The withdrawal was a humiliation for the Israeli Defence Forces. To the world, Sharon presented the withdrawal from Gaza as a contribution to peace based on a two-state solution. But in the year after, another 12,000 Israelis settled on the West Bank, further reducing the scope for an independent Palestinian state. Land-grabbing and peace-making are simply incompatible. Israel had a choice and it chose land over peace.

The real purpose behind the move was to redraw unilaterally the borders of Greater Israel by incorporating the main settlement blocs on the West Bank to the state of Israel. Withdrawal from Gaza was thus not a prelude to a peace deal with the Palestinian Authority but a prelude to further Zionist expansion on the West Bank. It was a unilateral Israeli move undertaken in what was seen, mistakenly in my view, as an Israeli national interest. Anchored in a fundamental rejection of the Palestinian national identity, the withdrawal from Gaza was part of a long-term effort to deny the Palestinian people any independent political existence on their land.

Israel's settlers were withdrawn but Israeli soldiers continued to control all access to the Gaza Strip by land, sea and air. Gaza was converted overnight into an open-air prison. From this point on, the Israeli air force enjoyed unrestricted freedom to drop bombs, to make sonic booms by flying low and breaking the sound barrier, and to terrorise the hapless inhabitants of this prison.

Israel likes to portray itself as an island of democracy in a sea of authoritarianism. Yet Israel has never in its entire history done anything to promote democracy on the Arab side and has done a great deal to undermine it. Israel has a long history of secret collaboration with reactionary Arab regimes to suppress Palestinian nationalism. Despite all the handicaps, the Palestinian people succeeded in building the only genuine democracy in the Arab world with the possible exception of Lebanon. In January 2006, free and fair elections for the Legislative Council of the Palestinian Authority brought to power a Hamas-led government. Israel, however, refused to recognise the democratically elected government, claiming that Hamas is purely and simply a terrorist organisation.

America and the EU shamelessly joined Israel in ostracising and demonising the Hamas government and in trying to bring it down by withholding tax revenues and foreign aid. A surreal situation thus developed with a significant part of the international community imposing economic sanctions not against the occupier but against the occupied, not against the oppressor but against the oppressed.

As so often in the tragic history of Palestine, the victims were blamed for their own misfortunes. Israel's propaganda machine persistently purveyed the notion that the Palestinians are terrorists, that they reject coexistence with the Jewish state, that their nationalism is little more than antisemitism, that Hamas is just a bunch of religious fanatics and that Islam is incompatible with democracy. But the simple truth is that the Palestinian people are a normal people with normal aspirations. They are no better but they are no worse than any other national group. What they aspire to, above all, is a piece of land to call their own on which to live in freedom and dignity.

Like other radical movements, Hamas began to moderate its political programme following its rise to power. From the ideological rejectionism of its charter, it began to move towards pragmatic accommodation of a two-state solution. In March 2007, Hamas and Fatah formed a national unity government that was ready to negotiate a long-term ceasefire with Israel. Israel, however, refused to negotiate with a government that included Hamas.

It continued to play the old game of divide and rule between rival Palestinian factions. In the late 1980s, Israel had supported the nascent Hamas in order to weaken Fatah, the secular nationalist movement led by Yasser Arafat. Now Israel began to encourage the corrupt and pliant Fatah leaders to overthrow their religious political rivals and recapture power. Aggressive American neoconservatives participated in the sinister plot to instigate a Palestinian civil war. Their meddling was a major factor in the collapse of the national unity government and in driving Hamas to seize power in Gaza in June 2007 to pre-empt a Fatah coup.

The war unleashed by Israel on Gaza on 27 December was the culmination of a series of clashes and confrontations with the Hamas government. In a broader sense, however, it is a war between Israel and the Palestinian people, because the people had elected the party to power. The declared aim of the war is to weaken Hamas and to intensify the pressure until its leaders agree to a new ceasefire on Israel's terms. The undeclared aim is to ensure that the Palestinians in Gaza are seen by the world simply as a humanitarian problem and thus to derail their struggle for independence and statehood.

The timing of the war was determined by political expediency. A general election is scheduled for 10 February and, in the lead-up to the election, all the main contenders are looking for an opportunity to prove their toughness. The army top brass had been champing at the bit to deliver a crushing blow to Hamas in order to remove the stain left on their reputation by the failure of the war against Hezbollah in Lebanon in July 2006. Israel's cynical leaders could also count on apathy and impotence of the pro-western Arab regimes and on blind support from President Bush in the twilight of his term in the White House. Bush readily obliged by putting all the blame for the crisis on Hamas, vetoing proposals at the UN Security Council for an immediate ceasefire and issuing

Israel with a free pass to mount a ground invasion of Gaza.

As always, mighty Israel claims to be the victim of Palestinian aggression but the sheer asymmetry of power between the two sides leaves little room for doubt as to who is the real victim. This is indeed a conflict between David and Goliath but the Biblical image has been inverted – a small and defenceless Palestinian David faces a heavily armed, merciless and overbearing Israeli Goliath. The resort to brute military force is accompanied, as always, by the shrill rhetoric of victimhood and a farrago of self-pity overlaid with self-righteousness. In Hebrew this is known as the syndrome of *yorim ve-bokhim*, "shooting and crying".

To be sure, Hamas is not an entirely innocent party in this conflict. Denied the fruit of its electoral victory and confronted with an unscrupulous adversary, it has resorted to the weapon of the weak – terror. Militants from Hamas and Islamic Jihad kept launching Qassam rocket attacks against Israeli settlements near the border with Gaza until Egypt brokered a six-month ceasefire last June. The damage caused by these primitive rockets is minimal but the psychological impact is immense, prompting the public to demand protection from its government. Under the circumstances, Israel had the right to act in self-defence but its response to the pinpricks of rocket attacks was totally disproportionate. The figures speak for themselves. In the three years after the withdrawal from Gaza, 11 Israelis were killed by rocket fire. On the other hand, in 2005-7 alone, the IDF killed 1,290 Palestinians in Gaza, including 222 children.

Whatever the numbers, killing civilians is wrong. This rule applies to Israel as much as it does to Hamas, but Israel's entire record is one of unbridled and unremitting brutality towards the inhabitants of Gaza. Israel also maintained the blockade of Gaza after the ceasefire came into force which, in the view of the Hamas leaders, amounted to a violation of the agreement. During the ceasefire, Israel prevented any exports from leaving the strip in clear violation of a 2005 accord, leading to a sharp drop in employment opportunities. Officially, 49.1% of the population is unemployed. At the same time, Israel restricted drastically the number of trucks carrying food, fuel, cooking-gas canisters, spare parts for water and sanitation plants, and medical supplies to Gaza. It is difficult to see how starving and freezing the civilians of Gaza could protect the people on the Israeli side of the border. But even if it did, it would still be immoral, a form of collective punishment that is strictly forbidden by international humanitarian law.

The brutality of Israel's soldiers is fully matched by the mendacity of its spokesmen. Eight months before launching the current war on Gaza, Israel established a National Information Directorate. The core messages of this directorate to the media are that Hamas broke the ceasefire agreements; that Israel's objective is the defence of its population; and that Israel's forces are taking the utmost care not to hurt innocent civilians. Israel's spin doctors have been remarkably successful in getting this message across. But, in essence, their propaganda is a pack of lies.

A wide gap separates the reality of Israel's actions from the rhetoric of its spokesmen. It was not Hamas but the IDF that broke the ceasefire. It did so by a raid into Gaza on 4 November that killed six Hamas men. Israel's objective is not just the defence of its population but the eventual overthrow of the Hamas government in Gaza by turning the people against their rulers. And far from taking care to spare civilians, Israel is guilty of indiscriminate bombing and of a three-year-old blockade that has brought the inhabitants of Gaza, now 1.5 million, to the brink of a humanitarian catastrophe.

The Biblical injunction of an eye for an eye is savage enough. But Israel's insane offensive against Gaza seems to follow the logic of an eye for an eyelash. After eight days of bombing, with a death toll of more than 400 Palestinians and four Israelis, the gung-ho cabinet ordered a land invasion of Gaza the consequences of which are incalculable.

No amount of military escalation can buy Israel immunity from rocket attacks from the military wing of Hamas. Despite all the death and destruction that Israel has inflicted on them, they kept up their resistance and they kept firing their rockets. This is a movement that glorifies victimhood and martyrdom. There is simply no military solution to the conflict between the two communities. The problem with Israel's concept of security is that it denies even the most elementary security to the other community. The only way for Israel to achieve security is not through shooting but through talks with Hamas, which has repeatedly declared its readiness to negotiate a long-term ceasefire with the Jewish state within its pre-1967 borders for 20, 30, or even 50 years. Israel has rejected this offer for the same reason it spurned the Arab League peace plan of 2002, which is still on the table: it involves concessions and compromises.

This brief review of Israel's record over the past four decades makes it difficult to resist the conclusion that it has become a rogue state with "an utterly unscrupulous set of leaders". A rogue state habitually violates international law, possesses weapons of mass destruction and practises terrorism – the use of violence against civilians for political purposes. Israel fulfils all of these three criteria; the cap fits and it must wear it. Israel's real aim is not peaceful coexistence with its Palestinian neighbours but military domination. It keeps compounding the mistakes of the past with new and more disastrous ones. Politicians, like everyone else, are of course free to repeat the lies and mistakes of the past. But it is not mandatory to do so.

This piece was originally published under the title "How Israel brought Gaza to the brink of humanitarian catastrophe" in The Guardian, *7 January 2009.*

— 2019 —

SABOTAGING A CEASEFIRE

Operation Cast Lead killed 1,417 people. Chillingly, the generals call their repeated bombardments "mowing the lawn".

This month marks the 10th anniversary of the first major military assault on the 2 million Palestinians of the Gaza Strip. After its unilateral withdrawal from Gaza in 2005, Israel turned the area into the biggest open-door prison on Earth. The two hallmarks of Israel's treatment of Gaza since then have been mendacity and the utmost brutality towards civilians.

On 27 December 2008, Israel launched Operation Cast Lead, pounding the densely populated strip from the air, sea and land for 22 days. It was not a war or even "asymmetric warfare" but a one-sided massacre. Israel had 13 dead; the Gazans had 1,417 dead, including 313 children, and more than 5,500 wounded. According to one estimate 83% of the casualties were civilians. Israel claimed to be acting in self-defence, protecting its civilians against Hamas rocket attacks. The evidence, however, points to a deliberate and punitive war of aggression. Israel had a diplomatic alternative, but it chose to ignore it and to resort to brute military force.

In June 2008 Egypt had brokered a ceasefire between Israel and Hamas, the Islamic resistance movement that rules Gaza. The agreement called on both sides to cease hostilities and required Israel to gradually ease the illegal blockade it had imposed on the Gaza Strip in June 2007. This ceasefire worked remarkably well – until Israel violated it by a raid on 4 November in which six Hamas fighters were killed. The monthly average of rockets fired from Gaza on Israel fell from 179 in the first half of 2008 to three between June and October.

The story of the missed opportunity to avoid war was told to me by Robert Pastor, a professor of political science at the American University in Washington DC and a senior adviser on conflict resolution in the Middle East at the Carter Center NGO. Here is what Pastor told me over the phone and later confirmed in an email to Dr Mary Elizabeth King, another close associate of President Carter, on 8 December 2013, a month before Pastor's death.

[continues after "Metaphorical Presence"]

METAPHORICAL PRESENCE

Peter Rhoades: A Visceral Process.

These drawings were originally made in response to the Israeli attack on Gaza in 2008-2009, called "Operation Cast Lead" by the Israel Defense Forces. At the time I preserved a file of press material including photographs. I later revisited these images and, quite spontaneously, began a series of drawings in response to them. I value drawing with traditional media for its physicality; the image is processed and formed through the body. The photograph is consumed by the mind and directly affects my metabolism; making a drawing in response with graphic materials rather than on a screen is a visceral process involving the active participation of my whole being. I chose to work with media which were difficult to control; it seemed appropriate that the horrors of the topic should be depicted in a graphic language which, to some degree, risked appearing chaotic. Some of the photographs were so soaked in pain they were difficult to contemplate and the responsive drawings became more abstract and detached. I hope that, whatever their various characteristics, the drawings achieve a metaphorical presence; they are intended as a protest against unjustified and illegal brutality.

September 2024

The following drawings were first reproduced in Gaza: An Artist's Response, *with a Foreword by Professor Avi Shlaim, and published by Skyscraper in 2016.*

Peter Rhoades is an artist, teacher and lecturer. The major part of his teaching career has been with the University of Oxford. He was a longstanding member of staff at the Ruskin School of Art and the University Faculty of Fine Art, and recently retired from being a tutor at Christ Church College.

VIII

XVI

Pastor met Khaled Mashaal, the Hamas politburo chief, in Damascus in December 2008. Mashaal handed him a written proposal on how to restore the ceasefire. In effect, it was a proposal to renew the June 2008 ceasefire agreement on the original terms. Pastor then travelled to Tel Aviv and met Major General (Ret) Amos Gilad, head of the defence ministry's political affairs bureau. Gilad promised that he would communicate the proposal directly to defence minister Ehud Barak, and expected to have an answer either that evening or the following day. The next day, Pastor phoned Gilad's office three times and got no response. Shortly afterwards, Israel launched Operation Cast Lead.

In the email he dictated to his son on his deathbed, Pastor authorised me to publicise this story and to attribute it to him because "it's an important moment in history that Israel needs to accept because Israel had an alternative to war in December 2008". It was indeed a critical moment and it conveyed a clear message: if Israel's real purpose was to protect its civilians, all it needed to do was to follow Hamas's example by observing the ceasefire.

Israel's conduct during the first Gaza war was placed under an uncompromising lens by the UN Human Rights Council's independent fact-finding mission headed by Richard Goldstone, the distinguished South African judge who happened to be both a Jew and a Zionist. Goldstone and his team found that both Hamas and the Israel Defence Forces had committed violations of the laws of war by deliberately harming civilians. The IDF received more severe strictures than Hamas on account of the bigger scale and seriousness of its violations.

The Goldstone team investigated 36 incidents involving the IDF. It found 11 incidents in which Israeli soldiers launched direct attacks against civilians with lethal outcomes; seven where civilians were shot leaving their homes waving white flags; a "direct and intentional" attack on a hospital; numerous incidents where ambulances were prevented from attending to the severely injured; and nine attacks on civilian infrastructure with no military significance, such as flour mills, sewage works, and water wells – all part of a campaign to deprive civilians of basic necessities. In the words of the report, much of this extensive damage was "not justified by military necessity and carried out unlawfully and wantonly".

In conclusion, the 575-page report noted that while the Israeli government sought to portray its operations as essentially a response to rocket attacks in the exercise of the right to self-defence, "the Mission itself considers the plan to have been directed, at least in part, at a different target: the people of Gaza as a whole". Under the circumstances "the Mission concludes that what occurred in just over three weeks at the end of 2008 and the beginning of 2009 was a deliberately disproportionate attack designed to punish, humiliate and terrorise a civilian population, radically diminish its local economic capacity both to work and to provide for itself, and to force upon it an ever-increasing sense of dependency and vulnerability."

The claim that the operation was designed to "terrorise a civilian population" needs underlining. Terrorism is the use of force against civilians for political purposes. By this definition Operation Cast Lead was an act of state terrorism. The political aim was to force the population to repudiate Hamas, which had won a clear majority in the elections of January 2006.

Operation Cast Lead is emblematic of everything that is wrong with Israel's approach to Gaza. The Israeli-Palestinian conflict is a political conflict to which there is no military solution. Yet Israel persists in shunning diplomacy and relying on brute military force – and not as a last resort but as a first resort. Force is the default setting. And there is a popular Israeli saying that goes with it: "If force doesn't work, use more force!"

Operation Cast Lead was just the first in a series of Israeli mini-wars on Gaza. It was followed by Operation Pillar of Defence in November 2012 and

Operation Protective Edge in the summer of 2014. The fancy names given to these operations were fraudulent, dressing up offensive attacks on defenceless civilians and civilian infrastructure in the sanctimonious language of self-defence. They are typical examples of Orwellian double-speak. UN secretary general Ban Ki-moon called the Israeli attack on 1 August 2014 on Rafah, in which a large number of civilians sheltering in UN schools were killed, "a moral outrage and a criminal act". This description applies equally to Israel's entire policy of waging war on the inmates of the Gaza prison.

Israeli generals talk about their recurrent military incursions into Gaza as "mowing the lawn". This operative metaphor implies a task that has to be performed regularly and mechanically and without end. It also alludes to the indiscriminate slaughter of civilians and the inflicting of damage on civilian infrastructure that takes several years to repair.

"Mowing the lawn" is a chilling euphemism but it provides a clue as to the deeper purpose behind Israel's steadfast shunning of diplomacy and repeated resort to brute military force in response to all manifestations of lawful resistance and peaceful protest on its southern border. Under this grim rubric, there can be no lasting political solution: the next war is always just a matter of time.

This piece was originally published as "Ten years after the first war on Gaza, Israel still plans endless brute force", in The Guardian, *8 January 2019.*

— 2019 —

ISRAEL, HAMAS AND THE CONFLICT IN GAZA: AN OVERVIEW

(Report to the ICC)

On 30 March 2018, a campaign of protest was launched by Palestinian activists in the Gaza Strip along the perimeter fence with Israel. It was called the Great March of Return. The protesters demanded the UN-sanctioned right of return of the 1948 Palestinian refugees and their descendants to their homes in present-day Israel and the lifting of the illegal Israeli blockade of Gaza. It was a mostly peaceful act of civil resistance to the Israeli occupation which was later endorsed and supported by Hamas. Underlying the protest was a Palestinian shift away from violence towards non-violent forms of resistance. Israel's response to the demonstrations, however, was swift and savage and included the use of live ammunition against unarmed civilians. In one year of protests the Israeli security forces killed 260 protesters – including women and children, journalists and paramedics – and wounded more than 20,000. Israel's disproportionate use of force raised serious international concern and was condemned by the United Nations General Assembly. In late February 2019 an independent commission of the UN Human Rights Council found that of 489 cases of Palestinian deaths or injuries analysed, only two were possibly justified. In all the other cases, the use of live ammunition was unlawful and possibly constituted war crimes or crimes against humanity. Israel, having obstructed the investigation, dismissed the report as biased, rejected its recommendations, and refused to alter its open-fire policy.

Israeli violence during the Great March of Return resulted in the deadliest days in the Israeli-Palestinian conflict since the 2014 Gaza War. "Operation Protective Edge" in the summer of 2014 was Israel's third major military campaign in the Gaza Strip in six years. It followed "Operation Cast Lead" of 2008-9 and "Operation Pillar of Defence" of November 2012. The name "Operation Protective Edge", like the names of so many of its predecessors, was intended to imply that it was a legitimate act of self-defence. The argument of self-defence is regularly cited by Israeli spokesmen to justify the resort to military force. It needs to be examined on a case-by-case basis. The evidence advanced for regarding "Operation Protective Edge" as a measure of self-defence is thin to non-existent. Like the invasion of Lebanon in 1982, the second Lebanon war of 2006, and the first two mini-wars in Gaza, it was an act of aggression, an offensive war undertaken by Israel in pursuit of broad but undeclared geopolitical objectives.

— ZIONISM AND THE ARABS —

To make sense of Israel's recurrent resort to lethal force in Gaza, it is necessary to place it within the context of the Israeli-Palestinian conflict and in the wider context still of the emergence of Israel as a colonial settler-state. The State of Israel is the principal political progeny of the Zionist movement which was itself a product of the age of nationalism in late nineteenth century Europe. Zion is one of the biblical names for Jerusalem and the Zionist movement's ultimate goal was to gather the Jews from "the four corners of the earth" and to build an independent Jewish state in Palestine in which Jews would constitute the majority. The principal problem with this project was that Palestine was already home to an Arab population that had lived there for centuries. There were two peoples and one land, hence the conflict.

Alongside the conflict on the ground in Palestine, there was the battle to win the hearts and minds of people in the world at large. Here the Zionist movement had a decisive edge over its rival. Zionist spokesmen skilfully presented their movement not as the ally of European colonialism but as the national liberation movement of the Jews, disclaiming any intention of hurting or dispossessing the indigenous Arab population. A famous slogan in the struggle for statehood was "a land without a people for a people without a land". The founding fathers of Zionism promised that their movement would adhere to universal values like freedom, equality, and social justice. Based on these ideals, they claimed to aspire to develop Palestine for the benefit of all the people who lived there, regardless of their religion or ethnicity.[33]

A huge gap, however, separated the proclaimed ideals of the founding fathers from the reality of Zionist treatment of the indigenous Arab population of Palestine. This gap was filled by Zionist spokesmen with hypocrisy and humbug. Even as they were colonizing Palestine and dispossessing the Palestinians, the Zionists continued to claim the moral high-ground. In the face of overwhelming evidence to the contrary, they persisted in portraying Zionism as an enlightened, progressive, and peace-loving movement and its opponents as irrational and implacably hostile fanatics.

From the early days of the Zionist movement, its leaders were preoccupied with what they euphemistically called "the Arab question" — the presence of an Arab community on the land of their dreams. And from the beginning, the Zionists developed a strategy for dealing with this problem. This was the strategy of the "iron wall", of dealing with the Arabs from a position of unassailable military strength.

In 2000 I published a book under the title "The Iron Wall: Israel and the Arab World".[34] It covered the first 50 years of statehood, from 1948 to 1998. A second, updated edition was published in November 2014.[35] This edition is 900 pages long but the main conclusion can be summarised in one sentence: Israel's leaders have usually preferred force to diplomacy in dealing with the Arabs. Ever since its inception, Israel has been strongly predisposed to resort to military force and reluctant to engage in meaningful diplomacy in order to resolve its political dispute with the local Arabs.

The main architect of the iron wall strategy was Ze'ev Jabotinsky, an ardent Jewish nationalist and the spiritual father of the Israeli Right. In 1923 Jabotinsky published an article "On the Iron Wall (We and the Arabs)" with an analysis of "the Arab question" and recommendations on how to confront it. He argued that no nation in history ever agreed voluntarily to make way for another people to come and create a state on its land. The Palestinians were a living people, not a rabble, and Palestinian resistance to a Jewish state was therefore an inescapable fact. Consequently, a voluntary agreement between the two parties was unattainable. The only way to realize the Zionist project of an independent Jewish state in Palestine, Jabotinsky concluded, was unilaterally and by military force. A Jewish state could only be built behind an iron wall of Jewish military power. The Arabs would hit their heads against the wall, but eventually they would despair and give up any hope of overpowering the Zionists. Then, and only then, would the time come for stage two, negotiating with the leaders of the Palestine Arabs about their rights and status in Palestine.[36]

The "iron wall" was a national strategy for overcoming the main obstacle on the road to statehood. The Arab revolt of 1936-1939 seemed to confirm the premises of this strategy. The point to stress is that this was not the strategy of the right, or of the left, or of the centre. Based on a broad consensus, it became the national strategy for dealing with the Arabs from the 1930s onwards. Regardless of the political colour of the government of the day, this was the dominant strategy under successive Israeli Prime Ministers from David

Ben-Gurion, the founder of the state, to Binyamin Netanyahu, the current incumbent. If any one document can be regarded as the bible of Zionist foreign policy, Jabotinsky's article was it.

In 1925 Jabotinsky broke away from the mainstream labour-Zionist movement led by Ben-Gurion to form the World Union of Zionist Revisionists. While the two movements were in agreement on the strategy for achieving a Jewish state, they differed in their territorial aims. Labour Zionists were deliberately vague about the borders of the state-in-the-making whereas the Revisionist Zionists insisted that it should stretch over the entire Mandate Palestine from the Jordan River to the Mediterranean Sea. When the Peel Commission of Inquiry first proposed the partition of Palestine in 1937, the Zionist movement was split but the official leadership eventually accepted it. Palestinian rejection sealed the fate of the plan. In 1947 the General Assembly of the United Nations voted for resolving the conflict by partitioning Mandate Palestine into Arab and Jewish states. *(See Portfolio of Maps, II)*.

Once again the Zionist movement accepted partition while the Palestinians, the Arab states, and the Arab League rejected it as illegal and immoral and went to war to nullify it. The first Arab-Israeli war was, in fact, two wars rolled into one. The first phase, from the passage of the UN partition resolution on

29 November 1947 to the expiry of the British Mandate on 14 May 1948, was the war between the Jewish and Arab communities in Palestine and it ended with a crushing defeat for the Palestinians and in the decimation of their society. The second phase began with the invasion of Palestine by the regular armies of the neighbouring Arab states on 15 May 1948 and it ended with a ceasefire on 7 January 1949. This phase, too, ended with an Israeli triumph and a comprehensive Arab defeat.

The main losers in 1948 were the Palestinians. Around 730,000 Palestinians, over half the total population, became refugees and the name Palestine was wiped off the map. Israelis call this "the War of Independence" while Palestinians call it the Nakba, or catastrophe. In 1949, after the guns fell silent, Israel concluded armistice agreements with all its Arab neighbours: Lebanon, Syria, Jordan, and Egypt. These are the only internationally recognised borders that Israel has ever had.

The armistice agreements were intended as a first step towards contractual peace agreements but the latter did not materialize. Gradually, despite intermittent violence on all fronts, the armistice lines gained wide international recognition as normal inter-state borders. In the course of the June 1967 War, popularly known as the Six-Day War, Israel captured the Sinai Peninsula, the West Bank, and the Golan Heights. *(See Portfolio of Maps, III)*. UN Security Council Resolution 242 of November 1967 proposed a package deal, the trading of land for peace. But the convergence of religious and secular nationalism set Israel on an expansionist course. Soon after the ending of hostilities Israel started building civilian settlements in the Occupied Territories. These settlements are illegal, and they constitute the main obstacle to peace. Refusal to relinquish the fruits of its military victory turned little Israel into a colonial power, ruling over a large and recalcitrant Arab population. As a result, Israel began to lose its legitimacy while the PLO began to gain in international legitimacy.

It is arguable that the history of the state of Israel is the vindication of the strategy of the iron wall at the inter-state level. First the Egyptians, in 1979, then the Jordanians, in 1994, negotiated peace agreements with Israel from a position of palpable weakness. So the strategy of "negotiations from strength" worked. But when it came to the Palestinians, the Israelis had a blind spot. They were unable to see that as a direct result of their own colonial regime, an authentic Palestinian national movement began to grow in the Occupied Territories. The first Israeli Prime Minister with the courage to move on the Palestinian front from stage one, the building of military power, to stage two, serious negotiations, was Yitzhak Rabin. He did so by concluding the Oslo accord with Yasser Arafat, the chairman of the PLO, on 13 September 1993.[37]

— THE OSLO ACCORD —

For all its shortcomings and ambiguities, the Oslo accord achieved three things: the PLO recognized the State of Israel; Israel recognized the PLO as the representative of the Palestinian people; and the two sides agreed to resolve their outstanding differences by peaceful means. Mutual recognition replaced mutual rejection. In short, the accord promised at least the beginning of an accommodation between two bitterly antagonistic national movements. And the hesitant handshake between Yitzhak Rabin and Yasser Arafat on the White House lawn clinched the historic compromise.

Critical to the architecture of Oslo was the notion of gradualism. The text did not address any of the key issues in this dispute: Jerusalem; the right of return of the 1948 Palestinian refugees; the status of the Jewish settlements built on occupied Palestinian land; or the borders of the Palestinian entity. All these "permanent status" issues were deferred for negotiations towards the end of the five-year transition period. Basically, this was a modest experiment in Palestinian self-government starting with the Gaza Strip and the West Bank town of Jericho. The text did not promise or even mention an independent Palestinian state at the end of the transition period. The Palestinians believed that in return for giving up their claim to 78 per cent of Mandate Palestine, they would gain an independent state in the remaining 22 per cent with a capital city in Jerusalem. They were to be bitterly disappointed.[38]

In 2000 the Oslo peace process broke down following the failure of the Camp David summit and the outbreak of the second intifada. Israelis claim that the Palestinians were responsible for the breakdown of the Oslo peace process because they made a strategic choice to return to violence and, consequently, there was no Palestinian partner for peace. Palestinian violence was indeed a contributory factor to the breakdown but not the main cause. The fundamental reason was that Israel reneged on its side of the deal following the assassination of Yitzhak Rabin. The Jewish fanatic who murdered Rabin also succeeded in derailing the peace train.[39]

In 1996 the right-wing Likud Party returned to power under the leadership of Binyamin Netanyahu Netanyahu had been elected leader of the Likud in March 1993. That year, before the Oslo accord was concluded, he published a major book under the title

A Place among the Nations: Israel and the World. The book was inspired by the teaching of Ze'ev Jabotinsky and by the fiercely nationalistic education he received from his father, the historian Benzion Netanyahu, who had been an adviser to Jabotinsky. The central element in Netanyahu junior's worldview was the right of the Jewish people to the whole Land of Israel. History was rewritten from a Revisionist perspective in order to demonstrate that it was not the Jews who usurped the land from the Arabs, but the Arabs who usurped it from the Jews. Britain was portrayed as no friend of the Jews, and the chapter on the British Mandate in Palestine was simply called "The Betrayal". The whole world was perceived as hostile to the State of Israel, and anti-semitism was said to be at the root of this hostility.

Netanyahu viewed Israel's relations with the Arab world as one of permanent conflict, as a never-ending struggle between the forces of light and the forces of darkness. His image of the Arabs was consistently and comprehensively negative and did not admit the possibility of diversity or change. His book did not contain a single positive reference to the Arabs, their history, or their culture. Much of Netanyahu's vehemence and venom was reserved for the Palestinians and especially for the notion that the Palestinian problem constituted the core of the Middle East conflict. For him the

Palestinian question was not a genuine problem but an artificially manufactured one. He denied that the Palestinians had a right to national self-determination and argued that the primary cause of tension in the Middle East was inter-Arab rivalry. For Netanyahu, compromise with the PLO was completely out of the question because its goal was the destruction of the State of Israel, and this goal allegedly defined its very essence.[40]

The change of government from Labour to Likud had profound implications for the peace process. The Labour Party is a pragmatic party whose position towards the West Bank is determined primarily by security considerations. The Likud is an ideological party which upholds the right of the Jewish people to the whole "Land of Israel".[41] Its position on the West Bank is shaped primarily by ideological rather than security considerations. Likud regards the West Bank — Judea and Samaria in its terminology — as an integral part of the historic homeland. In line with this view, it is opposed in principle to partition and in its electoral manifesto it explicitly rejects the idea of an independent Palestinian state alongside Israel.[42]

As leader of the Opposition, Netanyahu made no effort to conceal his deep antagonism to the Oslo accords. He denounced them as incompatible with Israel's right to security and with the historic right of the Jewish people to the whole Land of Israel. Ever the opportunist, during the 1996 electoral campaign he toned down his criticism of the Oslo accords because they were highly popular with the Israeli public. Netanyahu won the elections by a margin of less than one per cent. Once ensconced in the Prime Minister's chair, however, he revealed his true face. And he spent his first term in office in a largely successful attempt to arrest, undermine, and bypass the peace accords concluded by his Labour predecessors. Rabin had been the builder of dreams; Netanyahu is the destroyer of dreams.

Netanyahu also did irreparable damage to Israel's relations with Jordan by ordering the Mossad, in September 1997, to assassinate Hamas official Khalid Mash'al, a Jordanian citizen, in the Jordanian capital. King Hussein of Jordan was Israel's best ally in the Arab world. Whereas the peace with Egypt was a cold peace, Hussein did everything in his power to cultivate a warm peace with Israel. He was the only Arab leader with an active interest in normalizing relations with the Jewish state. In Yitzhak Rabin Hussein found a genuine partner on the road to peace. In Binyamin Netanyahu he saw the negation of everything he had worked for. Following the signing of the peace treaty, a strategic dialogue was institutionalized between the two countries. In the context of this dialogue, Hussein conveyed to Netanyahu an offer from Hamas for a thirty-year truce. Netanyahu's response was the abortive attempt to assassinate a Jordanian citizen in Amman. Hussein was forced to conclude that the Likud leader was not a partner for peace but a saboteur and a menace to the Hashemite Kingdom of Jordan.[43]

Particularly destructive of the prospects of peace with the Palestinians was the policy of expanding Israeli settlements in the Occupied Territories. All Israeli governments, both Labour and Likud, built settlements in the Occupied Territories before and after 1993. But whereas Labour leaders tended to permit settlements mainly in areas of strategic importance that they hoped to keep permanently, Likud leaders took the view that Jews are entitled to settle anywhere they like in the Land of Israel. Although this was not explicitly stated, they also hoped that the settlements would become so firmly entrenched as to make territorial compromise impossible in the event of Labour returning to power.[44]

Building civilian settlements beyond the Green Line (the 1949 armistice lines) does not violate the letter of the Oslo accord but it most decidedly violates its spirit. As a result of settlement expansion the area available for a Palestinian state has been steadily shrinking to the point where a two-state solution is barely conceivable. For the Palestinian population, these settlements are not only a symbol of the hated occupation, but also a source of daily friction and a constant reminder of the danger to the territorial contiguity of their future state.

For Raja Shehadeh, a Palestinian human rights lawyer and writer from Ramallah, the hills of the West Bank used to provide the setting for tranquil walks where he felt more freedom than anywhere else in the world. As a result of the Israeli incursion they became "confining, endangered areas and a source of constant anxiety".[45] For many years, Shehadeh conducted exhausting legal battles in Israel's military courts to save the hills of Palestine from Jewish settlements:

> Now some twenty-five years later those times seem aeons away. How complicated and dismal the future has turned out, with the land now settled by close to half a million Israeli Jews, living in hundreds of settlements scattered throughout our hills and connected by wide roads crossing through the wadis. And more recently a wall has looped around the "settlement blocs", destroying the beauty of our hills, separating our villages and towns from each other and annexing yet more of our land to Israel, demolishing the prospect for a viable peace.[46]

The so-called "security barrier" that Israel has been constructing on the West Bank since 2003 is not only a blight on the Biblical landscape and a barrier to peace but also a blatant violation of international law. It was condemned by the International Court of Justice and by the UN General Assembly but construction continues regardless. Its declared purpose is to prevent terrorist attacks on Israel and its West Bank settlements but it is as much about land-grabbing as it is about security. By building the Wall, Israel is unilaterally redrawing the borders at the expense of the Palestinians. The Wall separates children from their schools, farmers from their land, and whole villages from their medical facilities.

The rate of settlement growth in the West Bank and Israeli-annexed East Jerusalem is staggering. At the end of 1993 there were 115,700 Israeli settlers in the Occupied Territories. Their number doubled during the following decade. Today the number of Israeli settlers on the West Bank exceeds 400,000. Another 300,000 Jews live in settlements across the pre-1967 border in East Jerusalem. Thousands more settlement homes are planned or under construction.

The Oslo accord had many faults, chief of which was the failure to proscribe settlement expansion while peace talks were in progress. But the agreement was not doomed to failure from the start as its critics allege.

Oslo faltered and eventually broke down because Likud-led governments negotiated in bad faith. This turned the much-vaunted peace process into a charade. It was all process and no peace. While failing to advance the cause of peace, it provided Israel with just the cover it was looking for to continue to pursue its illegal and aggressive colonial project on the West Bank.

— THE UNILATERAL — — DISENGAGEMENT FROM GAZA —

In August 2005 a Likud government headed by Ariel Sharon staged a unilateral Israeli pullout from Gaza, withdrawing all 8,000 settlers and destroying the houses that they had left behind. Hamas, the Islamic resistance movement, had conducted an effective campaign to drive the Israelis out of Gaza. The withdrawal was a victory for Hamas and a humiliation for the Israeli Defense Forces (IDF). To the world, Sharon presented the move as a contribution to peace with the Palestinians. But in the year after the withdrawal, another 12,000 Israelis settled on the West Bank, further reducing the scope for an independent and territorially contiguous Palestinian state.

The real purpose behind the move was to redraw unilaterally the borders of Greater Israel by incorporating the main settlement blocs on the West Bank into the state of Israel.[47] Withdrawal from Gaza was thus not a prelude to a peace deal with the Palestinian Authority but a prelude to further Zionist expansion on the West Bank. It was a unilateral Israeli move undertaken in what was seen as an Israeli national interest. Anchored in deep-rooted hostility to Palestinian national aspirations, the withdrawal from Gaza was part of the determined right-wing Zionist effort to prevent any progress towards an independent Palestinian state. American support was a major argument used in marketing the disengagement plan to the Israeli public. In an interview with *Ha'aretz*, Dov Weissglas, Sharon's closest aide and confidante, explained the motives behind the disengagement from Gaza:

> The significance is the freezing of the political process. And when you freeze that process you prevent the establishment of a Palestinian state and you prevent a discussion about the refugees, the borders and Jerusalem. Effectively, this whole package that is called the Palestinian state, with all that it entails, has been removed from our agenda indefinitely. And all this with authority and permission. All with a presidential blessing and the ratification of both houses of Congress ...With the proper

management we succeeded in removing the issue of the political process from the agenda. And we educated the world to understand that there is no one to talk to.[48]

Weissglas resorted to clinical terms to explain how precisely the peace process would be frozen. The disengagement plan was the preservative, he said, of the sequence principle, which stated that there will be no political process until the Palestinians reform. The disengagement is "the bottle of formaldehyde within which you place the president's formula so that it will be preserved for a very lengthy period. The disengagement is actually formaldehyde. It supplies the amount of formaldehyde that's necessary so that there will not be a political process with the Palestinians." A lawyer by profession, Weissglas took particular pride in having secured American commitments in writing. "We receive a no-one-to-talk-to certificate", he claimed. "The certificate says: (1) There is no one to talk to. (2) As long as there is no one to talk to, the geographic status quo remains intact. (3) The certificate will be revoked only when this-and-this happens – when Palestine becomes Finland. (4) See you then and Shalom."[49]

Israel's spin-doctors repeatedly claimed that by withdrawing they gave the inhabitants of the Gaza Strip an opportunity to turn it into the Singapore of the Middle East. Gaza's inhabitants, however, saw no sign of this much-vaunted generosity. They were not freed from Israel's military grip nor were they given a chance to prosper. Israel's settlers were withdrawn but Israeli soldiers continued to control all access to the Gaza Strip by land, sea and air. Gaza was converted overnight into an open-air prison. From this point on, the Israeli air force enjoyed unrestricted freedom to drop bombs, to pursue with impunity the illegal practice of targeted assassinations, to make sonic booms by flying low and breaking the sound barrier, and to terrorise the defenceless inhabitants of the prison.[50]

Israel likes to portray itself as an island of democracy in a sea of authoritarianism. But it has not done anything to promote democracy on the Arab side and it has actively undermined Palestinian democracy. Israel has a long history of secret collaboration with reactionary Arab regimes to suppress Palestinian nationalism.[51] Appropriately enough, it also likes to play the old imperial game of "divide and rule" between rival Palestinian factions. In the late 1980s, it had supported the nascent Hamas in order to weaken Fatah, the secular nationalist movement led by Yasser Arafat. Despite all the handicaps of labouring under military occupation, the Palestinians succeeded in developing one of the few democracies in the Arab world. A major element in this success was the decision by Hamas to enter the political process.

In January 2006, free and fair elections were held in the West Bank and the Gaza Strip and Hamas unexpectedly won a decisive victory over Fatah. Numerous international observers confirmed that the elections had been both peaceful and orderly.[52] Hamas won a clear majority (74 out of 132 seats) in the Palestinian Legislative Council and it proceeded to form a government. Israel refused to recognize the new government; the United States and European Union followed its lead. Israel resorted to economic warfare by withholding tax revenues while its western allies suspended direct aid to the Hamas-led Palestinian Authority. Their commitment to democracy apparently had its limits. They were in favour of democracy in theory but not when the people voted for the wrong party.

With Saudi help the warring Palestinian factions managed to reconcile their differences. On 8 February 2007, Fatah and Hamas signed an agreement in Mecca to stop the clashes between their forces in Gaza and to form a government of national unity. They agreed to a system of power-sharing, with independents taking the key posts of foreign affairs, finance, and the interior. And they declared their readiness to negotiate a long-term ceasefire with Israel. Israel did not like this government either and refused to negotiate.[53] Israel and the US secretly plotted with Fatah officials and Egyptian intelligence to undermine it.[54] They hoped to reverse the results of the parliamentary election by encouraging Fatah to stage a coup in order to recapture power.[55]

As revealed by the "Palestine Papers", a cache of 1,600 diplomatic documents of the Israel-PA negotiations leaked to Al Jazeera, Israel and America armed and trained the security forces of President Mahmoud Abbas with the aim of overthrowing Hamas.[56] Aggressive American neoconservatives participated in the sinister plot to instigate a Palestinian civil war. Hamas pre-empted a Fatah coup with a violent seizure of power in Gaza in June 2007. At this point the Palestinian national movement became fractured, with Fatah ruling the West Bank and Hamas ruling the Gaza Strip.

Israel responded to the Hamas move by declaring the Gaza Strip a "hostile territory". It also enacted a series of social, economic, and military measures designed to isolate and undermine Hamas. By far the most significant of these measures was the imposition of a blockade. The stated purpose of the blockade was to stop the transfer of weapons and military equipment to Hamas but it also restricted the flow of food, fuel, and medical supplies to the civilian population. One American Senator was outraged to discover that pasta was on the list of proscribed items. The boycott applied not only to imports but, perversely, also to exports from Gaza. Why prevent the export of agricultural products and other non-lethal goods? It is difficult to avoid the conclusion that the hidden motive was to cripple Gaza's economy and to inflict poverty, misery, and unemployment on its inhabitants.

In its non-military aspects, the blockade constituted a form of collective punishment that is clearly proscribed by international law.[57] Given the scale of the suffering inflicted by the blockade on the million and a half inhabitants of the strip, Israel could be considered guilty of "depraved indifference". The concept of "depraved indifference" in American law, or "depraved heart" under English common law, refers to conduct that is so wanton, so callous, so reckless, so deficient in a moral sense of concern, so lacking in regard for the lives of others, and so blameworthy as to warrant criminal liability.

As so often in the tragic history of Palestine, the victims were blamed for their own misfortunes.[58] Israel's propaganda machine persistently purveyed the notion that the Palestinians are terrorists, that they reject coexistence with the Jewish state, that their nationalism is little more than anti-Semitism, that Hamas is just a bunch of religious fanatics, and that Islam is incompatible with democracy. But the simple truth is that the Palestinian people are a normal people with normal aspirations. They are no better but they are no worse than any other national group. What they aspire to, above all, is to live in freedom and dignity on roughly a fifth of Mandate Palestine.

Like other radical movements, Hamas began to moderate its political programme following its rise to power. It persisted in its refusal to recognise the Jewish state. But from the ideological rejectionism of its Charter and its call for an Islamic state over the whole of mandatory Palestine, it moved step by step towards pragmatic accommodation to a two-state solution.[59] Its spokesmen repeatedly offered a long-term truce and they stated, in addition, that they would accept a Palestinian state within the 1967 borders if the peace deal is endorsed by a national referendum.[60]

— OPERATION CAST LEAD —

Ehud Olmert succeeded Ariel Sharon as Prime Minister and leader of Kadima, the party they formed after breaking away from the Likud. On 27 December 2008, the Olmert government ordered a major military operation against Hamas – "Operation Cast Lead". The thinking behind it was to weaken Hamas, cow the people of Gaza into submission, and crush the Islamic resistance to the Israeli occupation. The idea was to make life for the inhabitants of Gaza so hellish that they would revolt against their Hamas rulers, causing internal turmoil.[61] Another objective was to restore the deterrent power of the Israeli army which had been severely damaged by the Second Lebanon War of 2006. Israel was intent on crippling Hamas because it knew that its leadership, unlike that of Fatah, would stand firm in defence of the national rights of the Palestinian people and refuse to settle for an emasculated Palestinian state on Israel's terms.

The Israeli authorities presented the Gaza war as an act of self-defence to protect their civilians against Hamas rocket attacks.[62] The right to self-defence is enshrined in Article 51 of the United Nations Charter. Implicit in this article is that a member state will use military means as a last resort to defend itself. For Israel, however, because of its broader political aims, military force was not the last resort but the preferred option. There was another, peaceful, option for stopping the rocket attacks from Gaza but Israel chose not to exercise it.

Rocket attacks had effectively ended in June 2008 as a result of an Egyptian-brokered truce between Hamas and Israel. The key element of the truce was that, on 19 June, the Gaza authorities would halt attacks by Palestinian armed groups against Israel and Israel would cease its military operations in Gaza. Another key element was an Israeli commitment to gradually ease the blockade of Gaza. The truce was due for renewal in December. The impact of the truce was dramatic. In the first six months of 2008, the monthly average of rockets fired from Gaza into Israeli territory had been 179. Between July and October the monthly average dropped to three. Hamas observed the truce but was unable to prevent other armed groups from firing the occasional rocket. Hamas officials explained that most of these rockets were fired by small militant groups and one group associated with Fatah, and Israeli officials did not dispute this explanation. On 4 November the IDF launched a raid into Gaza and the official reason given was to prevent the construction of a tunnel. But the tunnel was 540 metres inside the Gaza Strip. Building a tunnel was not a breach of the ceasefire but the armed incursion into Gaza definitely was. A fire-fight developed and six Hamas fighters were killed. Hamas retaliated to the unprovoked Israeli raid by renewing the rocket attacks.

Nor did Israel live up fully to its pledge to ease the blockade of Gaza. From July through September it permitted 200 trucks per day into Gaza. This was less than one third of the number of trucks promised in the Egyptian-brokered agreement. As the December deadline approached, Israel insisted that the rocket fire stop and Hamas demanded that Israel open the crossings to allow legitimate produce to go into and leave Gaza. Hamas offered to renew the truce on the basis of the original terms but Israel ignored the offer. On 27 December the IDF launched a massive air attack on Gaza and this was followed by a ground invasion on 3 January 2009. The stated aims were to stop rocket and mortar fire into Israel and to prevent the smuggling of weapons into the Gaza Strip. The first aim, however, could have been achieved by pursuing the Hamas offer to renew the ceasefire. The conclusion is inescapable: the invasion of Gaza was not a legitimate act of self-defence but a disproportionate response to rocket attacks that were provoked by Israel in the first instance. Israel had a diplomatic option for defending its citizens but it made a deliberate decision to resort to military force.

Operation Cast Lead was not a war in the usual sense of the word but a one-sided massacre. For twenty-two days, the IDF shot, shelled, and bombed Hamas targets and at the same time rained death and destruction on the defenceless population of Gaza. Statistics tell only part of the grim story. Israel had 13 dead; the Gazans had 1,417 dead, including 313 children, and more than 5,500 wounded. According to one estimate, 83 per cent of the casualties were civilians.

Along with the heavy civilian death toll, there were serious economic, industrial and medical consequences. Gaza lost nearly $2 billion in assets. Four thousand homes were totally demolished and another 20,000 were damaged. The IDF destroyed 600–700 factories, small industries, workshops and business enterprises, 24 mosques, and 31 security compounds. Eight hospitals, 26 primary health care clinics, and over 50 United Nations facilities sustained damage during the assault. Overall, the savage assault drove Gaza to the brink of a humanitarian catastrophe. The indifference to the fate of the civilian population is difficult to comprehend unless it was motivated by a punitive streak.

The war crimes, allegedly committed by both sides, were another deplorable feature of this campaign. Israel's leaders claimed to target only Hamas activists and to make every effort to spare the life of innocent civilians.[63] Yet throughout the war, the number of civilian casualties kept escalating. This was no accident but the direct result of applying a new IDF doctrine, the Dahiya Doctrine, which sought to avoid losses among its soldiers by the ruthless destruction of everything in their path.[64] War crimes were investigated by an independent fact-finding mission appointed in April 2009 by the UN Human Rights Council and headed by Richard Goldstone, the distinguished South African judge who happened to be both a Jew and a Zionist.

Goldstone and his team found that Hamas and the IDF had both committed violations of the laws of war. The IDF received more severe strictures than Hamas on account of the scale and seriousness of its violations.

Hamas and other Palestinian armed groups were found guilty of launching rocket and mortar attacks with the deliberate aim of harming Israeli civilians: "These actions would constitute war crimes and may constitute crimes against humanity." The Goldstone team investigated 36 incidents involving the IDF. It found 11 incidents in which Israeli soldiers launched direct attacks against civilians with lethal outcomes; seven incidents where civilians were shot leaving their homes waving white flags; a "direct and intentional" attack on a hospital; numerous incidents where ambulances were prevented from attending to the severely injured; nine attacks on civilian infrastructure with no military significance, such as flour mills, chicken farms, sewage works, and water wells – all part of a campaign to deprive civilians of basic necessities.[65] In the words of the report, much of this extensive damage was "not justified by military necessity and carried out unlawfully and wantonly."[66]

In conclusion, the 575-page report noted that while the Israeli government sought to portray its operations as essentially a response to rocket attacks in the exercise of the right to self-defence, "the Mission itself considers the plan to have been directed, at least in part, at a different target: the people of Gaza as a whole."[67] Under the circumstances the Mission concluded that what occurred just over three weeks at the end of 2008 and the beginning of 2009 was "a deliberately disproportionate attack designed to punish, humiliate and terrorize a civilian population, radically diminish its local economic capacity both to work and to provide for itself, and to force upon it an ever increasing sense of dependency and vulnerability."[68]

In the opinion of Goldstone and his colleagues, the grave breaches of the Fourth Geneva Convention committed by the Israeli armed forces in Gaza gave rise to individual criminal responsibility. They recommended that the UN Human Rights Council should formally submit their report to the Prosecutor of the International Criminal Court. But joint Israeli-American pressure on the Palestinian Authority and at the UN ensured that no further action was taken. There can be no doubt, however, that the Gaza war constituted a massive moral defeat for Israel and its army.[69]

Most of the political objectives of Operation Cast Lead were not achieved. While the military capability of Hamas was damaged, its political standing was enhanced. The assault on the people of Gaza also had the immediate effect of radicalising mainstream Muslim opinion. The images shown by Arab and Muslim television stations of dead children and distraught parents kept fuelling rage against Israel and its superpower patron, effectively silencing critics of Hamas and legitimizing the radical resistance movement in the eyes of many previously sceptical observers. More than any previous Arab-Israeli war, this one also undermined the legitimacy of the pro-Western Arab regimes like Egypt, Jordan, and Saudi Arabia in the eyes of many of their citizens. These regimes stood accused of inaction or even complicity in Israel's crimes against the Palestinian people.

Internationally, the main consequence of the Gaza War was to generate a powerful wave of popular sympathy and support for the long-suffering Palestinians. As always, mighty Israel claimed to be the victim of Palestinian violence, but the sheer asymmetry of power between the two sides left little room for doubt as to who was the real victim. This was indeed a conflict between David and Goliath but the Biblical image was inverted – a small and defenceless Palestinian David faced a heavily armed, merciless, and overbearing Israeli Goliath. While leaving the basic political problem unresolved, the war thus helped to turn Israel into an international pariah. At home, however, Operation Cast Lead enjoyed the support of 90 per cent of the population who saw it as a necessary act of self-defence. This high level of popular support translated into a further shift to the right in the parliamentary election held the following month.

THE NETANYAHU GOVERNMENT

Likud returned to power under the leadership of Binyamin Netanyahu. With the emergence of a Likud-dominated government, the prospects of a negotiated settlement with the Palestinians virtually vanished. Netanyahu appointed as Foreign Minister Avigdor Lieberman, the leader of Yisrael Beiteinu, who had not only set his face against any compromise with the Palestinians but also favoured subjecting Israel's one and a half million Arab citizens to an oath of loyalty to Israel as a Jewish state – a move rejected by the Labour opposition and seen as borderline "fascist" and damaging to Israel's reputation.[70] Netanyahu's coalition in his second term in office was arguably among the most aggressively right-wing and racist governments in Israel's history. It was led by a man whose ambition is to go down in history not as a peacemaker but as the leader who secured Greater Israel. The majority of the ministers were also wedded to an agenda of Greater Israel which was fundamentally at odds with the idea of a two-state solution.

In the worldview of Netanyahu, the brash scion of Revisionist Zionism, and of his even more extreme religious-nationalist partners, only Jews have historic rights over what they call "Judea and Samaria". The main thrust of their policy is the expansion of Jewish settlements on the West Bank and the accelerated Judaization of East Jerusalem. With such a focus, the government ensured that no progress could be made on any of the key issues in the Israeli-Palestinian conflict. Jerusalem, as always, lay at the heart of the dispute. By putting Jerusalem at the forefront of their expansionist agenda, ministers knowingly and deliberately blocked progress on any of the other "permanent status" issues.

Like his mentor Yitzhak Shamir, Netanyahu's game is to play for time and to extend Israel's reach into the West Bank to the point where a viable Palestinian state would become utterly impossible. Like Shamir, he is a procrastinator par excellence in the diplomatic arena. And like Shamir, his position is based on the premise that "the Arabs are the same Arabs, and the sea is the same sea". In short, Netanyahu is a rigid and reactionary politician who believes that the status quo is sustainable and who is imperious enough to think that it is the job of the United States and of the Arab dictators to sustain it. He is unable or unwilling to grasp that there is nothing static about a status quo which has already provoked two full-scale uprisings against Israeli rule.

Violence was the defining characteristic of the second Netanyahu government's approach to Hamas. Like its predecessors it shunned diplomacy and relied heavily on brute military force. In doing so, it missed one opportunity after another to end the cycle of violence. In November 2012, it ordered the extra-judicial assassination of Ahmed Jabari, the chief of Hamas's military wing in Gaza, while he was reviewing the terms of a proposal for a permanent truce from Israeli peace activist Gershon Baskin.[71] The timing of the assassination suggests a deliberate attempt to pre-empt the threat of a diplomatic solution. At any rate, Israel broke the informal ceasefire to launch Operation Pillar of Defence, its second major military operation against Gaza following disengagement. In eight days of intense aerial bombardment, 132 Palestinians were killed. The operation ended with a ceasefire brokered by Egypt. This specified that Israel and the Palestinian factions would stop all hostilities and that Israel would open the border crossings to allow the movement of people and the transfer of goods.

The sequel is described by Nathan Thrall, senior Middle East analyst of the International Crisis Group:

> During the three months that followed the ceasefire, Shin Bet recorded only a single attack: two mortar shells fired from Gaza in December 2012. Israeli officials were impressed. But they convinced themselves that the quiet on Gaza's border was primarily the result of Israeli deterrence and Palestinian self-interest. Israel therefore saw little

incentive in upholding its end of the deal. In the three months following the ceasefire, its forces made regular incursions into Gaza, strafed Palestinian farmers and those collecting scrap and rubble across the border, and fired at boats, preventing fishermen from accessing the majority of Gaza's waters.

The end of the closure never came. Crossings were repeatedly shut. So-called buffer zones – agricultural lands that Gazan farmers couldn't enter without being fired on – were reinstated. Imports declined, exports were blocked, and fewer Gazans were given exit permits to Israel and the West Bank....The lesson for Hamas was clear. Even if an agreement was brokered by the US and Egypt, Israel could still fail to honour it.[72]

— OPERATION PROTECTIVE EDGE —

Hamas for its part continued to abide by the ceasefire to the satisfaction of Israel's securocrats for another eighteen months. But in April 2014 it committed what Israel considered an unforgivable transgression: it reached a reconciliation agreement with Fatah and proceeded, on 2 June, to form a unity government with responsibility to govern the Gaza Strip as well as the West Bank. Netanyahu immediately went on the offensive, denouncing the move as a vote not for peace but for terror and threatening Palestinian President Mahmoud Abbas with a boycott of the incoming government.[73] For him any sign of Palestinian unity or moderation poses a threat to the existing order and to Israeli hegemony.[74] The unity government produced by the accord was in fact remarkably moderate both in its composition and in its policies. It was a government of Fatah officials, technocrats, and independents without a single Hamas-affiliated member. To escape isolation and bankruptcy, Hamas handed over power to the Fatah-dominated, pro-Western Palestinian Authority in Ramallah. The unity government explicitly accepts the three conditions of the Quartet (the United States, Russia, the United Nations, and European Union) for receiving Western aid: recognition of Israel; respect for past agreements; and renunciation of violence.[75]

Israel responded to this promising development by what can only be described as economic warfare. It prevented the 43,000 civil servants in Gaza from moving from the Hamas payroll to that of the Ramallah government and it tightened the siege round Gaza's borders thereby nullifying the two main benefits of the merger. Israel followed up its propaganda offensive and economic measures with a military assault on Gaza on 8 July 2014. It portrayed the attack as an act of self-defence in response to Hamas rockets launched against its civilian population. But these rocket attacks were themselves a response to a violent crackdown against Hamas supporters on the West Bank following the abduction and murder of three Israeli teenagers on 12 June.

Netanyahu stated that Hamas was responsible for the abduction and that Hamas will pay the price.[76] He produced no evidence, however, to support the charge because there was no evidence. The murder was committed by a lone cell without the knowledge of the Hamas leadership. The Israeli authorities knew that the teenagers were killed soon after their abduction but they did not announce the death until eighteen days later. They used the intervening period to launch a powerful, worldwide propaganda offensive to denounce Hamas as a murderous organisation. At the same time, the IDF initiated Operation Brother's Keeper, ostensibly to search for the teenagers but in reality to deal a body blow to Hamas. As part of the operation, 350 Palestinians were arrested, including nearly all of Hamas's leaders on the West Bank. Netanyahu seemed to see an opportunity to destabilise the newly-established unity government and to undermine President Mahmoud Abbas. Reluctantly rising up to the challenge, Hamas responded with rockets.[77] The sequence of events clearly indicates that the murder of the three Israeli teenagers was the pretext, not the cause, for the next onslaught on Gaza.

What were Israel's aims in launching this deadly attack? This question has no single, straightforward answer because the official war aims kept changing. First, in phase one of the war, which began with airstrikes on 8 July, the stated aim was to halt the rocket and mortar attacks from Gaza; then in phase two of the war, commencing in the late evening of 17 July with a full ground invasion lasting until 5 August, it was to destroy the "terror tunnels" that Hamas had dug under the border to launch raids inside Israeli territory; and subsequently it was said that war would continue until Hamas is completely disarmed.[78] Behind these tactical objectives lurked undeclared geopolitical aims. First and foremost was the desire to reverse the trend towards Palestinian reconciliation and to undermine the unity government. This was in keeping with the policy of "divide and rule" and of keeping the two branches of the Palestinian family geographically separate. The aggressive practice of *"divide et impera"* in this instance demonstrates the falsity of the self-defence argument. Then there was the urge to punish the people of Gaza for electing Hamas and for continuing to support it in defiance of Israel's repeated warnings. Related to this was the irresistible urge to display Israel's raw military power.[79] The overriding aim, however, was to defeat the struggle for Palestinian independence, to maintain the colonial status quo, and to preserve Israel's position as the imperial overlord.

The late Israeli sociologist Baruch Kimmerling coined a word to describe this policy: "politicide". Politicide is defined in a book with that title as "a process that has, as its ultimate goal, the dissolution of the Palestinians' existence as a legitimate social, political, and economic entity."[80] In simpler language politicide means denying the Palestinians any independent political existence in Palestine. The idea is to make the Palestinians so vulnerable, divided, and exhausted by the struggle for physical survival that they would cease to constitute a coherent political community capable of asserting its right to sovereignty on even a fraction of historic Palestine.

Operation Protective Edge was the third Israeli attack on Gaza in six years, the fiercest in the firepower it deployed, and the most devastating in its impact.[81] The aerial and naval bombardment of the enclave was followed by a large-scale land invasion. The toll on the Palestinian side after 50 days of intermittent fighting was over 2,200 dead, mostly civilians, and 12,656 wounded. 577 children were among the dead. 520,000 people, over a quarter of Gaza's population, were displaced. On the Israeli side the death toll was 67 soldiers and five civilians. Whereas the great majority of

Hamas's victims were soldiers, most of Israel's victims were civilians.

The unleashing of the full might of the IDF against the 1.8 million captive inhabitants of the densely-populated enclave suggests that the purpose of the operation went well beyond the targeting of Palestinian militants. Otherwise, how is one to explain the bombing of schools, universities, mosques, factories, hospitals, health clinics, ambulances, fire stations, and UN sanctuaries or the destruction of thousands of private homes and the flattening of whole neighbourhoods? Nor does the official line account for the deliberate targeting and destruction of the fragile civilian infrastructure that has not yet fully recovered from the damage done by the IDF in the 2008-9 attack.

Taken together the three wars in Gaza reflect a profoundly militaristic outlook, a stubborn refusal to explore avenues for peaceful coexistence, habitual disregard for the laws of war and international humanitarian law, and utter callousness towards enemy civilians. Israeli generals talk about their recurrent military incursions into Gaza as "mowing the lawn".[82] By this they mean weakening Hamas, degrading its military capability, and impairing its capacity to govern. This operative metaphor implies a task that has to be performed regularly and mechanically and with no end. It also alludes to indiscriminate slaughter of civilians and inflicting the kind of damage on the civilian infrastructure that takes several years to repair.[83] Under this grim rubric, there is no lasting political solution: the next war is always just a matter of time. "Mowing the lawn" is a chilling euphemism but it provides another clue as to the deeper purpose behind Israel's steadfast shunning of diplomacy and repeated resort to brute military force on its southern border.

The conduct of the IDF during its 50-day military campaign in Gaza gave rise to questions about war crimes. Navi Pillay, the UN High Commissioner for Human Rights, pointed to a strong possibility that international law was violated in a manner that could amount to war crimes. She believed that Israel deliberately defied the obligations imposed by international law and demanded that the world powers should hold it accountable. The UN Human Rights Council appointed a three-member panel to investigate the allegations. Israel's past record left little room for hope that it would cooperate with any UN investigation. After Operation Cast Lead it denied access to the UN team headed by Judge Goldstone and, following the publication of their damning report, it engaged in character assassination of the principal author. Similar ad hominem attacks were launched to discredit Navi Pillay, the UN's then most senior human rights official.

These attacks were indicative of a general feeling among Israelis that the UN is biased, that the whole world is against them, that Israeli security overrides all other considerations, and indeed that Israel is above the law. To understand this attitude one has to delve into the political psychology of Israelis. Basically, despite their staggering military power, despite possessing the eleventh strongest army in the world and the strongest army in the Middle East, Israelis regard themselves as victims.[84] As Uri Avnery, the veteran Israeli peace activist, wrote: the Israeli army is filled with "teenagers who are indoctrinated from the age of three in the spirit of Jewish victimhood and superiority."[85] The same is true of much of the rest of Israeli society with the exception of individuals like Uri Avnery and courageous human rights groups. Feeling themselves to be the victims tends to blind the Israeli majority to the suffering they inflict on the real victims in this conflict – the Palestinians.

The subjective feeling of victimhood also blurs the distinction between enemy combatants and innocent civilians. Retired Major General Giora Eiland, the former head of Israel's National Security Council, published an article in Ynet News, claiming that there is no such thing as "innocent civilians" in Gaza and arguing that the citizens of Gaza share responsibility with their Hamas leaders for the violence against Israel.

He even went as far as to compare Gaza under Hamas rule with Nazi Germany: "They are to blame for this situation", Eiland wrote, "just like Germany's residents were to blame for electing Hitler as their leader and paid a heavy price for that, and rightfully so."[86] Eiland was not reprimanded for expressing publicly these extreme views which are widely shared by the defence establishment and by the Israeli public at large.

The sense of permanent persecution, not to say paranoia, is understandable in the context of Jewish history. The American Jewish historian Salo Baron, spoke of "the lachrymose version of Jewish history" which sees the past as a world-wide and endless series of pogroms, culminating in the Holocaust. But this very preoccupation with security makes Israelis susceptible to politicians who are unscrupulous enough to manipulate the sense of threat and to inflate it for political advantage. The arch manipulator is Binyamin Netanyahu. He is the high priest of fear who never stops harping on the existential threats facing the country. His rhetoric about Hamas posing an existential threat to Israel is absurd when one examines the military balance between the two sides but it achieved the desired psychological and political effects. Ninety five percent of Israelis supported the 2014 military campaign in Gaza with all its excesses, and many of them felt that it ended too soon. Netanyahu's popularity plummeted from 85 percent at the beginning of the operation to 38 percent when he agreed to a ceasefire "without finishing the job".[87]

— CONCLUSION —

The terms in which Netanyahu and his right-wing colleagues frame the conflict with Hamas are a mixture of half-truths, obfuscation, deception, and double-standards. Their narrative offers no peaceful way out of the conundrum. It is the problem, not the solution. It makes it impossible to tackle the real roots of the Israeli-Palestinian conflict. This is a political conflict for which, as the historical record conclusively demonstrates, there is no military solution.

It follows that if Israel adheres to its militaristic policy, the result would be more of the same: more violence, more bloodshed, more terror, more wanton destruction, more human suffering, more wars, and more war crimes. In short, the Israeli narrative revolves round the demonisation of Hamas and demonisation leads directly to diplomatic deadlock.

The international community has both a moral and a legal obligation to protect the Palestinian civilians living under Israel's military occupation and to hold Israel to account for its persistent violations of the laws of war and of international humanitarian law.

The Western policy of refusing to engage with Hamas, of supporting Israel's abuse of the right to self-defence, and of supplying it with weapons that are repeatedly used to bomb a defenceless people is morally indefensible and therefore ultimately unsustainable.

UN secretary-general Ban Ki-moon called the Israeli attack on 1 August 2014 on Rafah – in which a large number of civilians sheltering in UN schools were killed – "a moral outrage and a criminal act".[88] This description aptly sums up Israel's entire policy in the conflict with Gaza.

The historical record of the last fourteen years does not support Israel's argument that its resort to force in Gaza is justified by the right to self-defence. By its own actions Israel has undermined any claim it might have had to dictate the terms in which the world should view its confrontation with Hamas and with the civilian population of Gaza. The international community urgently needs to develop a new narrative for addressing the conflict in Gaza, one based on the real facts of this tragic situation, international law, international humanitarian law, the norms of civilized international behaviour, and common human decency. And within this broader context, it is the specific duty of the International Criminal Court to hold Israel to account for the alleged war crimes committed by its security forces in the ongoing conflict in Gaza.

28 May 2019

This piece was published as Annex A to Mishana Hosseinioun's submission to the ICC, Article 15 Communication submitted to the ICC Prosecutor requesting initiation of an investigation into the alleged crimes committed in the Occupied Palestinian Territory, including East Jerusalem, since 13 June 2014, submitted 2019. This first partly appeared in Irish Pages *in the issue "Israel, Islam & the West" (Volume 9, Number 2).*

— 2024 —

ISRAEL'S WAR ON GAZA

When Israel withdrew from Gaza in 2005, it turned the tiny enclave into an open-air prison. Israel's response to the Hamas attack of October 7, 2023 – the incessant bombardment of Gaza by land, sea, and air – turned this open-air prison into an open graveyard, a pile of rubble, a desolate wasteland.

António Guterres, the Secretary-General of the United Nations (UN), said in his address to the Security Council, that the Hamas attack, in which 1,200 Israelis were killed and 250 taken hostage, did not happen in a vacuum. "The Palestinian people have been subjected to 56 years of suffocating occupation", he noted. He immediately added that "the grievances of the Palestinian people cannot justify the appalling attacks by Hamas. And those appalling attacks cannot justify the collective punishment of the Palestinian people."

Gilad Erdan, Israel's ambassador to the UN, responded with a vicious personal attack on the Secretary-General, claiming, falsely, that he accused Israel of blood libel, calling for his resignation, and topping it off with a call on members of the UN to stop funding the organization. Israeli antagonism to the UN and obstruction of its work is nothing new, but the contrast between the decency and humanity of the Secretary-General and the rudeness and crudeness of the Israeli representative was particularly striking on this occasion.

I propose to follow in the footsteps of the Secretary-General by stating the obvious: the Israel-Hamas conflict did not begin on October 7. It has to be placed in its proper historical context. The Gaza Strip is the name given to the southern part of the coastal plain of Palestine, adjoining Egypt. It was part of Palestine during the British Mandate which ended in May 1948. Under the 1947 UN partition plan this area was to form part of the Palestinian Arab State but this State did not materialize. During the 1948 war for Palestine the Egyptian army captured this semi-desert strip.

The 1949 Israeli-Egyptian Armistice Agreement left this area on the Egyptian side of the new international border. Egypt did not annex the territory but kept it under military rule, pending resolution of the Arab-Israeli conflict.

The strip is 25 miles long and four to nine miles wide with a total area of 141 square miles. In the course of the 1948 war more than 200,000 Palestinian refugees were added to a population of around 80,000, creating a massive humanitarian problem. UNRWA (the UN Relief and Works Agency) was set up to provide food, education, and health services to the refugees. Israel occupied the Gaza Strip in the course of the Suez War of October-November 1956 but was forced by international pressure to vacate it in March 1957. A large number of civilians were killed, and atrocities were committed by the Israel Defense Forces (IDF) during its short-lived occupation of the territory in what was a foretaste of things to come.

In June 1967, Israel occupied the Gaza Strip, the West Bank, including East Jerusalem, the Golan Heights, and the Sinai peninsula. In August 2005, Israel withdrew its soldiers and settlers from the Gaza Strip. Israeli spokespersons claimed that by withdrawing they gave the Gazans an opportunity to turn the enclave into the Singapore of the Middle East. This claim is utterly preposterous when compared with the grim reality, but it is quite typical of Israeli propaganda. The reality is that between 1967 and 2005, a classic colonial situation prevailed in the Gaza Strip. A few thousand

Israeli settlers controlled 25 percent of the territory, 40 percent of the arable land, and the largest share of the desperately scarce water resources.

The Gaza Strip is not backward and impoverished because its residents are lazy but because Israel's rapacious colonial regime did not give it a chance to flourish. Economic progress was thwarted by a deliberate Israeli strategy of "de-development". Sara Roy, a Jewish scholar at Harvard, the daughter of Holocaust survivors, is the leading expert on the Gaza Strip. She has written four books on Gaza. The first and ground-breaking book was called *The Gaza Strip: The Political Economy of De-development*. In this book she coined the term and formulated the pivotal concept of de-development. Her powerful thesis is that the dire state of Gaza is not the result of objective conditions but of a deliberate Israeli policy of keeping it under-developed and dependent. Despite considerable opposition from the scholarly community when she first introduced the concept, it has become widely used and part of the lexicon in political science and other disciplines. The book shows in detail the various measures by which Israel systematically thwarted the growth of industry in the Gaza Strip and exploited the enclave as a source of cheap labour as well as a market for its own goods.

There were three principal reasons for the decision of the right-wing Likud government, headed by Ariel

Sharon, to withdraw from Gaza in 2005. One is that Hamas, the Islamic Resistance Movement, launched attacks against Israel's settlers and soldiers and, as a result, the price of occupying Gaza outstripped the benefits. The game was no longer worth the candle. A second aim of the move was to sabotage the Oslo peace process. As Dov Weissglas, Sharon's chief of staff, explained in an interview with *Ha'aretz* on October 8, 2004:

> The significance is the freezing of the political process. And when you freeze that process you prevent the establishment of a Palestinian state and you prevent a discussion about the refugees, the borders and Jerusalem. Effectively, this whole package that is called the Palestinian state, with all that it entails, has been removed from our agenda indefinitely... The disengagement is actually formaldehyde. It supplies the amount of formaldehyde that's necessary so that there will not be a political process with the Palestinians.

The third reason for disengagement had to do with demography. Palestinians have a higher birth rate than Israelis and this is perceived as a threat, a "demographic time bomb" as some Israelis call it. To preserve the slim Jewish majority in areas claimed by Israel, the Likud government decided to withdraw unilaterally from Gaza. By withdrawing from Gaza, it removed, or thought it removed, in one stroke, 1.4 million Palestinians from the overall demographic equation. Sharon claimed that by withdrawing from Gaza, his government was making a contribution toward peace with the Palestinians. But this was a unilateral Israeli move undertaken solely in what was considered to be the Israeli national interest. The nature of the move was revealed by its official name: "the unilateral disengagement from Gaza." Disengagement from Gaza was not the prelude to further withdrawals from the West Bank and it most emphatically was not a contribution to peace. The houses that were abandoned in Gaza were demolished by bulldozers in what amounted to a scorched earth policy. The controlling consideration behind the move was to divert resources from Gaza in order to safeguard and consolidate the more significant Israeli settlements in the West Bank.

In the year after withdrawing its 8,000 settlers from Gaza, the Likud government introduced 12,000 new settlers into the West Bank. Today, there are over 700,000 settlers in the West Bank, including East Jerusalem. The 2005 move was not coordinated with the Palestinian Authority (PA). The long-term aim of the Sharon government was to redraw *unilaterally* the borders of Greater Israel. One step in this overall strategy was the disengagement from Gaza. The other step was the building of the so-called security barrier on the West Bank. The security barrier was in fact as much about land-grabbing as it was about security. It was said to be a temporary security measure, but it was intended to delineate the final borders of Greater Israel.

The two moves were anchored in a fundamental rejection of Palestinian national rights. They reflected a determination to prevent the Palestinians from ever achieving independence on their own land. Denying access between the Gaza Strip and the West Bank was a means of obstructing a unified Palestinian struggle for independence. At the tactical level, withdrawing from Gaza enabled the Israeli Air Force to bomb the territory at will, something they could not do when Israeli settlers lived there.

Following the Israeli withdrawal from Gaza, Hamas moderated its program and turned to the ballot box as the road to power. Its 1988 Charter was antisemitic and called for a unitary Islamic State from the Jordan River to the Mediterranean Sea. But in its platform for the January 2006 elections, it tacitly accepted Israel's existence and lowered its sights to an independent Palestinian State along the 1967 lines. However, Hamas did not agree to sign a formal peace treaty with Israel, and it insisted on the right of return of the 1948 refugees, widely seen as a codeword for dismantling Israel as a Jewish State. Hamas won a clear victory in a fair and free election not just in Gaza, but in the West Bank as well. Having won an absolute majority of seats in the Palestinian Legislative Council, Hamas proceeded to form a government in accordance with customary democratic procedure. The Hamas victory came as an unpleasant surprise for Israel and its Western supporters. Israel refused to recognize the new government and resorted to economic warfare to undermine it. The United States (US) and European Union, to their eternal shame, followed Israel's example in refusing to recognize the democratically elected government and joined Israel in economic warfare to undermine it.

This is just one example, one example among many, of Western hypocrisy on Israel-Palestine. The Western leaders claim that they believe in democracy and that their objective round the world is democracy-promotion. They invaded Iraq in 2003 in the name of democracy and ended up by destroying the country and causing hundreds of thousands of casualties. The Western military interventions in Afghanistan, Syria, and Libya also used democracy as a camouflage for imperial ambitions and all of them ended in dismal failure. Democracy needs to be built by the people from the ground up; it cannot be imposed by a foreign army from the barrel of a tank.

Palestine was a shining example of democracy in action. With the possible exception of Lebanon, it was the only genuine as opposed to sham democracy in the Arab world. Under the incredibly difficult conditions imposed by coercive military occupation, the Palestinians succeeded in building a democratic political system. The Palestinian people had spoken, but Israel and its Western allies refused to recognize the result of the election because the people had voted for the "wrong" party.

In March 2007, Hamas formed a national unity government with Fatah, the mainstream party that came second in the ballot box. It was a moderate government which consisted mainly of technocrats rather than politicians. Hamas invited its coalition partner to negotiate with Israel a long-term *hudna* or truce. Much more significant than the offer of a long-term truce was Hamas's acceptance of a two-State settlement (with the implicit de facto recognition of Israel). This acceptance was already hinted at in the Cairo Declaration of 2005, the "Prisoners' Document" of 2006, and the Mecca Accord between Hamas and Fatah of 2007. Hamas all-but-explicitly endorsed a two-State settlement and, as the then UN Middle East Envoy Álvaro de Soto observed, it could have evolved further – if only its overtures had not met with flat dismissal and rejection from Israel and its allies. Nevertheless,

Hamas leaders continued to make it clear, in countless subsequent statements, that they would accept a Palestinian State based on the 1967 borders.

Not content with dismissing Hamas's call for a *hudna* and its offer of negotiations for a two-State settlement, Israel entered into a plot to topple the national unity government and to oust Hamas from power. In 2008, a leak of memos from the Israel-Palestinian Authority negotiations showed that Israel and the US armed and trained the security forces of President Mahmoud Abbas with the aim of overthrowing the unity government. Later, the "Palestine Papers", a cache of 1,600 diplomatic documents leaked to Al Jazeera, provided more details. They revealed that a secret committee was formed called the Gaza Security Committee. It had four members: Israel, America, Fatah, and Egyptian intelligence. The aim of this committee was to isolate and weaken Hamas and to help Fatah stage a coup in order to recapture power.

Hamas decided to pre-empt the Fatah coup. It seized power violently in Gaza in June 2007. Since then, the two branches of the Palestinian national movement have been divided with Hamas ruling over the Gaza Strip from Gaza City and the Palestinian Authority, dominated by Fatah, governing the West Bank from Ramallah. The Palestinian Authority, funded mainly by the European Union and to a lesser extent by the

United States, functions essentially as a sub-contractor for Israeli security. It is corrupt, incompetent, and impotent. As a result, it enjoys little legitimacy in the West Bank and even less in the Gaza Strip.

Israel's response to the Hamas seizure of power was to intensify a blockade on Gaza. The US, United Kingdom (UK), and other European allies participated in this cruel blockade. The blockade has now been in force for seventeen years. It inflicts daily hardship on the inhabitants of the Strip. It involves Israeli control not only of the imports but also of all exports from Gaza, including agricultural goods. The blockade of Gaza is not only cruel and inhumane but plainly illegal. A blockade is a form of collective punishment which is explicitly proscribed by international law. And yet the international community has totally failed to hold Israel to account for this and the rest of its illegal actions. Israel denies that it is an occupying power of the Gaza Strip. However, the UN, the International Committee of the Red Cross (ICRC), Amnesty International, and Human Rights Watch have all concluded that Israel remains in "effective occupation" despite its physical withdrawal because it continues to control access to the territory by land, sea, and air.

Having been denied the fruits of its electoral victory, Hamas resorted to the weapon of the weak, to what Israel calls terrorism, and this took the form of rocket attacks from Gaza on southern Israel. The IDF retaliated by bombing Gaza; a tit-for-tat ensued and the inevitable escalation of hostilities. In June 2008, Egypt brokered a ceasefire between Israel and Hamas. The ceasefire worked remarkably well. In the six months before June, the average number of rockets fired on Israel was 179. In the following months, the average fell to three rockets a month. On November 4, 2008, the IDF launched a raid into Gaza, killed six Hamas fighters, and killed the ceasefire, leading to an immediate resumption of hostilities. Hamas offered to renew the ceasefire on its original terms which included the easing of the blockade. Israel refused the offer and prepared to renew the fight. In general, Hamas has a much better record than Israel of observing ceasefires.

Israel launched its first major military offensive in Gaza on December 27, 2008, naming it Operation Cast Lead. The reason given for the attack was self-defense. Israel, like any other country, it was claimed, has the right to defend itself and to protect its citizens. In other words, Israel claimed the right to self-defense against the people it occupied and oppressed. However, if all Israel wanted was to protect its citizens, it did not have to resort to force. All it had to do was to follow Hamas's good example and observe the ceasefire. Israel repeatedly invokes its right to self-defense but under international law self-defense does not apply if you are an illegal military occupier.

Operation Cast Lead was also the first major Israeli assault on the people of Gaza, and I use the words "people of Gaza" deliberately. Israel claims that Hamas uses civilians as a human shield and that this makes them legitimate military targets. In a crowded enclave, however, it is inevitable that some Hamas command centers, tunnels, and weapons stores are located near civilian buildings. That is not the same as using civilians as human shields. Many of the Israeli claims that Hamas uses schools, hospitals, mosques, and UNRWA buildings as cover for its operations have turned out to be untrue. On the other hand, the claim that the IDF goes to great lengths to avoid hurting innocent civilians is flatly contradicted by the evidence. Its offensive inflicted very heavy casualties and massive damage to the civilian infrastructure. It established a pattern of regular incursions to hit Hamas, incursions that invariably rain down death and destruction on the civilian population.

The United Nations Human Rights Council appointed a commission of inquiry into Operation Cast Lead. It was headed by the eminent South African Judge Richard Goldstone. The Goldstone team noted that both sides were guilty of war crimes but reserved its severest criticisms for Israel because of the scale and seriousness of its war crimes. To give just one example, Goldstone and his colleagues found seven incidents in which Israeli soldiers shot civilians leaving their homes, holding a white flag.

The conclusion of the report was that the attacks in 2008-2009 were directed, at least in part, at the people of Gaza as a whole. It was "a deliberately disproportionate attack designed to punish, humiliate, and terrorize a civilian population." During the second Lebanon war of 2006 the IDF Chief of General Staff Gadi Eizenkot enunciated a policy of deliberately harming enemy civilians which became known as the "Dahiya Doctrine". The doctrine was named after the Dahiya neighborhood of Beirut, where Hezbollah was headquartered during the war. It encompassed the destruction of civilian infrastructure in order to deny its use to the enemy and it endorsed the use of "disproportionate force" to achieve that end. Israel has repeatedly applied this criminal doctrine in Gaza to devastating humanitarian effect.

Operation Cast Lead was followed by further Israeli attacks on the Gaza Strip in 2012, 2014, 2018, 2021, 2022, and mid-2023. Operation Swords of Iron is the eighth Israeli military offensive in Gaza in fifteen years, and it has been by far the most lethal and destructive. After two months of fighting, the Palestinian death toll had risen to at least 17,700, including

7,729 children and 5,153 women, with over 48,700 injured – more than the total of the previous military offensives combined. A further 265 Palestinians were killed on the West Bank by the Israeli military and armed settlers. Nearly 1.9 million people in Gaza, equivalent to 85 percent of a population of 2.3 million, were internally displaced. Heavy IDF bombardment reduced entire neighborhoods to rubble and inflicted catastrophic damage on the civilian infrastructure and economy of Gaza. UN staff who assist the Palestinians were another casualty of this savage Israeli offensive. More than 130 UNRWA teachers, health workers, and aid workers were killed – the highest number in any conflict in the UN's history.

The United Nations Office for the Coordination of Humanitarian Affairs (OCHA) estimated that Israeli attacks destroyed more than 52,000 housing units and damaged more than 253,000. At least 60 percent of Gaza's homes were damaged or destroyed. By November 12, OCHA reported, 279 educational facilities had been damaged, more than 51 percent of the total, with none of Gaza's 625,000 students able to access education. More than half of Gaza's hospitals and nearly two-thirds of primary health care centers were out of service and 53 ambulances damaged. All thirteen hospitals in Gaza City and northern Gaza had received evacuation orders from the Israeli military.

Water consumption had fallen by 90 percent since the war started. People were queuing for an average of four to six hours to receive half the normal bread ration. Around 390,000 jobs had been lost since the start of the war. Before the war the jobless rate already stood at 46 percent, rising to 70 percent among youth. The socio-economic impact of the war has been nothing short of catastrophic. It is difficult to avoid the conclusion that, as in Operation Cast Lead, Operation Swords of Iron is "a deliberately disproportionate attack designed to punish, humiliate, and terrorize a civilian population."

Israeli generals frequently use the same phrase to describe their recurrent operations in Gaza: "mowing the lawn". What this means is that they have no political solution to the problem of Gaza. So every few years they move in with foot soldiers, tanks, artillery, navy, and aircraft, smash up the place, degrade the military capabilities of Hamas, pulverize the civilian infrastructure, and then go home and leave the political problem completely unresolved.

"Mowing the lawn" is a chilling metaphor because it describes a mechanical action that you do periodically every few years and with no end in sight. Under this template, there is no end to the bloodshed, and the next war is always around the corner. This is not a policy for dealing with Gaza; it is a non-policy. To put it differently, it is an inappropriate military response to what essentially is a political problem.

There is a popular Israeli saying: if force does not work, use more force. This is an asinine idea: if force does not work, it is because it is an unsuitable instrument for dealing with the problem at hand. It can also be counterproductive. Israel's disproportionate, excessive use of military force in the past ended up by encouraging the rise of Hezbollah in Lebanon and of Hamas in the Gaza Strip. Israel's policy of assassinating Hamas leaders with the aim of decapitating the organization has never worked. The dead leaders are quickly replaced by younger leaders who are usually more militant.

The government formed by Benjamin Netanyahu at the end of 2022 was the most radical, right-wing, xenophobic, expansionist, overtly racist – and the most incompetent government in Israel's history. It was also the most explicitly pro-settler, Jewish supremacist government. The policy guidelines of this government assert that "the Jewish people have an exclusive and inalienable right to all parts of the Land of Israel." In other words, only Jews have a right to the whole Land of Israel which includes the West Bank. Palestinians have no national rights. This extreme and uncompromising position makes bloodshed inevitable because it leaves the Palestinians no peaceful avenue for realizing their right to national self-determination.

After October 7, Israel announced a new war aim, namely, to eliminate Hamas altogether as a political and military force. Israeli leaders began to speak of "dismantling Hamas once and for all" or "eradicating" Hamas. To anyone familiar with the history of Israel-Gaza relations, this aim comes as a surprise. It definitely represents an abrupt reversal of Netanyahu's previous policy. Whereas some Israeli leaders prefer having a unified collaborator PA administration in Gaza and the West Bank, Netanyahu was content with the status quo of different regimes in Gaza and the West Bank. Here is what he reportedly said to his Likud colleagues in March 2019: "Anyone who wants to thwart the establishment of a Palestinian State has to support bolstering Hamas and transferring money to Hamas . . . This is part of our strategy – to isolate the Palestinians in Gaza from the Palestinians in the West Bank."

On October 7, the cynical policy of Netanyahu, of preserving the status quo in the occupied territories by a tactic of divide and rule, collapsed spectacularly. His policy was to keep the Palestinian Authority weak, to allow Israel a free hand to do whatever it liked on the West Bank, and to keep the Palestinians in Gaza cooped up in the open-air prison. It was a policy of containment that ultimately failed to contain.

On October 7, the inmates broke out of the prison. In the words of Norman Finkelstein, the breakout was akin to a slave rebellion. Fighters of Hamas and Islamic Jihad broke down the fence and went on a killing spree in southern Israel. First, they attacked a military base, then kibbutzim and settlements round the borders of Gaza. They killed about 350 soldiers, more than 800 civilians, and the carnage was accompanied by terrible atrocities. They also took 250 hostages, both soldiers and civilians. This was a game-changer: the first time Hamas conducted a large-scale attack by land inside Israel. It was a horrific and totally unexpected attack that traumatized the whole of Israeli society.

On the Israeli side, this was more than an intelligence failure; it was a policy failure of the highest magnitude. For years Netanyahu had been saying to the Israeli public that the Palestinians are finished, that they are defeated, that Israelis can do whatever they like on the West Bank, that they can forget Gaza, and achieve peace with the Arab States without making any concessions to the Palestinians.

The 2020-2021 Abraham Accords between Israel and Bahrain, the United Arab Emirates (UAE), Morocco, and Sudan seemed to vindicate Netanyahu. They yielded what he wanted: peace for peace without Israel having to make any concessions on the Palestinian issue. The Accords were a betrayal of the collective Arab position on the Palestinian issue. This position was adopted by the Arab League summit in Beirut in March 2002, and it became known as the Arab Peace Initiative. It offered Israel peace and normalization with all 22 members of the Arab League in return for agreeing to an independent Palestinian State along the 1967 lines with a capital city in East Jerusalem. Israel ignored the offer. The Abraham Accords amounted to a very different kind of a deal for Israel and a stab in the back to the Palestinian national movement. They were sponsored by the United States as part of a misguided policy of promoting stability in the Middle East by cooperating with authoritarian Arab regimes and Israel while bypassing the Palestinians.

The Hamas attack announced loud and clear that the Palestinian issue is not dead and that Palestinian resistance to the Israeli occupation is far from over. One of its aims was to deter Saudi Arabia from concluding a peace treaty with Israel. Under strong American pressure, Saudi Arabia came very close to signing an Abraham Accord with Israel. In the Arab world, as in the West, there is a disconnect between the governments and the people on Israel-Palestine. The governments value their relationship with America and Israel; the Arab street remains strongly pro-Palestinian regardless of the shifting geopolitics of the region. The Hamas attack, by rekindling popular support for the Palestinian cause throughout the Arab and Islamic worlds, forced the Saudis to think again.

The October 7 attack also highlighted the contrast between the craven subservience of the PA to Israel and America and the Islamic resistance to the occupation spearheaded by Hamas. The PA had been totally ineffective in protecting the people of the West Bank against Israeli land grabs, ethnic cleansing, escalating settler violence, and ever-increasing provocations in and around the al-Aqsa mosque in the Old City of Jerusalem, one of the three holiest sites of Islam alongside Mecca and Medina. Al-Aqsa is of the greatest importance to Muslims as a religious symbol and this is precisely why the encroachment by the Netanyahu government and its Jewish fundamentalist followers is so incendiary. By its attack of October 7 Hamas signaled to Israel that these provocations will no longer be tolerated. It was for this reason too that the operation was named the Al-Aqsa Deluge. All in all, it was a powerful assertion of Palestinian agency and leadership in the ongoing struggle against the Israeli occupation.

The Hamas attack left Netanyahu's entire policy in tatters, and he will probably pay the political price for the intelligence and security failures. Before October 7 there was massive protest in Israel against his plan for judicial overhaul. The protest did not cease altogether following the Hamas attack but the situation in Gaza became the dominant issue. It did not take long for families of the hostages to start a vigil outside the Prime

Minister's residence in Jerusalem. After the dust settles, all the anger will be redirected at Netanyahu. In the face of mounting international calls for an immediate ceasefire, he remains defiant. He knows that once the war against Hamas comes to an end, his days in office will be numbered. Politically speaking, Netanyahu looks like a dead man walking.

What is clear is that Netanyahu's new policy of eradicating Hamas has no chance of succeeding. Hamas has a military wing, the Izz ad-Din al-Qassam Brigades, which commits terrorist acts when it targets Israeli civilians. Even if all its commanders were killed, they would be quickly replaced by new recruits and more militant ones. But Hamas is also a political party with institutions and a social movement with many branches such as a women's association and a students' association. It is part of the fabric of Palestinian society. What is more: Hamas is a set of ideas, including the idea of freedom and self-determination for the Palestinian people. Military force can decimate an organization, but it cannot kill an idea.

With characteristic hubris, Netanyahu announced that he was determined to destroy Hamas not only to ensure his own country's security but also to free the people of Gaza from Hamas's tyranny. Israel's indiscriminate use of force, however, does not weaken Hamas; it strengthens it. By relying on brute military force alone,

Israel weakens those Palestinian leaders who advocate negotiations and believe that Palestinians need only behave nicely for the world to sit up and listen. Nor is Hamas identical to ISIS, as Netanyahu and an ever-increasing number of his ministers keep claiming. ISIS is a jihadist organization with a nihilist global agenda. Hamas, by contrast, is a regional organization with a limited and legitimate political agenda.

On June 2, 1948, Sir John Troutbeck, a senior official in the Foreign Office, wrote a memo to Foreign Secretary Ernest Bevin. He complained that by their support for the creation of Israel, the Americans helped to create a "gangster state with a thoroughly unscrupulous set of leaders." Whether Israel behaves like a gangster state is open to debate, but Netanyahu is without doubt a thoroughly unscrupulous leader. As he directed Israel's 2023 assault on Gaza, Netanyahu was also on trial for three serious corruption charges, and he knew that if convicted, he might end up in prison. The imperative of personal political survival helped to shape his conduct of the war.

Yet Netanyahu's motives for prolonging the war in Gaza went deeper than self-preservation. His life's mission has been to defeat the Palestinian national movement and to prevent the emergence of an independent Palestinian State alongside Israel. He grew up in a fiercely nationalistic Jewish home. His father,

Benzion Netanyahu, was the political secretary of Ze'ev Jabotinsky, the spiritual father of the Israeli Right and the chief architect of the strategy of the "iron wall". In 1923, Jabotinsky published an article under the title "On the Iron Wall (We and the Arabs)". In it he argued that the Zionist goal of an independent Jewish State in Palestine could only be achieved unilaterally and by military force. A Jewish State could only be established not by negotiations with the Arabs of Palestine but behind an iron wall of Jewish military power. The essence of the strategy was negotiations from strength. Once the Arabs gave up hope of defeating the Jews on the battlefield, then would come the time for stage two, for negotiating with them about their status and rights in Palestine. Israeli Prime Minister Yitzhak Rabin moved from stage one to stage two of the strategy by signing the Oslo Accord with the PLO in 1993 though he never conceded any Palestinian national rights.

Netanyahu came to power in 1996, following the assassination of Rabin, with the explicit mission of subverting the Oslo Accords and preventing the establishment of a Palestinian State. He was fixated on the first part of the iron wall strategy, on accumulating more and more military power, and avoiding stage two, negotiations of any kind. Until October 7, his strategy was to drive a firm wedge between Gaza and the West Bank and to allow a weak Hamas to govern Gaza. After October 7, he was determined to destroy Hamas but without allowing the PA to extend its writ to Gaza because that would strengthen the case for a two-State solution. This amounted to a crude version of Jabotinsky's strategy, using Jewish military power not to resolve the conflict but to keep the Palestinians in the West Bank and Gaza in a permanent state of subordination to a Jewish supremacist State. Netanyahu's declared aim is to ensure security for Israel for the long-term. His undeclared aim is to end forever the prospect of Palestinian independence.

One disturbing aspect of the Israeli response to the horrific Hamas attack is the dehumanizing of the Palestinian people. This is nothing new. On one occasion, Netanyahu famously suggested that it was Haj Amin al-Husseini, the leader of the Palestinian National Movement, who suggested to Hitler that instead of expelling the Jews from Germany, he should exterminate them. One of Netanyahu's most often repeated, and most morally repugnant claims is that Palestinian nationalism is a direct continuation of Nazi antisemitism.

Today, many Israeli ministers depict the Palestinians as Nazis. Yoav Galant, the defense minister, referred to the enemy as "human animals", and used this view to justify the inhuman siege that he imposed, the cutting off of electricity, food, water, and fuel to 2.3 million people. Particularly chilling in its cruelty, given the huge number of children killed, was the President of Israel Isaac Herzog's statement that the "entire nation" of Gaza "is responsible". Dehumanizing an entire people can have serious political consequences even if they are unintended. The Nazi dehumanization of the Jews was a major factor in paving the way for the death camps. Israeli demonization of the Palestinians is a similarly dangerous dynamic that can be used to justify the ethnic cleansing of Gaza.

The Western response to the crisis in Gaza has comprised the usual hypocrisy and brazen double standards, but this time taken to a new level. The Western love of Israel has always been accompanied by the denial of Palestinian history and humanity. Deep concern for Israel's security is reiterated all the time by all Western leaders, but no thought is spared for Palestinian security, let alone Palestinian rights. Evidently, the Palestinians are the children of a lesser God.

In the immediate aftermath of the Hamas attack, Western leaders undertook a pilgrimage to Jerusalem to demonstrate that they are standing by Israel. Palestinian resistance to the occupation, the most prolonged and brutal military occupation of modern times, has been decontextualized and de-historicized. The Palestinians are engaged in an anti-colonial struggle, possibly the last anti-colonial struggle in today's world. But their struggle is widely attributed by Western commentators to religious fanaticism and irrational hatred of Jews rather than to the normal, universal desire of all people to live in freedom and dignity on their land.

The Western stand with Israel carries an echo of the habitual colonial tendency to treat struggles for national liberation as proof of the savagery, barbarism, and terrorism of the indigenous population. This is how the "civilized world" responded to the liberation struggles of South Africans, Algerians, Kenyans, and Vietnamese. And this is how some Western leaders look upon Palestinian resistance today.

The US and UK have given Israel not only moral but material and military support as well as diplomatic protection. President Joe Biden said that the attack of October 7 was the worst attack on the Jewish people since the Holocaust. This is to trivialize the Holocaust. America sent two aircraft carriers to the Eastern Mediterranean and beefed up its forces in Saudi Arabia, Iraq, and Jordan. By shielding Israel from Hezbollah and Iran, the US enabled Israel to carry on the mass slaughter in Gaza. In effect, America and Britain gave Israel warrant to pursue its war on Gaza despite the humanitarian catastrophe it caused. They called for "humanitarian pauses" when what was desperately needed was a complete ceasefire. The seven-day pause in the fighting made it possible to send some humanitarian aid into Gaza and for the freeing by Hamas of some of the hostages in return for the release of three times the number of Palestinians from Israeli prisons. But as soon as the pause expired, on December 1, the IDF intensified the bombardment, killing 700 people in one day and exacerbating the utterly horrendous humanitarian crisis.

A UAE draft resolution to the Security Council for an immediate humanitarian ceasefire was defeated by an American veto on December 8 although it had the support of thirteen members with only the UK abstaining. Since 1948, the US has used its veto 34 times to defeat resolutions critical of Israel. The majority of these resolutions were drafted to provide a framework for resolving the Israel-Palestine conflict. The veto of the UAE draft resolution was widely denounced, especially in the global south, as tantamount to a free pass for Israel to continue the butchery and destruction of Gaza.

In his October 28 address to the nation, Netanyahu said that Israelis were fighting their second war of independence. This is preposterous: no one is threatening Israel's independence or existence today. It is Israel which is denying freedom and independence to the Palestinians. The statement may also have carried a veiled threat. In 1948 what Israelis call their "War of Independence" was accompanied by the Nakba, the catastrophe, the ethnic cleansing of Palestine. There have been ample signs that the Netanyahu government is in fact actively planning a second Nakba.

A leaked report of Israel's Intelligence Ministry, dated October 13, outlined three alternatives "to bring about a significant change in the civilian reality in the Gaza Strip in light of the Hamas crimes that led to the 'Iron Swords' war." The alternative deemed by the document's authors to best serve Israeli security involves moving Gaza's civilian population to tent cities in northern Sinai, then building permanent cities and an undefined humanitarian corridor. A security zone would be established inside Israel, on the border with Egypt, to block the displaced Palestinians from entering. The report did not say what would become of Gaza once its population is cleared out. History tells us that once Israel drives Palestinians from their homes, it does not allow them to return. This is what happened in the 1948 war and in the 1967 war and, despite strong Egyptian opposition, it could happen again.

These are not isolated actions but part of a pattern. They all serve the ultimate goal that the Zionist movement had set itself from the start: to build a Jewish State on as large a part of Palestine as possible with as few Arabs within its borders as possible. Operation Swords of Iron marks a new and utterly ruthless step in this direction. As Ahdaf Soueif, the Egyptian-British novelist, observed in the *Guardian* on December 4, 2023, "[w]hat the global south has known for 100 years, the people of the global north are understanding now: that the Zionists want all the land, with no Palestinian people, and will stop at nothing to get it."

In 1876, Liberal opposition leader William Gladstone published a pamphlet denouncing atrocities committed by soldiers of the Ottoman Empire against civilians in Bulgaria. Gladstone's indictment seared itself in my memory since I was an eighteen-year-old schoolboy in London doing A-Level British History. The key passage went as follows: "Let the Turks now carry away their abuses in the only possible manner, namely, by carrying off themselves. Their Zaphtiehs and their Mudirs, their Bimbashis and their Yuzbachis, their Kaimakams and their Pashas, one and all, bag and baggage, shall, I hope, clear out from the province they have desolated and profaned." This is rather how I feel about the atrocities perpetrated by the IDF in the Gaza province today.

Originally published as Chapter One in Jamie Stern-Weiner ed., Deluge: Gaza and Israel from Crisis to Cataclysm *(New York: OR Books, 2024).*

— 2024 —

ALL THAT REMAINS

On 7th January 2009, while Operation Cast Lead was in full swing, I wrote an article in the Guardian. "How Israel brought Gaza to the brink of humanitarian catastrophe." This was Israel's first major assault on the Gaza Strip after its unilateral withdrawal in 2005. Further major military offensives followed in 2012, 2014, 2021 and 2022, not counting minor flare-ups and nearly 200 dead during the border protests in 2018 known as the March of Return. By my count, the current war is the sixth serious Israeli assault on Gaza since the withdrawal, and by far the most lethal and destructive. And it also raises the ominous spectre of a second Palestinian Nakba.

The only way to make sense of Israel's cruel and self-defeating wars in Gaza is through understanding the historical context. From whatever perspective one chooses to view it, the establishment of the state of

Israel in May 1948 involved a monumental injustice to the Palestinians. Three quarters of a million Palestinians became refugees, and the name Palestine was wiped off the map. Israelis call it "The War of Independence"; Palestinians call it the Nakba, or the catastrophe. The most horrific event in the suffering-soaked history of the Jews was the Holocaust. In the history of the Palestinian people, the most traumatic event is the Nakba, which is not in fact a one-off event but the ongoing process of the dispossession and displacement of Palestinian people from their homeland that continues to this day, in the unspeakable horrors being visited by the Israeli Defence Forces (IDF) on Gaza.

The United Kingdom was the original sponsor of the Jewish state, going back to the Balfour declaration of 1917. But by 1948, the United States had replaced the UK as the principal backer. British officials bitterly resented American partisanship on behalf of the infant state, although they themselves had enabled and empowered the Zionist takeover of Palestine. The conditions that gave rise to the Nakba were made in Britain. Yet no British government has ever accepted any responsibility for the loss and suffering it brought upon the people of Palestine.

In the period since 1948 the western powers, led by the US, have given Israel massive moral, economic and military support, as well as diplomatic protection.

The US has used its veto power in the UN Security Council dozens of times to defeat resolutions that were not to Israel's liking. America also gives Israel around $3.8bn in military aid each year, with more this year to enable Israel to sustain its military offensive in Gaza. The trouble with American support for Israel is that it is not conditional on Israeli respect for Palestinian human rights or international law. As a result, Israel gets away, literally, with murder.

In August 2005, a Likud-led government headed by Ariel Sharon staged a unilateral Israeli pull-out from Gaza, withdrawing all 8,500 settlers and destroying the houses and farms they had left behind. Hamas, the Islamic resistance movement, conducted an effective campaign to drive the Israelis out of Gaza. To the world, Sharon presented the withdrawal from Gaza as a contribution to peace. But in the year that followed, more than 12,000 settlers moved into the West Bank, consolidating Israeli control, and further reducing the scope for an independent Palestinian state.

The real purpose behind the move was to redraw the borders of Greater Israel by incorporating the main settlement blocs on the West Bank to the state of Israel. Withdrawal from Gaza was thus not a prelude to a peace deal with the Palestinian Authority, but a prelude to further Zionist expansion on the West Bank. It was a unilateral Israeli move undertaken in what was seen as the Israeli national interest. Anchored in a fundamental rejection of Palestinian national identity, the withdrawal from Gaza was part of a long-term effort to deny the Palestinian people any independent political existence on their land. This did not stop Israeli spokespersons from making the preposterous claim that by quitting they gave the Gazans a chance to turn the strip into the Singapore of the Middle East.

In December 2008, Israel launched Operation Cast Lead, in breach of a six-month ceasefire that Egypt had brokered. This was not a war in the usual sense of the word but a one-sided massacre. For 22 days, the IDF shot, shelled and bombed Hamas targets and at the same time rained death and destruction on the defenceless civilian population. In all 1,417 Gazans were killed, including 313 children, and more than 5,500 wounded. Eighty-three per cent of the casualties were civilians.

War crimes were investigated by an independent fact-finding mission appointed by the UN Human Rights Council and headed by Richard Goldstone, a distinguished South African judge who happened to be both a Jew and a Zionist. Goldstone and his team found that Hamas and the IDF had both committed violations of the laws of war. The IDF received much more severe strictures than Hamas, on account of the scale and seriousness of its violations. Hamas and other Palestinian armed groups were found guilty of launching rocket and mortar attacks with the deliberate aim of harming Israeli civilians. The Goldstone team investigated 36 incidents involving the IDF. It found 11 incidents in which Israeli soldiers launched direct attacks against civilians with lethal outcomes (in only one case was there a possible "justifiable military objective"); seven incidents where civilians were shot leaving their homes "waving white flags and, in some of the cases, following an injunction from the Israeli forces to do so"; an attack, executed "directly and intentionally" on a hospital; numerous incidents where ambulances were prevented from attending to the severely injured; several attacks on civilian infrastructure with no military significance, such as flour mills, chicken farms, sewage works and water wells – all part of a campaign to deprive civilians of basic necessities. In the words of the report, much of this extensive damage was "not justified by military necessity and carried out unlawfully and wantonly."

In conclusion, the 452-page report noted that while the Israeli government sought to portray its operations as essentially a response to rocket attacks in the exercise of the right to self-defence, "the Mission itself considers the plan to have been directed, at least in part, at a different target: the people of Gaza as a whole."

Under the circumstances, the mission concluded that what occurred in just over three weeks at the end of 2008 and the beginning of 2009 was "a deliberately disproportionate attack designed to punish, humiliate and terrorize a civilian population, radically diminish its local economic capacity both to work and to provide for itself, and to force upon it an ever-increasing sense of dependency and vulnerability." Goldstone later published an op-ed in the Washington Post, saying that while Hamas had committed war crimes (its rockets were "purposefully and indiscriminately aimed at civilian targets"), "civilians were not intentionally targeted as a matter of policy" by Israel. The other three members of the fact-finding mission said that they stood by the conclusions, which were "made after diligent, independent and objective consideration of the information related to the events within our mandate, and careful assessment of its reliability and credibility."

Neither Israel nor Hamas was held to account nor made to pay any price for its war crimes. The Israelis resorted to a character assassination of the report's author rather than engaging with any of its findings. Although it did not lead to any action, the Goldstone report offers a deep insight into the pattern of Israeli behaviour in Gaza in this and all subsequent operations. The absence of sanctions also explains why Israel was able to continue to act with utter impunity and, yet again, to get away literally with murder.

While committing war crimes, Israel claims to be exercising its inherent right to self-defence, and its western cheerleaders repeat this claim parrot-fashion. In this most recent and most devastating attack on Gaza, Keir Starmer, the leader of the Labour party, outdid even Joe Biden and Rishi Sunak by stating that Israel's right to defend itself justified the denial of water, food and fuel to the civilian population. All three leaders persisted for eight weeks in their refusal to call for an immediate ceasefire, contenting themselves with feeble pleas to Israel for pauses in the fighting to allow humanitarian aid to reach the besieged civilian population.

Like most of its claims in this savage war, Israel's claim that it is simply exercising its right of self-defence is baseless – or at least hotly disputed. Francesca Albanese, the UN Special Rapporteur on human rights in the occupied Palestinian territories, has noted that under international law this right is only relevant in the case of an armed attack by one state against another state, or if the threat comes from outside. The attack by Hamas, however, was not by a state, nor did it come from outside. It came from an area for which, under international law, Israel is still the occupying power because after its withdrawal it continued to control access to Gaza by land, sea and air. Put simply, one does not have the right to self-defence against a territory that one occupies. In this case, therefore, the self-defence clause, Article 51 of the UN Charter, has no relevance. It is the people under occupation who have under international law the right to resist, including the right to armed resistance. And the Palestinian people are in a unique position: they are the only people living under military occupation who are expected to ensure the security of their occupier.

Taken together Israel's attacks on Gaza reflect a profoundly militaristic outlook, a stubborn refusal to explore avenues for peaceful coexistence, habitual disregard for the laws of war and international humanitarian law, and utter callousness towards enemy civilians. Israeli generals talk about their recurrent military incursions into Gaza as "mowing the grass". By this they mean weakening Hamas, degrading its military capability and impairing its capacity to govern. This dehumanising metaphor implies a task that must be performed regularly and mechanically and with no end. It also alludes to indiscriminate slaughter of civilians and inflicting the kind of damage on civilian infrastructure that takes several years to repair.

Under this grim rubric, there is no lasting political solution: the next war is always just a matter of time. "Mowing the grass" is a chilling metaphor but it provides another clue to the deeper purpose behind Israel's steadfast shunning of diplomacy and repeated resort to brute military force on its southern border.

The current Israeli bombardment of Gaza is a response to the Hamas attack on Saturday 7th October, or Black Saturday. This was a game changer. In the past, Hamas has fired rockets on Israel or engaged with Israeli forces inside its territory. On 7th October, Hamas and the more radical group Islamic Jihad used bulldozers to break down the fence round Gaza and went on a killing spree in the neighbouring kibbutzim and settlements, murdering about 300 soldiers and massacring more than 800 civilians, 250 of whom were at a music festival. They also captured 240 hostages, including some military personnel. The brutal, murderous attack on civilians was a war crime, and it was rightly denounced as such by international political leaders.

Whether the Hamas attack was totally unprovoked, as Israel and its friends claim, is another matter. The attack did not happen in a vacuum. The backdrop was 56 years of Israeli occupation of the Palestinian territories – the most prolonged and brutal military occupation of modern times. It constitutes daily violence against the residents of the West Bank and the Gaza Strip and a daily violation of their basic human rights.

Hamas is not a terrorist organisation pure and simple, as Israel and its western allies keep insisting. It is a political party with a military wing whose attacks on civilians constitute terrorist acts. Indeed, Hamas is more than a political party with a military wing. It is a mass social movement, a prominent part of the fabric of Palestinian society which reflects its aspiration to freedom and independence. It is the failure of the Palestine Liberation Organization (PLO) to achieve freedom and statehood that largely explains Hamas's growing influence.

In 1993 the PLO signed the first Oslo Accord with Israel. Mutual recognition replaced mutual rejection. For the Palestinian national movement this was a historic compromise: it gave up its claim to 78 per cent of Palestine as it existed between 1920 and 1948 under the League of Nations Mandate, in the hope of gaining an independent state in the remaining 22 per cent, in the West Bank and the Gaza Strip with a capital city in east Jerusalem. But it was not to be. The Oslo Accord turned out to be not a pathway to independence but a trap.

Following the assassination of Prime Minister Yitzhak Rabin in 1995, the hardline nationalist party Likud came back to power under the leadership of Benjamin Netanyahu. Netanyahu has spent the rest of his political career in a relentless and so far successful effort to prevent the establishment of a Palestinian state. He has never been a partner for peace with any Palestinian faction. His game is to play them off against one another in order to frustrate the Palestinian national struggle. "Anyone who wants to thwart the establishment of a Palestinian state has to support bolstering Hamas and transferring money to Hamas", he told his Likud colleagues in March 2019. "This is part of our strategy – to isolate the Palestinians in Gaza from the Palestinians in the West Bank." By weakening and discrediting the moderates in the West Bank, Netanyahu inadvertently assisted the rise of Hamas.

The 1988 Hamas Charter is antisemitic, denies Israel's right to exist and calls for a unitary Muslim state in the whole of historic Palestine, "from the river to the sea" as the slogan goes. But like the PLO before it, Hamas gradually moderated its political programme. Perhaps realising that the suicide bombings it carried out during the Second Intifada were both morally wrong and politically counter-productive, it opted for the parliamentary road to power. In January 2006, Hamas won an absolute majority in an all-Palestine election, in both Gaza and the West Bank, and proceeded to form a government. This was a more moderate, pragmatic government and it offered to negotiate a long-term ceasefire with Israel for 20, 30 or 40 years. Although the Charter was not revised until 2017, in a long series of speeches Hamas leaders indicated that they would accept a Palestinian state based on 1967 borders.

Israel refused to recognise the democratically elected Hamas government and turned down its offer of negotiations. The US and EU followed Israel's lead and joined it in measures of economic warfare designed to undermine it. The western powers claim to believe in democracy but evidently not when the Palestinian people vote for the "wrong" party. To paraphrase Bertolt Brecht, if the Israeli and western governments are dissatisfied with the Palestinian people, they should dissolve the people and elect another.

With Saudi help, the rival Palestinian factions managed to reconcile their differences. On 8th February 2007, Fatah and Hamas signed an agreement in Mecca to stop the clashes between their forces in Gaza and to form a government of national unity. They agreed to a system of power-sharing, with independents taking the key posts of foreign affairs, finance and the interior. And they declared their readiness to negotiate a long-term ceasefire with Israel.

Israel did not like this government either and again refused to negotiate. Worse was to follow. Israel and the US secretly plotted with Fatah officials and Egyptian intelligence to undermine the national unity government. They hoped to reverse the results of the parliamentary election by encouraging Fatah to stage a coup to recapture power.

In 2008, a leak of memos from the Israel-Palestinian Authority negotiations showed that Israel and the US armed and trained the security forces of President Mahmoud Abbas with the aim of overthrowing the Hamas government. (Later, the "Palestine Papers", a cache of 1,600 diplomatic documents leaked to Al Jazeera, would reveal more.) American neoconservatives participated in the sinister plot to instigate a Palestinian civil war. Hamas pre-empted a Fatah coup with a violent seizure of power in Gaza in June 2007. At this point the Palestinian national movement became fractured, with Fatah ruling the West Bank and Hamas ruling the Gaza Strip.

Israel responded to the Hamas move by declaring the Gaza Strip a "hostile territory". It also enacted a series of social, economic and military measures designed to isolate and undermine Hamas. By far the most significant of these measures was the imposition of a blockade. The stated purpose of the blockade was to stop the transfer of weapons and military equipment to Hamas, but it also restricted the flow of food, fuel and medical supplies to the civilian population. One American senator was outraged to discover that pasta was on the list of proscribed items. The boycott applied not only to imports but, perversely, also to some exports from Gaza. Why prevent the export of agricultural products, fish and other non-lethal goods? It is difficult to avoid the conclusion that the hidden motive was to cripple Gaza's economy and to inflict poverty, misery, and unemployment on its inhabitants.

In its non-military aspects, the blockade constituted a form of collective punishment that is clearly proscribed by international law. Given the scale of the suffering inflicted by the blockade on the inhabitants of the strip, if Israel were a person it could be considered guilty of "depraved indifference", a concept in American law (its equivalent under English common law is "depraved heart") that refers to conduct that is so wanton, so callous, so deficient in a moral sense of concern, so lacking in regard for the lives of others and so blameworthy as to warrant criminal liability.

The Israeli bombardment of Gaza since 7th October may undoubtedly be described as "depraved indifference" on account of the indescribable suffering it is inflicting on civilians. While the main enemy is Hamas, Israel keeps targeting civilian infrastructure, residential buildings, schools, mosques, hospitals, ambulances and UNRWA food depots. By the end of November, the death toll has risen to more than 15,000 dead and more than 30,000 injured – more than the total of the previous military offensives combined. An estimated 6,150 of the dead are children and 4,000 are women.

Slaughter of civilians on such an industrial scale may well have taken Israel to the verge of committing genocide, "the crime of all crimes".

There is one other aspect of this campaign that was not present in previous ones: the danger of ethnic cleansing. In previous campaigns Israel brought death and destruction to the people of Gaza but kept them cooped up in the enclave, "generously" allowing them to stay in their homes. This time Israel ordered the residents of the northern part of Gaza, nearly half the total population, to move to the southern part of the enclave. Some of those who obeyed the order were subsequently killed in Israeli air strikes. At the time of writing more than 1.8 million, out of a total of 2.3 million, have been internally displaced. As the Israeli military offensive moved into southern Gaza, the refugees were ordered to move out of the area to which they had fled. This amounts to a forced transfer of civilians: a war crime.

The upshot is that nowhere in Gaza is safe. Stretching the laws of war beyond credulity, Israel argues that civilians who disobey its orders and stay put in their homes in the north become legitimate military targets. In addition, Israel seems to be working on a plan to transfer people permanently from Gaza into northern Sinai. In a leaked document dated 13th October, the Israeli Ministry of Intelligence drafted a proposal for the transfer of the entire population of Gaza to Egypt's Sinai Peninsula. The Egyptian government has expressed strong objection to the plan as well as its determination to keep the Rafah crossing firmly closed – apart from to allow some aid into Gaza during the ceasefire. But the combined pressures of the massive bombardment by the IDF and its medieval-style siege on Gaza may result in a human avalanche across the border. One thing is certain: any civilians who leave Gaza will not be allowed to return to their homes. More than half of the houses in Gaza have already been destroyed or damaged in indiscriminate Israeli bombing. So nearly half the population do not have homes to return to. No wonder that the bleak legacy of 1948 haunts the Palestinian community.

While the martyrdom of over two million innocent Palestinian civilians continues, despite the temporary ceasefire and the exchange of hostages for Palestinian prisoners, a bigger question looms: who will run what remains of the Gaza Strip after the guns fall silent? Netanyahu has declared that he wants the IDF to keep indefinite security control of the strip but no one in Israel wants to assume all the responsibilities of an occupying power again. Meanwhile, his own grip on power at home is weakening. He faces strong popular opposition for his failure to prevent the horrendous Hamas attack and, more generally, for making Israel the most dangerous place in the world for Jews to live. He is also embroiled in a corruption trial on charges – all of which he denies – including fraud, breaching public trust and accepting bribes. Politically speaking, he is a dead man walking. His days in power are numbered and there is a chance that he will end up in prison. But he is still the Prime Minister, and his clearly stated aim is to eradicate Hamas and to prevent it from returning to power ever again. So, who will govern the Gaza Strip after the Israeli army leaves?

Early signs suggest that the Americans and the EU's foreign affairs chief, Josep Borrell, favour the return of the Palestinian Authority to Gaza. This is a totally preposterous proposition. The problem is not Hamas –which did not exist until 1987 – but the Israeli occupation of the Palestinian territories. Moreover, the Hamas that committed the massacre of 7th October is far more extreme than the Hamas that won the 2006 elections and formed a national unity government. By blocking the path to peaceful political change, Israel and its western supporters are largely responsible for this regression to fundamentalist positions. Hamas may not be to their liking, but it still commands broad popular support. If an election were held today, Hamas would almost certainly beat its Fatah rival again.

And what about the sclerotic Fatah-led Palestinian Authority? It is docile, weak, corrupt and incompetent, and can barely govern the West Bank. It receives funding from the EU and to a lesser extent from the US, essentially to serve as a subcontractor for Israeli security in the area. It has shown itself to be utterly incapable of resisting the expansion of Israeli settlements, the escalation of settler violence, the slow but steady takeover of the West Bank and East Jerusalem and the flagrant encroachment by fanatical religious Zionists on the Muslim holy places in Jerusalem. Fatah also lacks legitimacy because no parliamentary elections have been held since January 2006. It has stalled on holding another parliamentary election precisely because it realises that Hamas would win.

The idea that this discredited Palestinian Authority can be imposed on the proud and long-suffering people of Gaza on the back of Israeli tanks is completely detached from reality. But it is mildly interesting, in as much as it exposes the moral and political bankruptcy of the people who espouse it. It is not for Israel or its imperialist backers to tell the people of Gaza who should govern them. If the events of the last few weeks have demonstrated anything, it is that the old narrative of Israel having a right and a duty to defend itself against a terrorist organisation, no matter the human, civilian cost, can no longer be sustained. What is happening in Gaza today is the cruel manifestation of Israeli state terrorism. Terrorism is the use of force against civilians for political ends. The cap fits and Israel must wear it. The Israeli politicians and generals who orchestrate the criminal assaults on the people of Gaza are no better than riffraff.

This ghastly war has also exposed the ruthless hypocrisy of the western leaders, their blatant double standards, their indifference to Palestinian rights and their complicity in Israel's war crimes. Israel is an aggressive settler-colonial state and increasingly a Jewish-supremacist state intent on keeping the Palestinians in a permanent state of subordination. As long as Israel has western support, it will continue to act unilaterally, in violation of international law, in breach of a raft of UN resolutions and in defiance of the most basic norms of civilised international behaviour.

This is not a conflict between two equal sides but between an occupying power and a subjugated population. And there is absolutely no military solution to this conflict. Israel cannot have security without peace with its neighbours. A negotiated political compromise, as in Northern Ireland, is the only way forward. That settlement required external intervention, as does this one. Here, however, the US cannot serve as the sole broker because its pronounced bias in favour of Israel would make it a dishonest one. Ever since 1967, it has arrogated to itself a monopoly over the Israeli-Palestinian peace process but failed to put pressure on Israel to compromise. What is needed now is a new international coalition led by the UN which includes the US and EU but also Arab states and members of the global south. The priorities of such a coalition would be humanitarian relief, reconstruction and a long-term political plan that includes an independent Palestinian state on the Gaza Strip and the West Bank with a capital city in East Jerusalem.

Such a plan is eminently practical. All it would take to realise it is for Israel to shed its settler-colonial and Jewish-supremacist ambitions, for America to end its unconditional support for Israel, for the EU to morph from a payer to an active player, for the United Nations to overcome its self-imposed impotence, and a few similar trifles.

Originally published in Prospect *magazine, January-February 2024 issue.*

— 2024 —

ISRAEL'S ROAD TO GENOCIDE

Jamie Stern-Weiner and Avi Shlaim

> *Israel's actions have been driven by a genocidal logic integral to its settler-colonial project in Palestine, signalling a tragedy foretold.*
> — Francesca Albanese[89]

Doctrines of ethnic nationalism proliferated in nineteenth-century Europe. They divided humanity into primordial groups and advocated that political borders should so far as possible trace the boundaries separating these groups. Every extant nation should have its state and each state should be nationally homogeneous. Modern Zionism applied these premises to Europe's "Jewish Question" and reached an analogous conclusion. Zionist theoreticians argued that Jews in Europe were culturally stifled as well as physically persecuted on account of their anomalous position as a stateless nation. From this diagnosis it followed that the only viable remedy to the twin threats of assimilation and antisemitism was to normalise the Jewish condition by establishing a Jewish state. The Zionist mainstream settled on Palestine as the location of this state because of the territory's resonance in Jewish history and culture. How large should the state be, what should be its character, how could it be realised – such questions provoked heated controversies within the Zionist movement. But almost the full spectrum of Zionist opinion cohered around the essential goal of establishing a state in Palestine populated by an overwhelming Jewish demographic majority.[90]

This objective almost inevitably provoked conflict in Palestine between Zionist newcomers and the territory's existing inhabitants, who were overwhelmingly not Jewish. Palestinian Arabs had no political stake in an endeavour that sought, as the leading Zionist diplomat Chaim Weizmann put it, to render Palestine "as Jewish as England is English".[91] On the contrary, Palestinians reasonably feared that Zionism could succeed only by dispossessing them of house and homeland. Palestinian opposition to Zionism was therefore as comprehensive as it was consistent. This fundamental clash of interests was spotlighted by Ze'ev Jabotinsky, the ever-candid leader of Revisionist Zionism. In his seminal 1923 article, "The Iron Wall", Jabotinsky argued that Palestinians would never "voluntarily consent to the realisation of Zionism" because "every native population in the world resists colonists". This meant "Zionist colonisation must either stop, or else proceed regardless of the native population" behind "a power that is independent" of them.[92] Zionism for many Jews was a movement for collective assertion as well as defence through national self-determination. Zionism for Palestinians was a violent colonial imposition.

— JEWS IN, ARABS OUT —

Writing in 1965, the Palestinian scholar and diplomat Fayez Sayegh identified a "divergence of Zionism from the norm of European colonization". Whereas European settlers had often subjugated native peoples in order to exploit them, the Zionist project sought to evict the native inhabitants of Palestine in order to replace them.[93] The Australian historian Patrick Wolfe later drew this same distinction between franchise colonialism "dependent on native labour" and settler colonialism "premised on the elimination of native societies".[94] The Zionist movement was a case of settler colonialism because it ultimately prized Palestinian land not labour as it sought not to subordinate Palestinians but to supplant them. Mass expulsion (or "transfer") of the Palestinians was therefore, as the Israeli historian Benny Morris writes, "inbuilt into Zionism". On the one hand, "a Jewish state could not have arisen without a major displacement of Arab population"; on the other hand, "this aim automatically produced resistance among the Arabs which, in turn, persuaded" Zionist leaders "that a hostile Arab majority or large minority could not remain in place if a Jewish state was to arise or safely endure."[95]

In his presentation on Zionism before the November 1975 General Assembly of the United Nations, Sayegh conjured a vivid comparison. "As in the beating of a heart", he said, the Zionist project comprised "two inextricable rhythmic operations": the "pumping-in" of Jews to Palestine and the "pumping-out" of Palestine's non-Jewish inhabitants.[96] This twofold dynamic of Jewish expansion and Palestinian displacement has formed a relentless if irregular pulse animating more than a century of Zionist-Arab conflict. It began already under the British Mandate. Between 1917 and 1947, the Zionist movement brought hundreds of thousands of Jews from Europe into Palestine, increasing the Jewish presence there from below 10 percent to nearly one-third of the population. To facilitate Jewish colonisation,

Zionist organisations energetically purchased land in Palestine. By 1947, more than 10 percent of the cultivable area was in Jewish hands.[97] These territorial acquisitions often displaced Arab residents, usually to other locations in Palestine. Even as this "succession of microcosmic transfers" directly dislocated only a minority of Palestinians, still, the "piecemeal eviction" of tenant farmers both reflected "the underlying thrust" of Zionist ideology – the substitution of one people for another – and foreshadowed its catastrophic consummation.[98]

In a 1938 diary entry, the leader of the Jewish community in Palestine (the *Yishuv*) and later Israel's first prime minister, David Ben-Gurion, underlined the "necessity" of "removing the Arabs from our midst". But he recognised that timing was critical. "What is inconceivable in normal times", he wrote, "is possible in revolutionary times."[99] When the 1948 Arab-Israel War broke out, Zionist forces seized the opportunity to bring about what Ben-Gurion euphemistically referred to as "great changes in the composition of the population of the country".[100] During the war, some 700,000 Palestinians – two-thirds of the population – fled or were driven from their homes in what became Israel. Historians debate the extent to which this displacement unfolded according to a central plan. What cannot plausibly be denied is that Zionist massacres as well as expulsions were a major catalyst of Palestinian flight, that Zionist leaders welcomed the exodus, and that military commanders carried out evictions within an ideological context that had broadly legitimated population transfer as a strategic desideratum.[101]

After the dust settled, Israeli authorities moved to consolidate Jewish domination within the new state whose expanded boundaries (established by armistice agreements in 1949 and known as the "Green Line") encompassed 78 percent of historic Palestine. Israel refused to allow the return of Palestinians displaced during the war and killed thousands of unarmed refugees who made the attempt.[102] Multiple Arab communities within Israel were expelled long after the war was over,[103] while more than four hundred Palestinian villages, towns, and neighbourhoods inside Israel were destroyed to make way for Jewish settlement. Property owned by Palestinian refugees as well as Palestinians who remained to become citizens of Israel was systematically confiscated. This vast expropriation left the Israeli state in possession or control of fully 93 percent of the land within the Green Line, which authorities allocated almost exclusively for use by Jews. In the half-century after independence, the state established more than seven hundred Jewish localities and zero Arab localities, excepting several townships built to facilitate the concentration and dispossession of Bedouin Arabs.

Even as Israeli administrators relentlessly promoted Jewish immigration, they directed Jewish settlement strategically to encircle Arab villages and restrict the Arab minority to "small enclaves". The overarching policy was to "Judaize" the entire territory by "concentrating the Arabs and dispersing the Jews."[104]

— ROUND TWO —

Israel conquered the remaining 22 percent of Mandate Palestine in the June 1967 Arab-Israel War. The same dynamic of Jewish expansion, Arab displacement – Sayegh's "rhythmic operations" – then played out in the occupied West Bank (including East Jerusalem) and Gaza Strip. In the aftermath of the war, Israeli prime minister Levi Eshkol likened these occupied Palestinian territories (OPT) to a dowry and their Arab residents to a bride. "The trouble is", Eshkol lamented, "the dowry is followed by a bride whom we don't want."[105] The 1967 War lasted only six days and Israel did not initiate hostilities with the primary objective of territorial expansion.[106] Even so, by November 1967, about 200,000 Palestinians from the West Bank and 35,000 from Gaza – above 20 percent of the occupied Palestinian population – were in exile. The Israeli cabinet did not issue orders for an ethnic cleansing. But during the war and in its wake, Israeli leaders welcomed Palestinian flight and took measures calculated to expedite it, while military units directly cleared and demolished Palestinian settlements along the Green Line. "I hope they all go", Defence Minister Moshe Dayan enthused. The threat of international censure eventually compelled Israel to formally authorise the return of displaced West Bankers. In practice, authorities kept the vast majority out.[107] To the same demographic end, Israeli authorities refused to recognise as residents of the OPT approximately 270,000 Palestinians who were outside the West Bank and Gaza when the occupation began. Over the next half-century, Israel revoked the OPT residency rights of another quarter-million Palestinians, mostly after they travelled abroad.[108]

From 1967, Israel extended its Judaizing policy from the area within the Green Line to the occupied territories. Over nearly six decades, successive Israeli administrations implanted more than 700,000 Jews in some 350 colonies established across the OPT. Israeli planners recognised and the International Court of Justice (ICJ) affirmed that this policy was a flagrant violation of the Fourth Geneva Convention, which stipulated that an "Occupying Power shall not deport or transfer parts of its own civilian population into the territory it occupies." Jewish settlers benefited from government subsidies and the state allocated over 40 percent of the West Bank for their use. Meanwhile, Israel expropriated more than one-third of the West Bank from Palestinians, virtually barred Palestinians from building houses or infrastructure in nearly two-thirds of the West Bank, and pushed out Palestinian communities from areas earmarked for Jewish expansion. It was a similar story in Gaza, where Israel took control of nearly 60 percent of the land by 1990 and allocated one-quarter of the Strip for use by Jewish settlers even as they comprised just a half-percent of Gaza's population.[109] A formidable phalanx of Israeli civil and military institutions was deployed to maximise Jewish control in the OPT and, simultaneously, to concentrate and confine Palestinians in dozens of crowded enclaves, disconnected from one another, with development outside them effectively banned.[110] In July 2024, the ICJ found that Israel's "discriminatory policies and practices" in the West Bank and East Jerusalem – including its "settlement policy" and "encirclement of Palestinian communities into enclaves" – constituted unlawful "racial segregation and *apartheid*".[111]

From the outset, then, a central thrust of Zionist policy has been, as Human Rights Watch neatly summarises, to "maximise the number of Jews, as well as the land available to them" in areas desired for Jewish settlement, and at the same time to "minimise the number of Palestinians and the land available to them."[112] This demographic project unfolded inter alia through various forms of population transfer. Transfer was often preemptive, as when Israel prohibited Palestinians from entering, living in, or building on vast swaths of land in Palestine. Transfer was also retroactive, as when Israel demolished or expropriated the property of displaced Palestinians, prevented refugee return, and revoked Palestinian residency rights. And, on occasion, transfer was brutally direct, as in the wholesale expulsions of the 1948 Nakba. Israeli policy typically worked to concentrate Palestinians in dependent enclaves within Palestine, but when opportunities arose for displacement abroad, in 1948 and to a lesser extent in 1967, Israeli leaders exploited them. The endeavour to forcibly substitute one group of people for another is the essence of settler colonialism. In Israel – where a "virtual consensus" favouring transfer crystallised in the late 1930s, where almost all leaders after 1948 opposed Palestinian refugee return, where all governments since 1967 have participated in colonising the OPT, and where "almost all" civilian administration as well as military authorities are involved in enforcing "apartheid against Palestinians" – the settler-colonial impulse is not confined to one political party or ideological tendency but pervades and penetrates the state.[113]

— CONTAINING RESISTANCE —

As Jabotinsky prophesied, expanding Jewish settlement frequently provoked Palestinian opposition as well as resistance. Such opposition was typically overruled by means of discriminatory administration while resistance was suppressed by force. In the Mandate period, the Zionist leadership rejected the democratic principle of majority rule in Palestine so long as Jews comprised a minority, on the correct assumption that an Arab electoral majority would vote to end Jewish immigration and settlement. Between 1936 and 1939, British armed forces along with Jewish paramilitaries viciously crushed a Palestinian national revolt. After the 1948 War, Israel subjected some 90 percent of its Arab citizens to military rule. This emergency regime facilitated the destruction of Arab property and expropriation of Arab land until it was lifted in 1966, by which time the state's demographic objectives within the Green Line had been substantially accomplished.[114] The pattern repeated in the OPT from the following year. Palestinians in the West Bank and Gaza Strip have lived under Israeli military rule since 1967: three-quarters of Israel's lifespan as a state. The occupation has been enforced through harsh repression including deportation, arbitrary detention, collective punishment, and unlawful killings. By one estimate, Israel jailed more than 800,000 Palestinians from the OPT between 1967 and 2016; those detained were "routinely subjected to torture".[115]

From the mid-2000s, Israel's control policy in the West Bank relied on carrots as much as sticks. A subordinate "Palestinian Authority" (PA) patrolled and administered the main Palestinian population centres on Israel's behalf. The PA's economic dependence on Israel and the United States induced its political compliance, while broader public quiescence was purchased through foreign subventions – distributed by the PA to a bloated civil service and authoritarian security apparatus – as well as Israeli permits enabling tens of thousands of Palestinians to work for higher incomes in Israel.[116] In Gaza, the emphasis lay heavier on the stick. Israeli officials had long viewed the enclave – crowded with impoverished refugees from the 1948 expulsion and their descendants – as a hotbed of resistance. After a mass civil revolt against Israeli military rule spread from Gaza across the OPT, beginning in December 1987 (the first *intifada*), Israel crushed the uprising then strengthened its grip on Gaza through various forms of confinement. By 2004, the head of Israel's National Security Council could describe Gaza as "a huge concentration camp".[117] In January 2006, the Islamic Resistance Movement, Hamas, won parliamentary elections in Gaza and the West Bank. Israel and its allies responded by subjecting the occupied Palestinian population – already enduring the "worst economic depression in modern history" – to "possibly the most rigorous form of international sanctions imposed in modern times".[118] When Hamas seized control in Gaza the following year, Israel tightened the screws further as it put Gaza under a closure regime that has been enforced with varying degrees of intensity ever since.[119]

The siege extinguished Gaza's economy and reduced its people to penury. "The idea is to put the Palestinians on a diet", a senior Israeli official explained, "but not to make them die of hunger."[120] An Israeli officer stationed on the Gaza border distilled his mission there: "no development, no prosperity, only humanitarian dependency."[121] The unemployment rate soared to among the highest in the world, four-fifths of the population were forced to rely on humanitarian assistance, three-quarters became dependent on food aid, more than half faced "acute food insecurity", and over 96 percent of the groundwater became unsafe for human consumption. The head of the United Nations agency for Palestinian refugees, UNRWA, observed in 2008 that "Gaza is on the threshold of becoming the first territory to be intentionally reduced to a state of abject destitution, with the knowledge, acquiescence and – some would say – encouragement of the international community."[122] The UN warned in 2015 that the cumulative impact of this induced humanitarian crisis might render Gaza "unlivable" within a half-decade. Israeli military intelligence agreed, whereas a subsequent UN analysis judged the projection overly optimistic.[123] By 2018, Israel had reduced Gaza to what the UN high commissioner for human rights called a "toxic slum", in which above two million people – half of them children – were "caged" from "birth to death".[124] "If there is a hell on earth", UN Secretary-General António Guterres said in May 2021, "it is the lives of children in Gaza."[125]

Many in Gaza did not share this vision for their future, and so Israel found it prudent every few years to violently discipline them – what Israeli officials termed "mowing the lawn". Some of these onslaughts responded to resistance emanating from Gaza: armed, as when Hamas fired projectiles into Israel in May 2021 following settler encroachments in occupied East Jerusalem, or unarmed, as in early 2018, when Palestinians demonstrated peacefully along Gaza's perimeter fence – scores were killed and thousands injured by Israeli snipers arrayed on the other side. But Israel's most devastating offensives, in 2008 and 2014, were motivated by broader political objectives: to inspire fear in the Arab world and to thwart Hamas "peace offensives" that threatened to make Israel's rejectionist diplomatic posture – its refusal to withdraw from Palestinian territory in exchange for peace – untenable.[126] In the 2014 assault alone, Operation Protective Edge, approximately 1,600 civilians in Gaza were killed, including 550 children, and 18,000 homes were destroyed.

By October 2023, Israel had firmly entrenched what the Israeli human rights group B'Tselem characterised as a "regime of Jewish supremacy from the Jordan River to the Mediterranean Sea".[127] The coalition guidelines of the 37th Israeli government, formed the preceding year and led by Prime Minister Benjamin Netanyahu, stipulated that "the Jewish people have an exclusive and inalienable right to all parts of the Land of Israel" – including the OPT – and committed to Jewish "settlement" across this territory. Large parts of the West Bank had been formally or de facto annexed, Jewish colonies were expanding at an unprecedented rate, the people of Gaza were trapped in suffocating stasis behind a prison fence, their compatriots in the West Bank were squeezed into dependent enclaves, and the Palestinian cause had all-but-vanished from Arab and international diplomatic agendas. In his September 2023 address to the UN General Assembly, Netanyahu hailed the bilateral agreements reached in 2020 and 2021 between Israel and four Arab states – the United Arab Emirates, Bahrain, Sudan, and Morocco – as a "pivot of history", anticipated a "historic" treaty with Saudi Arabia, and ridiculed the "so-called experts" who had maintained that Israel-Arab normalisation was predicated on peace with the Palestinians. On the ground, Israeli officials knew the "humanitarian condition in Gaza" was "progressively deteriorating" – this being an intended policy outcome – and could predict that, "if it blows up, it'll be in Israel's direction."[128] But they apparently believed that, by oscillating "between [military] operations and providing that level of aid to Gaza" sufficient to prevent its complete "collapse", Palestinian eruptions could be contained within tolerable limits. Hamas will "rise up from time to time and hit us", Israel's former national security advisor acknowledged in 2018, but it can't do any "real damage".[129] The people of Gaza could be left to fester in their cage. Netanyahu boasted that Israel was entering a new "age of peace" without compromise, and Palestinians – who made up "only 2% of the Arab world" – had no "veto over the process".

— "WHAT WAS WILL NOT BE": —
— GAZA CRISIS AND OPPORTUNITY —

On 7 October 2023, Netanyahu's confidence was revealed as complacency when Hamas-led militants burst the gates of Gaza, overwhelmed multiple military installations, then rampaged across southern Israel.[130]

Unaffiliated residents of Gaza joined in. The operation was shocking in its boldness, the ensuing massacre for its brutality. Analysis by the Agence France-Presse (AFP) found that nearly 1,200 people were killed in the attack, overwhelmingly civilians, and 250 were taken hostage. If these figures are correct, this means Palestinians killed more Israelis in one day than during the five years of the second intifada, inclusive of the bloody suicide bombings. The shock of the casualties was compounded by the military and intelligence vulnerabilities Hamas exposed. A poorly resourced militia, constrained within a besieged and intensely surveilled ghetto, brushed past Israel's high-tech ramparts, overpowered the Israel Defence Forces (IDF) Gaza Division, and ran rampant for hours unimpeded by any coordinated military response. "We spend billions and billions on gathering intelligence on Hamas", a former senior official on Israel's National Security Council rued. "Then, in a second… everything collapsed like dominoes."[131] The Hamas assault marked the first time since Israel's war of independence that Israeli territory was seized in battle and, all told, the "most traumatic day" in Israel's seventy-five-year history.[132]

In retaliation for the Hamas operation and massacre, Israel turned Gaza into a howling wasteland. The onslaught was dubbed Operation Swords of Iron. Between October 2023 and July 2024, Israeli forces killed upward of forty thousand people, most of them women, children, and the elderly.[133] The reported death toll included almost as many children as were killed across all the world's conflict zones over the preceding three years combined.[134] Gazan hospitals developed the acronym "WCNSF" – Wounded Child No Surviving Family – as hundreds of extended family units were wiped out.[135] Fully 90 percent of the population – 1.9 million people, including an estimated 800,000 children – was internally displaced, most multiple times and some up to ten times.[136] Gazans were being shunted around like "human pinballs", UN Secretary-General Guterres decried, "ricocheting between ever-smaller slivers of the south, without any of the basics for survival".[137] Israel set records for killing UN staff, health workers, and journalists;[138] littered Gaza with more unexploded bombs than anywhere in the world since the Second World War;[139] and, according to former UN assistant secretary-general for human rights Andrew Gilmour, probably inflicted the "highest kill rate" of any military since the 1994 Rwandan genocide.[140] Gaza became "the most dangerous place in the world to be a child" (UNICEF), "the most dangerous place for aid workers in the world" (International Crisis Group), "the most dangerous place to be a civilian" (International Rescue Committee), and, indeed, "the most dangerous place in the world" period (ACLED).[141]

Targeting Palestinian civilians and civilian infrastructure was not in itself a novelty. A UN inquiry found that Israel's 2008 offensive, which visited upon Gaza what Amnesty International described as "22 days of death and destruction", was a "deliberately disproportionate attack designed to punish, humiliate and terrorise a civilian population."[142] Five years later, Israeli soldiers confessedly inflicted "destruction on a whole other level" in Gaza as they unleashed "an insane amount of firepower" while "shooting at anything that moves – and also at what isn't moving".[143] In 2018, IDF snipers responded to overwhelmingly unarmed demonstrations along Gaza's perimeter fence by intentionally targeting children, journalists, health workers, and disabled persons with live ammunition.[144] Indeed, long before October 2023, every political and military official in charge of Operation Swords of Iron – Prime Minister Netanyahu, Defence Minister Yoav Gallant, IDF Chief of Staff Herzi Halevi, Emergency War Cabinet member Benny Gantz, and their key advisors – was on record endorsing the intentional targeting of civilians as a tenet of Israel's military doctrine.[145] After October 2023, however, the scale of destruction qualitatively increased: from 100–120 targets bombed per day (2014) to 430 targets bombed per day (October 2023),[146] from 305 buildings damaged per day (2014) to 743 buildings damaged per day (October

2023–January 2024),[147] and from 2.5 million tonnes of rubble generated (2014) to over 39 million tonnes of rubble generated (May 2024) – thirteen times the combined debris generated by all previous conflicts in Gaza since 2008.[148] The American military historian Robert Pape concluded in January 2024 that Israel's ongoing assault amounted to "one of the most intense civilian punishment campaigns in history".[149]

This radical ramping up of violence reflected a qualitative change in Israeli policy. Israel had previously sought to contain Hamas within an impoverished Gaza sealed off from the West Bank, Israel, Egypt, and the wider world. The 7 October assault made this "conflict management" approach a dead letter. But with crisis came opportunity. Israeli leaders had long been alive to the need for calibrating Israel's use of force to the political limits set by international public opinion. In 2008, Israel moved to break an unwanted ceasefire with Hamas on 4 November, when Americans were preoccupied with the presidential election of Barack Obama.[150] More generally, a 2018 study found, "Israel authorities appear to time their attacks" on Palestinians so as to minimise the likelihood of coverage in US newscasts.[151] Netanyahu himself is acutely sensitive to these dynamics. "Israel, when it fights, is subject to international pressures", he explained in a 2006 interview. "In the televised age", the "kinds of wars that we fight" are "not sustainable beyond a few weeks".[152] Following the Tiananmen Square massacre in 1989, Netanyahu – then deputy foreign minister – lamented that Israel had not carried out "large-scale" expulsions of Palestinians from the OPT while global media focused elsewhere.[153] And during Israel's summer 2014 assault on Gaza, Netanyahu seemingly decided to launch a ground invasion when international attention was diverted by the downing of a Malaysian airliner over Ukraine.[154]

The unqualified support extended Israel by the US, Britain, and the European Union following the Hamas attack signalled an unbuckling of external constraints. It was interpreted by Israeli planners as a green light to transform the "strategic reality" in Gaza and "change the Middle East".[155] Former national security advisor Meir Ben Shabbat argued that "the scale of the attack by Hamas provides legitimacy for Israel to take extraordinary measures."[156] An influential military think-tank advised that strong "international legitimacy and freedom of offensive action for Israel" now "enables high aggressiveness".[157] An unnamed political source informed veteran correspondent Ben Caspit that Israel "must take advantage of the opportunity" to "go all out".[158] And former parliamentarian Ofer Shelah, considered a dove, urged that Israel exploit the unprecedented "global legitimacy for any type of action" to unleash an "unprecedented degree of power".[159]

Israeli leaders had long despaired of their Gaza headache – Prime Minister Yitzhak Rabin famously wished it would "sink into the sea"[160] – and after 7 October saw the prospect of a permanent cure. Israel's strategy accordingly shifted from mowing the lawn in Gaza to salting the earth; from perpetually deferring the Gaza question to definitively resolving it. Israel would "act with full force" to "change the face of reality in the Gaza Strip for the coming fifty years", Defence Minister Gallant pledged. "What was will not be."[161]

— FROM DISPLACEMENT —
— TO DESTRUCTION —

Since 2008, almost every escalation in Gaza had been triggered by Israel. By contrast, the 2023 hostilities, like the so-called Unity Intifada of May 2021, were initiated by Hamas, which by all accounts caught Israel unprepared. The Israeli response was accordingly characterised by an unusual degree of dissensus and improvisation. But a broad spectrum of elite opinion soon converged around two basic options. At the more extreme end were calls for annihilation. A British jurist representing Israel subsequently attempted to downplay examples of bloodthirsty statements by Israeli officials as a few "random quotes" of merely "rhetorical" significance.[162] In truth, as researchers like Yaniv Cogan have diligently catalogued, demands for the destruction of Gaza echoed across Israel's political spectrum and down through civil society.[163] Lawmakers from Israel's governing coalition called for "crushing Gaza on all its inhabitants" and "flattening" Gaza "without mercy". They demanded that the "civilian population" in Gaza "leave the world" and that the IDF impose "one sentence for everyone there – death".[164] Senior politicians underscored that "there are no innocents" in Gaza; "it's an entire nation out there that is responsible."[165] A deputy speaker of Israel's parliament bluntly enjoined, "Burn Gaza now nothing less!" while a parliamentarian from the ruling Likud Party – and former minister of public diplomacy – urged her followers to "invest your energy on one thing: wiping Gaza off the face of the earth." Those "Gazan monsters" who do not flee abroad, she clarified, should "die horribly" at the hands of "a vengeful and cruel IDF...Anything less than that is immoral".[166] Opposition legislators chimed in: "there are no innocents in Gaza", "the children in Gaza have brought this upon themselves!"[167]

Israeli media, meanwhile, were saturated with demands to "erase" Gaza and turn it into a "slaughterhouse", its inhabitants "without exception...exterminated".[168] One prominent television presenter enthused that "there are already more refugees and more dead in the Gaza Strip than there were in the original Nakba in 1948" and urged that "this important process must not be interrupted". A journalist for one of Israel's most widely circulated newspapers opined that "every baby [in Gaza] will grow to become a terrorist. Erase, kill, destroy, annihilate." A TV talking head defined "victory" in Gaza as "annihilation + deportation + occupation + judahization of the area + annexation." An award-winning news anchor informed viewers that "Gaza should be erased".[169] "Do not leave a stone upon a stone in Gaza", former Likud MK Moshe Feiglin fulminated in a nationally broadcast interview. "Complete incineration. No more hope... Annihilate Gaza now! Now!"[170] To be sure, Israel's Gaza policy also had its critics: a deputy mayor of Jerusalem charged that, if political leaders truly cared, "there would have been 150,000 dead already" in Gaza and "not a single building... left standing". One municipal leader fantasised that Gaza would end up resembling Auschwitz.[171]

Popular songs released in Israel since October 2023 featured such lyrics as "Good morning Gaza, another day, another dead Nazi... no survivors" and "We got into Gaza, we'll get out only when it's gone... you have no bread or water. Oh, and you don't have a home either." One ditty on "turning Gaza into a parking lot" was performed for schoolchildren; another promising that "within a year we will annihilate everyone" was sung by children in a video circulated online by Israel's national broadcaster.[172] The IDF Operations Directorate ran a social media channel entitled "72 Virgins – Uncensored" which published hundreds of posts in Hebrew. These included images of Palestinian captives and corpses captioned "exterminating the roaches"; footage of an Israeli soldier allegedly dipping machine gun bullets in pork fat, captioned "you won't get your virgins"; and video of an Israeli vehicle repeatedly driving over the body of a Palestinian militant, captioned "flatten them".[173] Likud MK Moshe Sa'ada observed a shift in Israeli public opinion with respect to Palestinians. Even left-wing kibbutzniks, he said, "are telling you to exterminate them".[174] The decimation of Gaza was no secret – Israel being a small country with a civilian army that is representative of and entrenched in civil society, whose soldiers effectively livestreamed the ransacking on social media[175] – yet nine-tenths of Israeli Jews surveyed answered that Israel's operation was "about right" or had "not gone far enough".[176]

Amidst this "genocide fever",[177] Prime Minister Netanyahu repeatedly invoked the Biblical injunction to "Remember… Amalek"[178] – referencing a divine command to "smite" the enemy of Israel "and utterly destroy all that they have, and spare them not; but slay both man and woman, infant and suckling, ox and sheep, camel and ass."[179] According to B'Tselem, this was "a dog whistle that anyone who has gone through Israel's educational system will recognise" as an order to "wipe out Gaza".[180] Netanyahu's colleagues followed his lead as they evoked Amalek to oppose "any humanitarian gesture" for Gaza's civilians, demand the "total annihilation" of population centres, and advocate that Gaza be targeted with nuclear weapons.[181] In July 2024, long after he and other senior officials had been censured by the ICJ for their dehumanising language, Defence Minister Gallant hailed the indiscriminate demolition of a Palestinian town as indexing the achievements of Israel's war against "Amalek".[182] It would seem that IDF forces operating in Gaza received the message loud and clear: one group in uniform filmed themselves chanting "we know our motto: there are no uninvolved civilians" and "wipe off the seed of Amalek"; another soldier recorded a video thanking God "we killed tens of thousands of Amalekites".[183]

Alongside this chorus for annihilation, many officials advocated that Gaza's population be evicted. Thinning Gaza's population had long been an Israeli desideratum. After Israel conquered the Strip in 1967, the Eshkol government attempted to transfer large numbers of refugees from Gaza to Jordan, Egypt, the Gulf, and Latin America. Officials relied on economic incentives – keeping unemployment and poverty in Gaza high, then paying individuals to leave – for fear that a directly forced expulsion would put in jeopardy US support. The scheme foundered in the face of Jordanian obstruction as well as the emergence of popular resistance in Gaza.[184] More generally, as the first part of this chapter showed, Zionist institutions have consistently employed various forms of population transfer to facilitate Jewish colonisation in Palestine. This process was typically gradual and piecemeal, while Palestinian opposition was usually overcome through a combination of economic appeasement and military repression. Whenever Palestinian resistance escalated above a tolerable threshold, however, as during the second intifada, the idea of expelling Palestinians en masse regained salience in Israeli public and political discourse.[185] This pattern became visible again after 7 October. Just as Ben-Gurion in 1938 foresaw emptying Palestine of its Arab population amid the fog of war, so the Netanyahu government in 2023 attempted to exploit global indignation over the Hamas attacks to drive out the people of Gaza.

Calls for ethnic cleansing came from the highest echelons of Israel's political and military establishments. Cabinet ministers argued for encouraging Palestinians in Gaza "to leave" (Jerusalem Affairs and Heritage Minister Amichai Eliyahu), "the voluntary emigration of Gaza Arabs to the countries of the world" (Finance Minister Bezalel Smotrich), the "voluntary resettlement" of Gazans "outside of the Strip" (Intelligence Minister Gila Gamliel), and "the emigration of Gaza residents" (Interior Minister Itamar Ben Gvir).[186] Prime Minister Netanyahu himself commanded "the residents of Gaza: Leave now", reportedly instructed a close advisor to prepare a plan to reduce Gaza's population to the "minimum possible", and affirmed he was working to find countries willing to absorb Gaza refugees.[187] Lawmakers from Israel's governing coalition urged a "Nakba" that would "scatter" Gazans around the world or else to a "refuge city" in the Sinai desert. "It must be emphasised that relocation is for those in Gaza who desire to leave", a senior Likud figure winkingly caveated – albeit "anyone who stays", his parliamentary colleague clarified, "bears full responsibility for what will happen to him". For any bleeding-hearts who objected, another coalition Knesset member pointed out that expulsion was a venerable Zionist tradition: "you fled? Don't come back. Just like in Tel Aviv, just like in many more places in the State of Israel."[188] One is almost nostalgic for the days when Israeli spokespeople denied the 1948 expulsion instead of braying for its sequel. On 13 October 2023, Israel's Ministry of Intelligence produced an official document recommending that Israel solicit US support for evacuating the civilian population of Gaza to Egypt.[189] "We may be about to see massive ethnic cleansing", one EU diplomat warned.[190] As Israel drove the entire population of northern Gaza toward the Egyptian border, Israeli officials reportedly proposed that Egypt's World Bank debt be forgiven in exchange for hosting Gazan refugees while US Secretary of State Antony Blinken attempted to procure Arab government support for establishing "humanitarian corridors" into the Sinai. Egyptian authorities in particular refused to cooperate and, as of July 2024, continued to obstruct Palestinian flight.

One frequently cited rationale for these policies was the need to restore Israel's "deterrence capacity" vis-á-vis its regional adversaries, notably Hezbollah in Lebanon. Gaza has often served Israel as a demonstrative punching bag. In August 1955, IDF Chief of Staff Moshe Dayan argued that even "minor" Israeli reprisal operations in Gaza and elsewhere along the border were "very important" because of "their impact on the Arab assessment of Israel's strength – and on Israel's belief in her own strength".[191] More recently, then-foreign minister Tzipi Livni bragged that Israel went "wild" in its 2008–2009 assault on Gaza. In so doing, a former senior Israeli security official explained, Israel showed "Hamas, Iran and the region" that it could be "as lunatic as any of them".[192] After the debacle of 7 October, Israeli officials sought to revive regional terror – if not of the IDF's military prowess, then at any rate of its deranged potency against civilians. "Hizbullah will only be deterred if it sees not only destruction in Gaza City, but a humanitarian disaster and absolute governmental chaos", one influential strategist argued. "We will obliterate civilian infrastructure", an IDF officer promised, because "Hezbollah feeds off our apprehension to land a decisive strike". The whole of Gaza "has to look like Beit Hanoun", an IDF company commander explained, referring to a town in northern Gaza levelled by Israel, so "there will be fear [among] all the surrounding nations".[193]

A cruder motivation was revenge. On 7 October, Prime Minister Netanyahu pledged that Israel "will forcefully avenge this dark day" and quoted from Haim Bialik's poem on the Kishinev pogrom: "Revenge for the blood of a little child has [not] yet been devised by Satan." Alas, Netanyahu omitted the poet's preceding line: "And cursed be the man who says: Avenge!" Netanyahu's wife, Sara, expressed "hope" for "a very great revenge", while an officer in the IDF 162nd Armoured Division hailed vengeance as an "important value". "I'll give it to you straight", another IDF soldier admitted. "We are all out for revenge."[194] Already on 10 October, B'Tselem warned that a "criminal policy of revenge is underway". Carmi Gillon, a former head of Israel's Shin Bet security service, agreed that Israel had "embarked on a war of revenge" and considered this wholly legitimate.[195] Soldiers operating in Gaza justified everything from property destruction and looting to indiscriminate killing in these terms.[196] A third rationale, fringe at first but increasingly voluble as Israel's campaign dragged on, was a desire to re-establish the Jewish settlements in Gaza dismantled in the unilateral disengagement of 2005. Even as Netanyahu himself dismissed the prospect, one-third of his cabinet reportedly endorsed it while an energised minority of IDF soldiers appeared inspired by the vision.[197]

Whether Israeli decision-makers favoured annihilation or expulsion, and whether they did so for reasons of deterrence, vengeance, or settlement, the policy upshot and practical bottom-line was the same: Gaza was to be rendered permanently uninhabitable. Israel resolved to inflict what the IDF spokesperson termed a "massacre that collapses the Gaza Strip upon its residents" and reduce Gaza, as one Israeli defence official put it, "into a city of tents". "We are now rolling out the Gaza Nakba", Minister of Agriculture Avi Dichter explained. "Gaza Nakba 2023. That's how it'll end." Hamas's leader "made a mistake", Defence Minister Gallant declared, and sealed the "fate of Gaza". Even if Hamas agreed to return Israeli hostages, a former acting head of Israel's Civil Administration and counterterrorism advisor to multiple Israeli prime ministers assured, "Gaza will be turned into piles of ruins". "Nothing left", the Civil Administration's serving deputy head summarised. "Whoever returns here, if he returns here later, will see here scorched earth. No houses, no agriculture, no nothing. They have no future."[198] IDF Major General (Reserve) Giora Eiland – the former head of Israel's National Security Council, former IDF operations chief, and sometime advisor to Defence Minister Gallant – most clearly articulated the operative policy. In a series of articles and interviews, he argued that Israel should "create a humanitarian crisis in Gaza", compelling the "entire population" to flee into exile while rendering Gaza "temporarily, or permanently, unfit for living". Israel should impose "a dramatic, continuous, and strict siege" as well as systematically destroying critical health and water infrastructure so that Gaza will become "a place where no human being can exist". The civilian population would be given two choices: "to stay and to starve, or to leave".[199]

— GAZA APOCALYPSE —

B'Tselem observed that Eiland's prescriptions were "an accurate reflection" of "the strategy pursued" in Gaza, where Israel unleashed "one of the most intense bombing campaigns in history" upon a population of two million people, half of them children, trapped in a crowded enclave less than one-quarter the size of Greater London.[200] In the first week alone, Israel dropped more bombs on Gaza than the US did in Afghanistan each *year* between 2008 and 2019.[201] By June 2024, Israel had carpeted Gaza with more than seventy thousand tonnes of explosives, surpassing the combined weight of bombs dropped on London, Dresden, and Hamburg in all of World War II.[202] Every population centre was pulverised. North Gaza was left "an uninhabitable moonscape" as broad swaths of the territory were erased. "Beit Hanoun is not only dead", a correspondent for *Le Monde* reported in November. "Beit Hanoun no longer exists."[203] Some 70 percent of Jabaliya refugee camp was destroyed, according to Palestinian officials.[204] The largest urban concentration, Gaza City, became a "wasteland" stalked by "hunger and chaos" as critical infrastructure was "ravaged" and "whole districts" were "razed to the ground".[205] Among them were the upmarket Rimal quarter, substantially "reduced to rubble", and long-suffering Shujai'ya, where "nearly every building" for "block after block" was "flattened". Nine months into the onslaught, Israel continued to bombard Gaza City neighbourhoods long since reduced to "disaster zones with 85 percent of buildings destroyed".[206] Farther south, the city of Khan Younis was "flattened", "utterly destroyed", "devastated". "The damage to infrastructure is insane", one UN official based in Gaza reported. "In Khan Younis, there is not one building untouched."[207] In May 2024, "Gaza's last refuge" became "Israel's next target" as Israel defied international outrage to assault Rafah. The southern border city was "shredded" as Israeli forces left it "unrecognizable", "an empty husk", a "flattened wasteland".[208]

By mid-2024, between 40 and 60 percent of all structures in Gaza had been damaged or destroyed,[209] including more than 60 percent of homes, 85 percent of school buildings, 80 percent of health facilities, 80 percent of commercial facilities, 60 percent of cultural heritage sites, 60 percent of cropland, and every university. Some 60 percent of Gaza's roads, electricity distribution network, and water infrastructure was damaged or destroyed, including two-thirds of waste treatment and management facilities.[210] In Gaza City, three-quarters of all buildings, 90 percent of water wells, and all brackish or seawater desalination plants were damaged or destroyed.[211] "There is no Gaza", a right-wing Israeli pundit who embedded with IDF forces in the Strip reported back. "Everything is in ruins, everything is over." Israeli troops operating in Gaza also expressed satisfaction with the wreckage inflicted: "Gaza is in fucking ruins. What a wonderful view", "Shujai'ya should remain in ruins for eternity", "Shujai'ya – rest in peace... 30 houses [gone]... How beautiful." "Tell me, when you see Gaza like this, up in flames, what do you feel?" a commander stationed in Jabaliya was asked. "That we are finally destroying Hamas", he replied. "Everyone here is an enemy!"[212] "I can count on one hand the cases we were told not to shoot", an officer who served in the IDF Operations Directorate attested. "Even with sensitive things like schools, [approval] feels like only a formality."[213] "Yes, we set fire to houses. To as many as possible", the director of one of Israel's governing parties who did active duty in Gaza after 7 October acknowledged. "And we are proud of it."[214]

In what might have been a first in the annals of modern warfare, Israeli forces systematically targeted hospitals as they "completely obliterated" Gaza's healthcare infrastructure.[215] In northern Gaza, CNN reported, at least twenty of twenty-two hospitals were damaged or destroyed over the first two months of Israel's offensive. Fourteen were directly hit.[216] Foreign doctors volunteering in Gaza returned with horror stories about Israel "deliberately targeting" healthcare workers, vehicles, and buildings.[217] As the indiscriminate bombing of Gaza caused unrelenting "mass casualty events"[218] – including from weapons designed to maximise injuries and deaths[219] Israeli restrictions on fuel and humanitarian aid forced medics to perform brain surgeries, amputations, and C-sections without anaesthetic, sedatives, gloves, disinfectant, or even clean water.[220] "We do surgeries while the injuries are covered with flies", a doctor in Beit Lahiya testified. "The whole hospital is full of blood and insects."[221] By January 2024, more than one thousand children had undergone the amputation of one or both legs, many without anaesthetic.[222] Already in October, Giora Eiland had warned that Israeli fuel restrictions would cause babies in Gazan hospitals to "die in incubators" and urged that Israel "not give in on this issue". The authorities proved their mettle as premature babies in Al-Shifa Hospital duly perished.[223] This still did not satisfy one Likud lawmaker who lamented that, while soldiers were rounding up "150 terrorists" in Al-Shifa's orthopaedic department, "300 terrorists were born in the maternity ward."[224] As headlines like "UN Rights Chief 'Horrified' by Mass Grave Reports at Gaza Hospitals" (BBC), "Gaza's Largest Hospital Is 'Death Zone' With Mass Grave at the Door" (Sky News), and "A Senior Gazan Doctor Died During Israeli Detention. Officials Refuse to Explain How" (*Ha'aretz*) became routine, the UN World Health Organisation (WHO) informed in March 2024 that only ten of thirty-six large-scale hospitals across Gaza were even "minimally functional".[225] After the IDF "systematically dismantled hospital after hospital", Medicins Sans Frontieres (MSF) reported in July, "there is no health system to speak of left."[226]

The incessant bullets, bulldozing, and bombardment were accompanied and compounded by a lethal blockade. At the outset of Israel's offensive, Defence Minister Gallant announced "a complete siege" on Gaza. "There will be no electricity, no food, no water, no fuel…We are fighting human animals and we are acting accordingly."[227] "Israel has imposed a total blockade on Gaza: no electricity, no water, just damage", the Coordinator of Government in the Territories (COGAT) echoed. "Hamas became ISIS and the citizens of Gaza are celebrating… Human beasts are dealt with accordingly."[228] Israel blocked all aid as well as commercial traffic into Gaza until 21 October and "vastly reduced" it thereafter. When supplies did enter their effective distribution was prevented by repeated Israeli strikes on civilians gathered to receive them and, more generally, by the hellish conditions Israel had wrought.[229] These restrictions were "catastrophic" for a population that – thanks to decades of economic strangulation by Israel – relied on imports as well as external aid to survive.[230] The amount of water available for each person per day in Gaza shrunk by 94 percent to less than one-third the internationally accepted minimum standard for basic survival in emergencies.[231] By April 2024, international agencies reported that famine was "imminent" in northern Gaza while the entire population was experiencing acute food insecurity – the "highest share" ever recorded.[232] Conditions improved somewhat the following month when Israeli restrictions loosened in concession to international pressure,[233] but a "high risk of Famine" persisted.[234] Meanwhile, by obstructing humanitarian assistance, dismantling critical sewage, water, and health infrastructure, and concentrating hundreds of thousands of people in "overcrowded spaces" that were "unfit for human habitation", Israel created in Gaza the "perfect environment" for the transmission of disease.[235] Giora Eiland had again anticipated this scenario when he enthused, back in November, that "severe epidemics in the south of the Strip will hasten our victory." Finance Minister Smotrich circulated Eiland's comments and endorsed their "every word".[236] By the end of June 2024, nearly one million cases of acute respiratory infection and over half a million cases of diarrhoea had been reported. Poliovirus – an infectious disease that can cause fatal paralysis – was detected in multiple sewage samples the following month.[237] UN experts repeatedly warned that spreading disease could eventually increase the death toll in Gaza by "multiples".[238]

— THE CRIME OF CRIMES —

In the opening weeks of Israel's offensive, UN human rights officials as well as academic experts sounded the alarm that a genocide was unfolding.[239] This concern came to global notice in December 2023, when the government of South Africa instituted historic proceedings at the ICJ accusing Israel of "committing genocide".[240] The following month, in a decision as politically remarkable as it was devastating for Israel's international legitimacy, the Court found by fifteen votes to two that South Africa's charge of genocide was plausible.[241] South Africa brought its case on the basis of the 1948 Genocide Convention. This defined the crime of genocide as "any of the following acts committed with intent to destroy, in whole or in part, a national, ethnical, racial or religious group, as such: (a) Killing members of the group; (b) Causing serious bodily or mental harm to members of the group; (c) Deliberately inflicting on the group conditions of life calculated to bring about its physical destruction in whole or in part; (d) Imposing measures intended to prevent births within the group; (e) Forcibly transferring children of the group to another group." The Convention definition has been widely criticised by scholars on various grounds, including that its roster of victim groups is arbitrarily narrow, that it focuses on "physical" to the omission of cultural and social destruction, and that its drafters excluded acts of population transfer for purely opportunistic reasons.[242] Furthermore, ICJ jurisprudence has established that, "in order to infer the existence" of genocidal intent "from a pattern of conduct", this must be "the *only* inference that could reasonably be drawn from the acts in question."[243] This is a formidable threshold to meet when genocide unfolds in the context of war, since posited military objectives can almost always be adduced as providing alternative rationales.

Beyond the legal context, the *Oxford English Dictionary* provides a more intuitive grasp of the concept. It defines genocide as the "deliberate and systematic killing or persecution of people from a particular group identified as having a shared ethnicity, nationality, etc., with the intention of partially or wholly destroying that group."[244] Israel has spent more than seventy-five years progressively confining Palestinians within, and when possible displacing them from, their homeland. After 7 October, Israel seized the political opportunity created by the Hamas atrocities to drive out Gaza's population. To this end, Israel unleashed unprecedented firepower with the candid objective of making Gaza permanently uninhabitable. By systematically destroying the prerequisites for human civilisation in Gaza while corralling its desperate population into unliveable encampments along the southern border, Israel hoped to force civilians to flee en masse across the border. When Egypt refused to open the gates, Israel did not significantly change course but continued its onslaught. Put otherwise, Israel continued to indiscriminately target civilians and civilian infrastructure with overwhelming force in order to render uninhabitable an area most of whose inhabitants were unable to leave. How else to describe this policy except as a "deliberate and systematic killing or persecution" intended to "partially or wholly destroy" the people of Gaza?

The conclusions of the Independent International Commission of Inquiry into Israel's conduct in Gaza merit careful consideration in view of the *OED* definition quoted above. The Commission found that Israel had "intentionally" directed "attacks against the civilian population" of Gaza, including "children" as well as displaced persons sheltering in "designated safe zones"; "intentionally" caused "the near total destruction of civilian objects across the densely populated Gaza Strip"; "forcibly transferred the civilian population" from northern Gaza to the south with a view to its permanent displacement; "destroyed the water and electricity infrastructure in the Gaza Strip and much of the other key infrastructures... indispensable to the survival of the civilian population there"; and employed "starvation of civilians as a method of warfare" by "cutting off access to food, water, shelter and medical care and wilfully impeding relief supplies." Israel's "victims were overwhelmingly civilians", in an attack that "was directed against the civilian population" as a whole, as Israel committed against part of Gaza's civilian population "the crime against humanity of extermination".[245] By July 2024, more than 100,000 Gazans, and perhaps three times as many, had fled to Egypt.[246] Disease was spreading. Correspondence published in prestigious medical journal *The Lancet* conservatively estimated that direct and indirect deaths from the conflict to that point could eventually reach 186,000, or 8 percent of Gaza's population.[247] The "extensive destruction" inflicted meant there was "no prospect of the return of the great majority of displaced residents of northern Gaza and Khan Younis in the foreseeable future."[248] Indeed, UN agencies estimated it would take fifteen years just to clear the rubble.[249] A senior UN aid official summarised Israel's achievement thus: "Gaza has simply become uninhabitable."[250]

"The question of genocide", Patrick Wolfe observed, "is never far from discussions of settler colonialism."[251] The project to establish a state for newcomers in an area already populated by others inherently presumes a displacement of the indigenous inhabitants. Where expulsion fails, elimination offers an alternative route to the same end. As the legal scholar William Schabas writes, "genocide is the last resort of the frustrated ethnic cleanser."[252] The first part of this chapter showed that Israel is constitutionally antagonistic toward the Palestinian presence in Palestine; has continuously resorted to demographic engineering to reduce, contain, and overwhelm that presence; and has reflexively resorted to lethal repression to overcome the resistance such measures almost inevitably provoked. Given this record, it was not surprising when, as the chapter's second part documented, Israel responded to the 7 October massacre by inflicting overwhelming force on Gaza's civilian population with the intention of expelling it abroad. That response was consonant with, and rooted in, decades of consistent state practice and ideology. This is not to say the Gaza genocide was inevitable. Had the people of Gaza resigned themselves from despair to life in an open-air prison, or proven unable to muster the resources and ingenuity to challenge this fate, Israel would doubtless have been content to let them rot there in perpetuity. Meanwhile, the Zionist quest for a stable Jewish majority has at times led Israeli leaders as well as public opinion to oppose territorial expansion or support a political resolution of the conflict through partition.[253]

Brigadier General Shlomo Brom, a former deputy to Israel's national security advisor, interpreted the events of 7 October as proof that Israel's strategy of force vis-à-vis the Palestinians had failed. "It is absurd to hope that Israel can indefinitely contain with its military might… millions of Palestinians who claim the right to self-determination and a free, normal life", Brom wrote in the immediate aftermath of the Hamas attack. "Eventually the oppressed will rise against their oppressor." But Brom's was an isolated voice. In general, the policy combining territorial expansion with ethnic supremacy was not discredited but doubled down on. As the IDF laid waste to Gaza, a large majority of lawmakers in the Knesset voted to classify "the establishment of a Palestinian state" as "an existential threat to the State of Israel" while government authorities accelerated land expropriation, Jewish settlement, and the forcible transfer of Palestinian communities in the West Bank.[254] After 7 October, as before it, Israel appeared determined to render its conflict with the Palestinians zero sum. In the long run, this could only end by reducing the sum of either Palestinians or Israelis in Palestine to zero, one way or the other.

31 July 2024

Jamie Stern-Weiner has a PhD in Middle East Studies from the University of Oxford. His most recent edited book is Deluge: Gaza and Israel from Crisis to Cataclysm *(OR Books, 2024).*

— 2024 —

GREEN LIGHT TO GENOCIDE: JOE BIDEN AND ISRAEL'S WAR IN GAZA

In 1967, Israeli Defence Minister Moshe Dayan, in triumphalist mood following Israel's victory in the Six-Day War, said to Nahum Goldmann, the veteran American Zionist leader: "Our American friends offer us money, arms and advice. We take the money, we take the arms, and we decline the advice." The statement reflected the widely held belief that Israel could take US support for granted. "What would happen if ever America were to tell you: you can have the aid only if you also take the advice?" Goldmann asked him. After a moment's reflection, Dayan replied: "Then we would have to take the advice, too."

Here, in a nutshell, is the basic flaw in the US approach to Middle East peace-making since 1967:

the unconditional nature of its economic, military, and diplomatic support for Israel. The United States has posed as an honest broker, but in practice it has acted as Israel's lawyer. This has made its policy for resolving the Israeli-Palestinian conflict incoherent, contradictory, and self-defeating.

Since 1967, Washington has arrogated to itself a monopoly over the diplomacy surrounding the Israeli-Palestinian conflict, marginalizing the United Nations, the European Union, the Soviet Union, and the Arab League. It ultimately failed, however, because it was unable or unwilling to use its massive leverage to push Israel into a peace deal.

The United States and Israel have what is almost invariably described as a "special relationship". This special relationship enjoys bipartisan support. What is unique about this special relationship is that it runs so deep as to make Israel an issue in America's domestic politics rather than an ordinary foreign policy matter. Another prominent feature of this special relationship is that, despite the huge asymmetry of power between the two allies, it is the junior partner who usually calls the shots. The tail wags the dog.

What is the explanation for the extraordinary hold that Israel has over American politics? At its core, the special relationship is supposedly based on common values, such as freedom and democracy. Israel used to be seen as the only democracy in the Middle East, as an island of democracy in a sea of Arab authoritarianism. Much of the international sympathy and support that Israel enjoyed after 1948 derived from this perception. Even after Israel became a fully-fledged colonial power in the aftermath of the June 1967 war, this image of Israel persisted. The steady shift of Israeli politics to the right played a part in eroding the ideational foundations of the special relationship. The coalition government formed by Benjamin Netanyahu in December 2022 is the most right-wing, xenophobic, territorially expansionist, and overtly racist government in Israel's history. It includes messianic religious extremists, like Itamar Ben-Gvir and Bezalel Smotrich, who openly advocate ethnic cleansing of Palestinians and the formal annexation of the West Bank. Popular support for Israel in America has been declining as a result of this shift to the right, and as a result of Israel's mounting oppression of the Palestinians in the occupied territories. American Jewish opinion, especially among the younger generations, has also been moving steadily against Israel and in support of the Palestinians. But so far this shift in public opinion has had only negligible impact on American foreign policy.

One reason for the support that Israel continues to enjoy at the official level is the conviction, shared by politicians from the two main political parties, that

Israel is a strategic asset. During the Cold War, American policy-makers could be divided into two schools of thought on the Arab-Israeli conflict: the "even-handed" and the "Israel first". Proponents of the even-handed approach argued that uncritical support for Israel undermined America's standing in the Islamic world, placed great strain on the pro-Western Arab regimes, and fed radical and Islamic fundamentalist movements. Israel's occupation of the Palestinian territories and its refusal to recognize their national rights was, according to this school of thought, the central problem in Middle East politics. America's best hope of bringing stability to the region as well as safeguarding its own interests lay in an active pursuit of Arab-Israeli reconciliation and, above all, a resolution of the Palestinian problem.

Proponents of the Israel first policy tended to see the Arab world as backward, undemocratic, prone to violence at home and abroad; as so seething with hostility towards Israel and the West, and so endemically volatile, as to preclude the possibility of a durable peace. Israel was said to be America's only rational, intelligent, competent, and reliable ally in the area. Under these circumstances, America's best bet was to maintain Israel's superiority over its adversaries through regular infusions of money and arms, so as to enable it not only to deal with threats to its own security but also to fend off challenges to American interests from radical,

Islamic and Soviet-backed forces. Complaints from Arab quarters about America's partiality towards Israel were dismissed as being of no practical consequence since the Arabs needed America more than America needed them. In short, Israel was seen as a strategic asset and, in less polite language, as a guard dog for American interests in the region.

The leaders of the American military-industrial complex threw their considerable weight behind this Israel first foreign policy. Arms manufacturers like wars because wars generate profits, huge profits. Israel is among their favourite clients because it is so often at war with either the Palestinian resistance or with its Arab neighbours. US military credits for Israel are paid for by the federal government. This means that American taxpayers' money goes to Israel and comes back as profits for the arms manufacturers. Moreover, Israel's advanced armoury generates demand for military hardware and services from the Arab states, especially Saudi Arabia and the United Arab Emirates, for which they pay the full market price. Israel thus helps to place the manufacturers of weapons and of related industries in a win-win position.

Another factor of substantial importance in the making of American foreign policy towards the Middle East is the Israel lobby. This lobby is a collection of organisations the most prominent of which is the

American Israel Public Affairs Committee (AIPAC). AIPAC is strongly allied with the Likud party of Israel, and the Republican Party in the US It acts as an agent of the Israeli state and its influence is considerable, especially in Congress. It has deep pockets and it plays hardball, rewarding pro-Israel candidates with campaign contributions and destroying the careers of anti-Israel candidates. So great is AIPAC's influence that Capitol Hill has been described as Israeli-occupied territory. Without doubt, it is the most powerful foreign policy lobby in Washington DC.

Senator Joe Biden was one of the most ardent advocates of the Israel first approach to the Middle East and one of AIPAC's most influential allies on Capitol Hill. He represented Delaware in the Senate from 1973 to 2009. During this period, he was a major beneficiary of AIPAC campaign funds and a consistent supporter of its agenda. Biden remained an unwavering supporter of Israel throughout his long political career. He had a consistent pro-Israel voting record in the Senate. Israel is "the best $3 billion investment we make", he declared in the Senate back in 1986. "Were there not an Israel", he added, "the United States of America would have to invent an Israel to protect our interests in the region." For him the bonds with Israel have always been "unbreakable" and "bone deep". Not only is Biden an ardent Zionist; he thinks that conditioning military aid to Israel is a "gigantic mistake" and "absolutely outrageous".

During his eight years as vice president under Barack Obama, from 2009 to 2017, Biden did much to burnish his already shining Zionist credentials. President Obama himself belonged to the even-handed school of thought on the Israeli-Palestinian conflict. He saw Israeli settlements on occupied Palestinian territory as a violation of international law and a major obstacle to peace. He tried to secure a settlement freeze to give diplomacy a chance. But all his efforts, and those of Secretary of State John Kerry, were sabotaged by Benjamin Netanyahu, Israel's right-wing prime minister.

Despite his sterling record of support for Israel and pride in his personal friendship with Netanyahu, Biden was not spared Israel's standard operating procedure of biting the hand that feeds it. In 2010, just as Biden arrived in Israel, he was greeted with the announcement that the cabinet had approved a new batch of illegal settlements in the West Bank. Biden meekly put up with the calculated insult, thereby confirming the Israelis in their belief that they could continue to repay American generosity with ingratitude and contempt without being made to pay any price.

In its last year in office, the Obama administration granted Israel a military aid package worth $38 billion over ten years. This was the biggest military aid package in history. In keeping with Biden's precepts, no conditions were attached to the aid. There was advice aplenty on the importance of moving forward towards a diplomatic solution to the Israeli-Palestinian conflict. But as in the days of Moshe Dayan, Israel took the money, took the arms, and ignored the advice.

On one issue, however, in the twilight of their administration, Obama overruled his malleable vice president: a U.N. Security Council resolution which strongly censured Israeli settlement expansion on the West Bank. The resolution was in line with long-standing US foreign policy. Biden wanted to wield the US veto to defeat the resolution. Obama chose to abstain and, with 14 votes in favour, the landmark Resolution 2334 was adopted. It condemned the settlements as a flagrant violation of international law and a major impediment to the achievement of a two-state solution.

When Biden entered the White House, on 20 January 2020, his first task was to confront the toxic legacy of Donald Trump, the most fanatically pro-Israel president in US history. Toward the Middle East as a whole, Trump did not have a coherent foreign policy so much as a series of impulsive and ill-considered moves, many of which breached international law.

On the Israeli-Palestinian conflict, however, Trump was entirely consistent – in his partiality towards Israel. His foreign policy was virtually indistinguishable from the agenda of the Israeli right: recognizing Israel's sovereignty over the occupied Syrian Golan Heights; moving the US Embassy from Tel Aviv to Jerusalem; abolishing the US Consulate General in Jerusalem, the United States' main channel of communication with the Palestinian Authority; cutting all US funding from the U.N. agency that looks after Palestinian refugees; withdrawing crucial US aid to the Palestinians; and closing down the office of the Palestine Liberation Organization (PLO) in Washington.

Trump's polarizing partisanship culminated in a plan for the future of Israel and the occupied territories, a plan he loudly trumpeted as the "deal of the century". In substance it was not a peace plan at all but a free pass for expanding Israel at the expense of the Palestinians. It invited Israel to formally annex around 30 percent of the West Bank, including the illegal settlement blocs and the Jordan Valley, the breadbasket of the Palestinian population.

Predictably, the Palestinian Authority rejected the plan and refused to even discuss it. Netanyahu welcomed the plan but took no action to implement it because he saw no advantage in formal annexation of parts of the West Bank. He was content, at that stage, with the status quo, which gives Israel a free hand to continue its creeping annexation without triggering international sanctions.

As a presidential candidate in the 2020 elections, Biden promised to reopen the office of the PLO that his rival shut down. He also undertook to reopen the US Consulate in East Jerusalem but pledged not move the US Embassy back to Tel Aviv. Once in office, however, Biden engaged only in damage limitation rather than the wholesale reversal of Trump's poisonous legacy. The Israeli-Palestinian conflict was not among Biden's top priorities as president. Unlike his immediate predecessors, he did not appoint a special envoy for Middle East peace, leaving this task to Anthony Blinken, his Jewish and Zionist Secretary of State.

Biden did take some modest steps on Israel-Palestine after entering the White House. He renewed communications with the Palestinian leadership in Ramallah. He restored American funding to the United Nations Relief and Works Agency (UNRWA) and to the humanitarian aid programmes serving the Palestinians in the West Bank and Gaza. But other foreign policy challenges, such as countering China in the Far East and then the Russian invasion of Ukraine, claimed Biden's attention. On Palestine it suited him to adopt a minimalist position. The consensus among his officials was that it was not worth investing much political capital in reviving the Israeli-Palestinian peace process because it would only anger the Israelis without yielding any tangible benefits. The PLO office in Washington was not allowed to resume its activities. Nor was the American consulate in East Jerusalem reopened. Another cause for disappointment to the Palestinians was the failure to reinstate the State Department declaration that the Israeli settlements on the West Bank are illegal. This four decades old declaration had been cancelled by Mike Pompeo, Trump's Christian Zionist Secretary of State. With the benefit of hindsight, it looks as if Biden missed a real opportunity to roll back Trump's actions and to develop a genuine strategic dialogue with the Palestinians by acknowledging that they have legitimate national rights, that they have international law on their side, and that they command overwhelming popular support across the entire Arab and Muslim world.

The one aspect of Trump's policies that Biden chose to energetically promote was the one that was most hurtful to the Palestinians: the Abraham Accords. These accords had been brokered by Trump as part of his policy of downgrading the Palestinian issue and forging a new alignment of Sunni Arab states and Israel against the Islamic Republic of Iran. The United Arab Emirates, Bahrain, Morocco, and Sudan signed these accords in 2020-21. These were not genuine peace agreements between societies but self-serving transactions between autocratic Arab rulers and the Israeli apartheid regime. They were intended to facilitate

Israel's integration into the region without expecting it to resolve the conflict with the Palestinians.

There was once a collective Arab position on the terms of peace with the Jewish state. It was enshrined in the Arab Peace Initiative (API) which was adopted at the Arab League summit meeting in Beirut in March 2002. Based on a Saudi proposal, it offered Israel full normalisation and peace with all 22 members of the Arab League in return for an end to occupation and the establishment of an independent Palestinian state on Gaza and the West Bank with the capital city in East Jerusalem. It also called for a "just settlement" of the Palestinian refugee problem based on U.N. Resolution 194.

The Abraham Accords meant the abandonment of the API by the countries that signed them. Palestinian leaders denounced the accords as a stab in the back. For Benjamin Netanyahu, on the other hand, they represented a major foreign policy victory; they seemed to support his claim that Israel could achieve peace with the Arab states without conceding anything to the Palestinians. The big prize, however, was Saudi Arabia. Unlike the smaller Gulf states, Saudi Arabia has much to lose from an open betrayal of the Palestinians. It risks a backlash at home and in parts of the Islamic world. It therefore resisted Trump's pressure to give official expression to its covert intelligence and security cooperation with Israel. And it stood by its commitment to the 2002 Arab Peace Initiative.

The API was the real "deal of the century". The Palestinian Authority under Yasser Arafat immediately embraced the initiative; the Israeli government under Prime Minister Ariel Sharon rejected it as a "non-starter". The Arab League re-endorsed the plan at its 2007 and 2017 summit conferences. But in 2018, Netanyahu rejected it again as a basis for future negotiations with the Palestinians. The US government welcomed the API but put no pressure on Israel to accept it.

Had Biden been interested in forging a peace settlement, he could have used the Arab Peace Initiative as the basis for US-led negotiations between Israel and the Palestinians. But he opted to use his diplomatic clout to persuade Saudi Arabia to sideline the Palestinians and join the club of the Abraham Accords. Washington offered various inducements for normalising relations with Israel, including acceptance of a peaceful Saudi nuclear program, the acquisition of advanced US weaponry and, perhaps most importantly, a defence pact to protect Saudi Arabia against an Iranian attack. Considerable progress was made in working out the details of the Saudi-Israeli accord. But when Hamas attacked on 7 October, Saudi Arabia suspended the negotiations. Shortly after 7 October, Biden said that though he didn't have proof, he was convinced that one of the reasons behind the Hamas attack was to impede progress on Israel's regional integration. "We can't leave that work behind," he added.

The Hamas attack called for an American response. Biden's instinctive reaction was to fly to Israel to demonstrate solidarity, to reassert the "unbreakable bond", and to pledge his country's total support for what he claimed was Israel's right to defend itself. The Hamas attack, he said, was "as consequential as the Holocaust". This remark not only ignored the context for the Hamas attack; it also trivialised the Holocaust in which six million Jews were slaughtered. Biden implied that Palestinians killed Israelis because they hated Jews. Their struggle was thus twisted from an anti-colonial one into an antisemitic one, from a normal desire to live in freedom and dignity on their land to an irrational hatred and thirst for Jewish blood.

Israel responded to the October 7 attack with a ferocious military offensive which was directed not just against Hamas but against the entire civilian population of Gaza. The declared aims of the war were to destroy Hamas as a political and military organisation, to maintain permanent Israeli security control over the Gaza Strip, to ensure that it could not pose another threat to Israel's security, and to bring back the hostages. The undeclared war aims were to ethnically cleanse Gaza by pushing its population into Egypt and to render the enclave uninhabitable. Firm Egyptian opposition prevented Israel from depopulating Gaza, but the IDF did succeed, through massive bombardment, in reducing large parts of Gaza to rubble.

President Biden supported the destruction of Hamas which is proscribed in the US as a terrorist organisation despite winning an absolute majority in a free and fair Palestinian election in January 2006. He regarded the destruction of Hamas as being not just in Israel's interest but in America's interest as well. This goal, however, is unattainable because Hamas is not just a political party with a military wing; it is a mass social movement, part of the fabric of Palestinian society. The US was thus dragged by its junior ally into a protracted but unwinnable asymmetric war. A much-vaunted strategic asset was beginning to look like a strategic liability.

Moreover, the way that Israel conducted the war in Gaza posed a serious problem for Biden. To justify the unprecedented violence and destructiveness of its own response, Israel's spin doctors exaggerated the scale of the Hamas atrocities and invented horror stories that had no basis in reality. Israeli spokesmen habitually told lies in previous conflicts but on this occasion they orchestrated a massive campaign of misinformation to paint their enemies as monsters in human form. The cruelty of Israel's soldiers was fully matched by the mendacity of its official spokesmen. Biden joined in the campaign against the common enemy, denouncing Hamas as "pure, unadulterated evil".

But his own credibility was called into question when he was caught regurgitating false Israeli propaganda. One famous story that made the rounds was that the Palestinian armed groups left behind forty decapitated babies in their killing spree of 7 October. Biden described seeing images of mutilated children during a meeting with Jewish leaders at the White House. His staff had to walk back on this claim when the lie was exposed. "The president based his comments about the alleged atrocities on the claims from Netanyahu's spokesman and media reports from Israel", admitted an embarrassed White House spokesman.

The manner in which Israel conducted the war in Gaza posed a much graver problem for Biden than its campaign of misinformation. Everything the IDF did after 7 October was justified in the name of self-defence. Biden himself repeatedly invoked Israel's right to self-defence. Under international law, however, an occupying power does not have the right to self-defence against the people it occupies. Even if Israel had the right to self-defence, its response to the Hamas attack had to be within the confines of international humanitarian law. The IDF conduct in Gaza, on the other hand, openly flouted the laws of war. If Hamas alone were the target, why inflict such indescribably horrific suffering on the civilian population? The IDF carried out in Gaza mass slaughter on an industrial scale, mostly of women and children; it destroyed or damaged 65 percent of the houses; it levelled much of the civilian infrastructure – hospitals, schools, universities, libraries, archives, and mosques; it forced 2 million out of a population of 2.3 million to evacuate their homes, often multiple times. These are not acts of self-defence; they are war crimes. As Israel's chief ally and armourer, the United States was inevitably implicated in these war crimes.

One of the worst crimes committed by Israel was to stop the flow of water, food, fuel, and medical supplies to the residents of Gaza in the immediate aftermath of the Hamas attack. This amounted to the use of starvation as a weapon of war. Having created a humanitarian catastrophe, Israel moved to disable UNRWA, the principal UN agency responsible for providing health, education, and welfare services to the Palestinian refugees. Israeli attacks on UNRWA schools and health centres housing fleeing homeless refugees were nothing new. But on this occasion Israel launched a political campaign to discredit and dismantle the organisation altogether. In early 2024, Israel alleged that twelve members of UNRWA staff in Gaza had participated in the Hamas-led attack, and that hundreds of them were members of militant groups. Seventeen countries reacted immediately by suspending aid to the organisation. Fifteen of them later reversed their decision when the Israeli allegations turned out to be unsubstantiated. Britain restored funding following the change from a Conservative to a Labour government. Only the United States, the organization's largest donor, continued to withhold funding.

Israel's obstruction of humanitarian aid from reaching the embattled people of Gaza was one of the most distressing but also constant features of this crisis. Most of the humanitarian aid used to reach Gaza by land from Egypt through the Rafah crossing. Israel introduced ever changing bureaucratic rules to impede the free flow of humanitarian aid to Gaza. In one case Israel bombed an aid convoy after being given its coordinates. Its drones targeted a three-car convoy belonging to the World Central Kitchen (WCK) in the Gaza Strip, killing seven aid workers. All three vehicles had the logo of the organisation clearly marked on their roofs, giving rise to suspicions that the attack was intentional and that it was aimed at discouraging other agencies delivering aid to Gaza. The attack occurred three days after a unanimous International Court of Justice ruling in the ongoing Genocide Convention case that ordered Israel to ensure the unhindered flow of aid into Gaza. The attack drew widespread international condemnation and led WCK and other humanitarian organizations to pause their operations in Gaza. This was at a time when the UN reported that virtually all of Gaza's 2.3 million people were struggling to find food and more than half a million were facing starvation.

President Biden did not join in the chorus of condemnation for the attack on the aid convoy. He had other ideas which helped Israel to persist in its bad old ways. In his March 2024 State of the Union address, he announced that the US military would construct a floating pier to hasten the delivery of aid to Gaza. He issued the directive although the experts in the US Agency for International Development (USAID) expressed concern that the plan would be difficult to implement and that it would undercut the effort to persuade Israel to open the far, far more efficient land crossings. The floating pier was a costly failure. A report by the inspector general of USAID, painted a scathing picture of a failed project, noting that political imperatives outweighed humanitarian considerations. The pier cost $230 million; it functioned intermittently for just 20 days; and it delivered only 8,100 metric tonnes of humanitarian assistance over that period, enough to feed 450,000 people for one month.

Relations between Joe Biden and Benjamin Netanyahu became progressively strained as the IDF committed more atrocities and more violations of international law without making much headway in its war against Hamas. Netanyahu, who has always boasted about his ability to manipulate American politicians, seized every opportunity to belittle and to undermine the American president, secure in the knowledge that he would not be made to pay a price. Netanyahu made no attempt to conceal his hope that Donald Trump would defeat Biden in the November elections. Nor was it a mere hope: Netanyahu has actively intervened in American domestic politics to bring about a Republican victory in the 2024 election.

While splits were beginning to appear in the US-Israel alliance, Biden's support for Israel as a Jewish nation remained firm. On 11 December 2023, at a Hannukah party at the White House, he said that "were there no Israel, there would not be a Jew in the world who is safe." He added: "You don't have to be a Jew to be a Zionist. I am a Zionist." But at the same time, he began to vent in public his frustration with Netanyahu, blaming him for the "indiscriminate bombing" that was going on in Gaza. In an interview with *Time* magazine on 4 June 2024, Biden suggested that Netanyahu was prolonging the war effort in Gaza for his own political survival.

Biden's rhetorical reprimands had little or no practical effect. Things came to a head in early May

2024 when Israel was making plans to go after Hamas in the southern city of Rafah where a million civilians were sheltering, having been ordered to go there by the IDF. American officials warned that without a credible plan for protecting civilians, a humanitarian disaster was bound to unfold. Biden said he was prepared to withhold certain types of weapons should Israel launch a major military operation in Rafah. It was the first time he drew a red line by threatening to curb arms supplies. In blatant defiance of Biden's warning, Israeli tanks rolled into Rafah, forcing a million displaced civilians to flee for their lives once again. Reminded of his red line in a TV interview, Biden responded "it is a red line, but I'm never going to leave Israel. The defense of Israel is still critical, so there's no red line I'm going to cut off all weapons so they don't have the Iron Dome to protect them." Biden was characteristically muddled and incoherent, but Anthony Blinken insisted on NBC's "Meet the Press" that his boss had not, in fact, drawn a red line at all. "Look, we don't talk about red lines when it comes to Israel", he said. That said it all. "Red lines applied to the US-Israel relationship have a habit of turning pink", observed Aaron David Miller, a former US negotiator on the Middle East.

At the United Nations the US continued to provide Israel with diplomatic protection by vetoing two

Security Council resolutions calling for a ceasefire. This was in the context of mounting international calls to stop the carnage and destruction. On 20 February 2024, the US used its veto for the third time to defeat a resolution for an immediate ceasefire, the release of all hostages, and unhindered humanitarian access. The reason given by the US ambassador to the UN was that Joe Biden was in the midst of negotiations aimed at a comprehensive hostage deal. But the veto was widely seen as giving a green light to the continued slaughter. The timing of the third veto was particularly embarrassing because Washington was seeking to build international solidarity in condemnation of Russia on the second anniversary of its invasion of Ukraine. The charge of double standards was difficult to refute.

Cast in the role of Israel's last diplomatic redoubt, Washington tried to reassert its diplomatic leadership role over Gaza. On 31 May 2024, the president announced a three-phase plan which he said Israel had accepted. Phase 1 called for temporary ceasefire, the release of hostages in return for Israel's release of Palestinian prisoners it held, and the withdrawal of the Israeli forces from the populated areas of Gaza. Phase 2 called for a permanent end to hostilities, the release of all other hostages, and a full withdrawal of all Israeli forces from Gaza. The third phase envisaged a multi-year reconstruction plan for Gaza. The Security

Council endorsed the plan on 10 June 2024 but insisted on a complete Israeli withdrawal from Gaza. On July 2, Hamas announced that it had agreed to restart ceasefire talks based on the framework outlined by the president. But Netanyahu, as was his wont, threw a spanner into the works. He publicly denied that this was an Israeli plan and added that any plan that did not achieve Israel's war aims, including the complete destruction of Hamas, was a "non-starter". The statement was designed to humiliate Biden. An experienced communicator like Netanyahu would know that the phrase "non-starter" would capture the headlines and undermine Biden's bid for a ceasefire.

Netanyahu's constant changing of the goal posts doomed to failure this and all subsequent attempts to wind down the war. Qatar and Egypt worked tirelessly to mediate between the two sides. They communicated on a regular basis with Hamas which was not present at the meetings. But the negotiations in Doha and Cairo failed to close the gap. The sticking point was Netanyahu's insistence that any agreement had to allow an Israeli presence along the Egypt-Gaza border, a strip of land known as the Philadelphi Corridor, and along a road that bisects the Gaza Strip horizontally, known as the Netzarim Corridor. Hamas rejected any such presence, pointing out it contravened Biden's three-stage plan, which envisaged a complete Israeli withdrawal from Gaza. Israeli security experts, and even defence minister Yoav Gallant, have declared that Israeli presence along the corridors is not crucial. Yet, to appease Netanyahu, Blinken subsequently came up with what he called a "bridging proposal" although it included Netanyahu's new demands.

Hamas refused to participate in the ceasefire and hostage release negotiations under the new US "bridging proposal". The group also charged the US of deceiving the public on the negotiations, saying it had backtracked from Biden's original proposal. Hamas was not alone in regarding Netanyahu as an inveterate liar. A survey conducted a few weeks after the 7 October attack, found that only four percent of the Israeli public trusted him. By siding with the mendacious Israeli prime minister and blaming Hamas for the diplomatic impasse, Blinken reduced his already very low credibility as a mediator to zero. What this sordid episode demonstrated, yet again, was that the US cannot serve both as Israel's lawyer and as an honest broker. This is a colonial game in which the US pretends to bring the Gaza war to an end but only provides its protégé with the diplomatic cover and munitions for continuing its genocidal campaign against the Palestinian people. The episode also reflects badly on the US for neutralising the UN, the proper organ for dealing with threats to international peace and security, and insisting on indirect negotiations on a ceasefire between a genocidal government and its victims, rather than imposed through the enforcement of international law.

Even outside the UN framework, Biden had a sure way of forcing Israel to heed his advice, namely, to stop the flow of arms. But he was almost congenitally incapable of using it. The US is by far the biggest arms supplier to Israel, with Germany as a distant second. Britain is a minor supplier by comparison to these two countries. Israel is also the largest beneficiary of US aid in the world, having received about $300bn since it was born. In May 2024, Biden boasted that he suspended the shipment to Israel of 3,500 large bombs capable of destroying whole neighbourhoods. But within days it became clear that he wanted Israel to be given a far larger shipment of arms. This instantly undermined Biden's strategy of preventing an Israeli land invasion of Rafah. It also created the clear impression that Biden was not prepared to back up his protestations of concern for Palestinian civilians with any effective action. His actions told a different story. At his insistent request, Congress voted, in April 2024, for $26bn in emergency support for Israel, including $14bn in unconditional military aid. On other occasions, the administration used loopholes to expedite arms deliveries to Israel and avoid congressional scrutiny. In the first ten months of the Gaza war, the Pentagon supplied Israel with 50,000 tons of arms and ammunition. A report by the State Department which raised doubts as to whether the IDF used American arms in accordance with international humanitarian law was brushed aside with the claim that the administration received written assurances to the contrary from Israeli officials which it considered "credible and reliable".

By its own murderous actions in Gaza, and systematic violations of international law, Israel has turned itself into an international pariah and helped to drag down the US with it. Biden's near unconditional support for Israel, and his attempts to shield it from being called to account for its actions, inevitably affect his own credibility and his country's standing in the world. But the wheels of international justice have been turning. On 26 January 2024, the International Court of Justice at The Hague issued a landmark ruling in response to a South African charge that Israel was committing genocide in Gaza. Anthony Blinken dismissed the South African case as "meritless". A spokesperson for the US National Security Council described the case as "meritless, counterproductive, completely without any basis in fact whatsoever". But the judges did find merit in the case. They concluded that Israel's actions in Gaza raise a plausible risk of genocide, and they ordered Israel to take steps to prevent genocidal acts, to prevent and punish incitement to genocide, and report back on its actions within a month. The court has few powers of enforcement. But it does have moral authority. Its ruling sends a clear message to Israel and to those who are ready to protect it from any and all criticism. In sharp contrast to the Biden administration's pick and choose approach to justice, the court reasserted the principle that unequal justice is no justice at all. The ICJ "advisory opinion" was all the more devastating for Israel because its whole national identity is intertwined with the Nazi genocide, just as South Africa's is indivisible from apartheid.

Another development of critical importance is the application by Karim Khan, the chief prosecutor at the International Criminal Court (ICC) at The Hague, for arrest warrants for war crimes and crimes against humanity against Prime Minister Netanyahu, Defence Minister Gallant, and the IDF chief of staff, Herzl Halevi. Khan also applied for arrest warrants for Hamas leaders. The US is not a member of the ICC, but it has been highly critical in the past of its attempts to hold either American or Israeli personnel to account for alleged war crimes. In this instance, Biden insisted that arraigning Israeli and Hamas leaders at the same time implies "moral equivalence". Khan considers that there are "reasonable grounds to believe" that both sides have committed grave criminal offences and that all those responsible must answer equally, whoever they may be. Biden evidently has difficulty with the concept of equality before the law even as he prattles about upholding the democratic, rules-based international order. His reaction to the chief prosecutor's application proves that he is in denial. "What's happening is not genocide", he said. But Khan is not saying it is. He only wants to apply the rules of international law without fear or favour. Biden backed the ICC arrest warrant against Vladimir Putin, but he denounced the arrest warrants against the Israeli leaders as "outrageous".

On one matter Netanyahu and Biden have been at odds since the beginning of the Gaza war: Netanyahu wants to extend the geographical scope of the conflict whereas Biden wants to contain it. The reason for Netanyahu's desire to prolong, extend, and escalate the war in Gaza is connected both to his need to survive in power and with his endgame. For decades Netanyahu believed that a major war could provide Israel with cover to carry out a mass expulsion of Palestinians from the West Bank. In 1977 he explained this precise idea to the British historian Max Hastings who was writing a biography of his older brother, Yoni Netanyahu. "In the next war", Netanyahu boasted, "if we do it right, we'll have a chance to get all the Arabs out ... We can clear the West Bank, sort out Jerusalem".

The war in Gaza gave Netanyahu just the opportunity he had been looking for to accelerate the ethnic cleansing of Palestine. Settler violence against the Palestinians on the West Bank was nothing new but after 7 October the settlers stepped up their attacks with the open support of the government and the army. So far the violent and racist settlers have succeeded in driving 19 Palestinian communities out of their homes. In early September 2024, with the world's attention fixed on the martyrdom of Gaza, the IDF moved on several Palestinian towns and refugee camps in the northern West Bank. "Operation Summer Camps" was the biggest military campaign in the West Bank in more than 20 years. It was described as a counter-terrorist operation, but it involved the deliberate destruction of civilian infrastructure that serves hundreds of thousands of Palestinians. The scale and destructiveness of the operation indicated that its broader aim was to drive out as many Palestinian civilians as possible. In the ten months since the Hamas attack, Israeli settlers and soldiers killed 662 people on the West Bank, including at least 140 minors. Several Israeli officials made it clear that they intended to do to the West Bank what they had been doing to Gaza.

Netanyahu and his far-right ministers make no attempt to conceal their ultimate aim: total control and permanent Jewish sovereignty over the whole of the West Bank. They seem intent on simultaneously escalating the clashes with Hizballah, Iran's powerful proxy in Lebanon. Two particularly provocative acts were the targeted assassination of Ismail Haniyeh, the political head of Hamas, while he attended a funeral in Tehran, and of Fuad Shukr, a top Hizballah commander. By preventing a ceasefire and waging a war on all fronts, Netanyahu and his hardcore nationalist ministers seem to be pushing for a regional war that would draw the US into a confrontation with Iran, Hizballah, and other regional groups allied with the Palestinian resistance. Biden constantly urged restraint on Israel but as the copious flow of arms continued, his pleas were simply ignored. Biden also ordered American aircraft carriers to the eastern Mediterranean, ostensibly to deter Iran and its proxies. But this move could also be interpreted as holding the ring for Israel while it proceeded with the systematic destruction of Gaza.

The double standards that Biden consistently displayed during the war in Gaza have not only diminished American influence in the world and its ability to lead; they have also undermined the entire rules-based international order that America traditionally claimed to uphold. Joe Biden will go down in history as a leader who had the power to restrain Israel but refused to use this power. His policy was a continuation of previous American policy on Israel-Palestine, an extension of the

"Israel first" approach, rather than a new departure or aberration. The basic flaw in America's foreign policy is that its support for Israel is unconditional. This means that Israel has been able to get away literally with murder. Where Biden stands out is in his dogmatic and rigid rejection of conditionality. Throughout his long political career, he has refused to make America's massive support conditional on Israeli respect for international law and Palestinian human rights. The war in Gaza has seen a dangerous escalation in Israel's brutality towards the Palestinians and in its disregard for international law. In Gaza, Israel is committing the crime of all crimes – genocide. The saddest irony is that a people once in need of protection from genocide is now committing it. The continuing flow of American arms for Israel's multi-pronged attack on Gaza and the West Bank, makes America complicit in its ally's war crimes. It is nothing less than a green light for genocide. It also makes President Biden personally complicit, if not a full partner, in Israel's genocidal war against the Palestinian people. This role has earned President Biden a new sobriquet – Genocide Joe.

8 September 2024

— 2021 —

THE TWO-STATE SOLUTION: ILLUSION AND REALITY

The idea of partitioning Palestine into two states as a way of satisfying both Palestinian and Zionist national aspirations is not a new one. It was first proposed at the official level by the Peel Commission of Inquiry in 1937, following the outbreak of the Arab Revolt.

The Arabs, under the leadership of Hajj Amin al-Husseini, rejected the plan, not least because the Arab state was to be merged with Transjordan. The Zionist movement was divided but the moderates, led by Dr. Chaim Weizmann, won the argument. "The Jews would be fools not to accept it", said Weizmann, "even if the Jewish state were the size of a tablecloth. *C'est le premier pas qui compte!*" – It is the first step that counts!

A decade later, in 1947, the United Nations General Assembly passed Resolution 181 which called for replacing the British Mandate for Palestine with two states, one Arab and one Jewish, with a special international regime for the City of Jerusalem. The logic of partition was now endorsed by the international community. Once again, however, the Partition Plan was accepted by the Jewish Agency and rejected by the Arabs.

The Arabs went to war in 1948 to resist partition and to liberate Palestine, but they suffered a resounding defeat. The winners in this war were Israel and Jordan; the greatest losers were the Palestinians: 750,000 Palestinians became refugees, and the name Palestine was wiped off the map of the Middle East. This was the *nakba*, the catastrophe. One of the reasons for the Arab defeat was a tacit understanding reached the previous year between King Abdullah of Jordan and the Jewish Agency to divide up Palestine between themselves at the expense of the Palestinians. This secret understanding laid the foundation for limiting the clashes of their armed forces during the war and continuing collaboration in its aftermath.[255]

In the course of the 1948 war, the newly born state of Israel enlarged its territory from the 55% proposed by the UN cartographers to 78% of Mandatory Palestine. Jordan captured, and two years later formally annexed, the West Bank, which would have been the heartland of the Palestinian state. The Palestinians were reduced from a nation in search of a state to a refugee problem, and a UN agency was created to cater to their basic needs as refugees. The two-state solution to the Zionist-Palestinian conflict remained in abeyance for the next four decades.

— JUNE 1967 MARKS A TURNING-POINT —

The next major turning point in the history of the Arab-Israeli conflict was the June 1967 War, popularly known as the Six-Day War. In the course of this war, Israel captured the remaining 22% percent of Mandatory Palestine: the Gaza Strip from Egypt and the West Bank from Jordan, including the Old City of Jerusalem, the jewel in the Hashemite crown.

In November 1967, the UN Security Council passed Resolution 242, which remained the basis for nearly all subsequent international plans for resolving the conflict. The resolution proposed a package deal: Israel was to withdraw from the territories it captured during the war in return for peace with its Arab neighbors. Resolution 242 did not acknowledge the Palestinians as a stateless nation or even mention them by name. All it called for was "a just solution to the refugee problem". The two-state solution thus disappeared from the international agenda. There was support for a Palestinian state alongside Israel in some left-wing quarters, but it was miniscule and politically insignificant.

The most prominent option for a settlement after the Six-Day War was the Jordanian option. This involved a peace agreement between Israel and the Hashemite Kingdom of Jordan based on a return to the pre-1967 territorial status quo. Given the previous history of collaboration between the Zionist movement and the Hashemites, the ruling Labor Party in Israel had a strong preference for Jordan over the Palestinians as a partner for peace. King Hussein was a willing, indeed an eager interlocutor. Back in 1963, he began a series of secret talks with Israeli officials, breaking the biggest Arab taboo. Immediately after the end of hostilities, he resumed the dialogue across the battle lines and offered Israel total peace in return for total withdrawal. But by this time Israel was drunk with victory and swept along a wave of religious and secular nationalism which militated against withdrawal.[256] Prime Minister Levi Eshkol summed up the national mood by telling his colleagues: "You like the dowry but not the bride", meaning you like the land but not the Arabs who lived on it.[257] In return for peace, Israel's leaders offered King Hussein only part of the West Bank without the Old City of Jerusalem. This he repeatedly rejected, so no agreement was reached, and the political deadlock persisted.

The Palestinian option as an alternative to the Jordanian option did not emerge until the late 1980s. In July 1988, following the outbreak of the first intifada, King Hussein severed Jordan's legal and administrative ties with the West Bank and made way for the PLO to represent its inhabitants in future negotiations with Israel. At that point, the Palestinian national movement moderated its political program. In November 1988, the Palestinian National Council (PNC) adopted a series of profoundly important resolutions. It recognized Israel's right to exist; it accepted all previous UN resolutions on the conflict going back to 181; and it opted unambiguously for a two-state solution to the dispute between the two peoples. These resolutions represented a revolution in PLO thinking. The architect of this revolution was Yasser Arafat. The PNC resolutions opened the door to a dialogue with the enemy. But a hard-line Likud government under Yitzhak Shamir adamantly refused to negotiate with the PLO, continuing to denounce it as a terrorist organization.

In the meantime, Israel continued to build civilian settlements or colonies on occupied Palestinian territory. These settlements are illegal and constitute a major obstacle to peace, yet Israel's two main parties promoted them, although with a difference in approach. Whereas the Labor-led governments built settlements mainly in areas of strategic importance that they intended to keep permanently, Likud governments built settlements across the length and breadth of the West Bank, partly for reasons connected with the ideology of "the Greater Land of Israel", and partly to block the path to withdrawal in the event of a Labor return to power.

— THE OSLO YEARS —

In 1992, Labor did return to power under the leadership of Yitzhak Rabin, and a year later it signed the Oslo Accord with the PLO. The Oslo Accord was preceded by an exchange of letters that denoted mutual recognition. The PLO recognized Israel's right to exist, while the Israeli letter only recognized the PLO as the representative of the Palestinian people without recognizing any Palestinian national rights. Nevertheless, to many optimistic observers, including the present writer, the accord looked like the first step on the long road towards a two-state solution.

On the Palestinian side, the Oslo Accord enjoyed broad support but was also subjected to fierce criticism. The most basic criticism was that the deal negotiated by Yasser Arafat did not carry the promise, let alone guarantee, of an independent Palestinian state at the end of the five-year transition period. One of the most hard-hitting critics was Edward Said. In a series of newspaper articles, he argued that the Oslo Accord compromised the basic national rights of the Palestinian people as well as the individual rights of the 1948 refugees. He lambasted Yasser Arafat for failing to coordinate his moves with the Arab states and for introducing appalling disarray within the ranks of the PLO. "The PLO", wrote Said, "has transformed itself from a national liberation movement into a kind of small-town government, with the same handful of people still in command." Arafat and his corrupt cronies, according to Said, had sacrificed principle to grab power.

Furthermore, this was not a deal between two equal parties: On the one hand there was Israel, a modern state and a military superpower; on the other hand there was the PLO, a leadership in exile with no maps, no technical expertise, no territorial base, and no friends. "All secret deals between a very strong and a very weak partner", wrote Said, "necessarily involve concessions hidden in embarrassment by the latter… The deal before us smacks of the PLO leadership's exhaustion and isolation, and of Israel's shrewdness."[258]

Rabin's shrewdness in foisting upon the PLO such an unequal, unfair, and unpromising deal was to no avail. He himself was assassinated by a Jewish fanatic in what turned out to be a highly successful attempt to derail the Oslo peace process. Following his death, Rabin was surrounded by the aura of a martyr who had sacrificed his life on the altar of peace. Rabin's supporters argued that had he lived, he would have proceeded step by step towards a two-state solution. There is no way, however, of knowing what might have happened had Rabin lived longer. History does not disclose its alternatives. All we know for a fact is that to his dying day, Rabin never agreed to a full-fledged Palestinian state alongside Israel. The most he was prepared to concede, and this rather grudgingly, was what he called "a state minus".

On October 31, three days before Rabin's murder, Yossi Beilin, Israel's militantly moderate deputy foreign minister, and senior PLO official Mahmoud Abbas (better known as Abu-Mazen) concluded the framework for a future Israeli-Palestinian peace deal. The basic premise of the Beilin-Abu-Mazen plan was that there would be a demilitarized Palestinian state. The plan envisaged the annexation by Israel of about 6% of the West Bank, where roughly 75% of the Jewish settlers resided. The Muslim holy places in East Jerusalem were to be given an exterritorial status, but the capital of the Palestinian state had to be just outside the municipal boundary of the city as defined by Israel. Hussein Agha, a Palestinian negotiator, dubbed the Beilin-Abu-Mazen plan "the deal of the century". But Shimon Peres, who succeeded Rabin as prime minister, could not be persuaded to adopt the plan as the Labor Party's platform in the coming elections. He was afraid he would be accused of dividing Jerusalem, and he wanted to retain the Jordan Valley as Israel's strategic border. When Peres was unexpectedly defeated by Benjamin Netanyahu in the May 1996 elections, the Beilin-Abu-Mazen plan became history.

— FAILURE OF CAMP DAVID —

Three years later, the Labor Party was back in power under the leadership of Ehud Barak. Barak was a former IDF chief of staff and Israel's most decorated soldier. He was a brave and brilliant soldier but an inept politician who lacked the courage to take the necessary risks for the sake of peace. The moment of truth came at the Camp David summit in July 2000, which Barak himself had asked President Bill Clinton to convene. Barak's advisers warned him that the Palestinians would not budge from their basic demand for an independent state in the Gaza Strip and the West Bank with a capital city in East Jerusalem. Barak believed that with Clinton's help, he could push Yasser Arafat into a corner and force him to settle for less.

What Barak set out to achieve at Camp David was not a peace treaty grounded in international legality, but a deal dictated by the acute asymmetry in the power of the two sides. His modus operandi was peace by ultimatum. For two weeks at the presidential retreat, Barak refused to meet with Arafat and to negotiate with him face-to-face. He used his own aides and the American president to convey offers to his opponent. Every time Arafat turned down an offer, Barak tried a slightly improved offer, the last of which included Gaza and 91% of the West Bank but no sovereignty over the Haram al-Sharif in the Old City of Jerusalem. When Arafat rejected this offer, the summit ended in spectacular failure.

Following the failure of the summit, Barak invented the myth that there is no Palestinian partner for peace. He claimed that at Camp David he had made the most generous offer imaginable to the Palestinians but that Arafat rejected it and made a strategic decision to return to violence, a decision that led to the outbreak of the second intifada four months later. The claim that Arafat planned and instigated the second intifada is utterly baseless. Instead of admitting his own fault, Barak sought to pin the blame for the impasse on the other side.

The problem with Barak's post-facto explanation, or more precisely the myth he invented, was that the great majority of Israelis believed it. This myth had dire consequences for the Labor Party, the peace camp, and the prospects of a peaceful settlement. For if there was no Palestinian partner for peace, it was only logical for Israelis to vote for a leader who was good at killing Palestinians rather than for a party that advocated negotiations with them. Ariel Sharon fitted the bill perfectly. Consequently, his Likud party was elected in February 2001, and right-wing parties have remained in power ever since.

— SHARON – UNILATERALIST — — "PAR EXCELLENCE" —

Sharon was an aggressive former soldier and an ardent Israeli nationalist who from the beginning rejected the notion that diplomacy could resolve the Israeli-Palestinian conflict. He was a proponent of the doctrine of permanent conflict and a champion of violent solutions. His long-term thinking was encapsulated in the slogan that "Jordan is Palestine". He maintained that a Palestinian state already existed on the East Bank of the Jordan River because the majority of its inhabitants were Palestinian, and he hoped that the Palestinians would topple the monarchy, transform the Hashemite Kingdom of Jordan into the Republic of Palestine, and thereby facilitate the absorption of the West Bank into Greater Israel.

Sharon's premiership provided further proof, if further proof was needed, that Israel was not ready for a genuine a two-state solution. On March 12, 2002, the Security Council adopted Resolution 1397, the first UN resolution to explicitly call for a two-state solution. Sharon rejected it. On March 27, the Arab League offered Israel peace and normalization with all its 22 members in return for a full withdrawal by Israel from the occupied territories (including the West Bank, Gaza, the Golan Heights, and Lebanon), a "just settlement" of the Palestinian refugee problem based on UN Resolution 194, and the establishment of a Palestinian state with East Jerusalem as its capital. The Arab Peace Initiative (API) was overshadowed by a Hamas suicide bombing that killed 29 Israelis and wounded 150. Sharon retaliated by launching "Operation Defensive Shield", the biggest and most destructive military operation in the West Bank since the Six-Day War. At no point subsequently was he willing to engage with the API.

Sharon was suspicious of diplomacy and addicted to violence. He even boasted that during his five years in power, there were no peace negotiations of any kind with the Palestinians. Yet, in rejecting an independent Palestinian state, Sharon faithfully represented the policy position of the Likud and more broadly of the Israeli right. Sharon fell out with his party over his plan to withdraw from Gaza in 2005. Sharon was the unilateralist *par excellence*. He envisaged disengagement from Gaza as a unilateral Israeli move to enhance Israeli security, not as a first step towards a negotiated settlement of the conflict. The plan was anchored in a fundamental rejection of Palestinian statehood. Yet the hard-liners in the Likud denounced the withdrawal from Gaza as a betrayal of the settlers and appeasement of Hamas, prompting Sharon to quit and form a new party, Kadima (Forward).

— DIFFERING ACCOUNTS OF — — OLMERT-ABBAS NEGOTIATIONS —

Ehud Olmert succeeded Sharon as leader of Kadima and prime minister in January 2006. Olmert's main claim to being a peacemaker rested on an offer he made at his residence in Jerusalem to Mahmoud Abbas, the Palestinian president, on September 16, 2008, 12 days before announcing his resignation. He resigned because of a police investigation into charges of corruption of which he was later convicted. After leaving office,

Olmert made the offer public, claiming he had been willing to place the entire Old City under an international regime, divide Jerusalem, give the Palestinians 93.5% of the West Bank with one-to-one swaps for the areas to be retained by Israel, and absorb 5,000 refugees inside the Green Line over a period of five years. This was certainly a far-reaching proposal for a two-state solution, which addressed all the "permanent status" issues. On Jerusalem and borders, Olmert went well beyond what Ehud Barak had been prepared to concede.

Yet Olmert's version of events is not entirely accurate. By his own account, Olmert demanded that Abbas meet him the very next day, together with map experts, in order to arrive at a final line for the border between Palestine and Israel. Abbas asked to take the Israeli map with him to show to his experts. Olmert declined, fearing the map would be used not for closure but as the starting point in future negotiations. Abbas was not prepared to be rushed by the "caretaker" prime minister on a matter of such supreme importance, and no meeting took place the following day. Olmert claimed that he never heard from Abbas again and that the most generous offer in Israel's history remained without a Palestinian answer. But Olmert and Abbas did negotiate subsequently, on more than one occasion. Far from ignoring the offer, the Palestinians requested clarifications, which they did not receive.

Palestinian doubts about Olmert's credibility were compounded by his deep unpopularity at home and his imminent political demise. He was a lame duck prime minister, and his constitutional right to sign the agreement he proposed was wide open to challenge. Abbas was advised by some Israelis not to sign an agreement with Olmert. Tzipi Livni, the foreign minister and number two in Kadima, reportedly sent messages to Abbas advising him to wait for her to become prime minister and promising to improve on Olmert's terms. Henry Kissinger famously said that Israel has no foreign policy, only internal politics. This was a classic example of internal rivalries obstructing peace-making.[259]

Even without the added complications of internal Israeli rivalries, Olmert's peace initiative faced an uncertain future. On a number of critical issues, the two sides remained far apart. The Palestinians were not told whether Olmert's percentages for the West Bank included or excluded the Jewish neighborhoods around Jerusalem, nor was there agreement on the West Bank settlements to be removed. Olmert, for example, insisted on keeping Ariel, which extended nearly halfway across the West Bank, and this was not acceptable to the Palestinians. Olmert demanded that Israel's armed forces be stationed on the territory of the future Palestinian state; this, too, was not acceptable to the Palestinians. Olmert offered to admit 5,000 refugees into Israel in five years; Abbas wanted 150,000 to return over a period of 10 years. So even if his hold on power had been much firmer, it is far from certain that Olmert could have reached an overall settlement on a two-state solution. He later accused Abbas of lacking guts, of being indecisive, and of missing a unique opportunity for peace. But under the circumstances, the Palestinian leader's caution was understandable.

— NETANYAHU WAS FIRMLY — — WEDDED TO THE STATUS QUO —

The Likud returned to power under Benjamin Netanyahu in 2009. Netanyahu was the longest serving prime minister in Israel's history. He served as prime minister in 1996-1999 and in three consecutive terms from 2009 until 2021. One of the myths surrounding his premiership was that he supported a two-state solution to the Israeli-Palestinian conflict. The only solid piece of evidence for this claim was a speech he made at Bar-Ilan University on June 14, 2009, two and a half months after he formed his second government. In that speech, Netanyahu stated: "We will be willing to accept a demilitarized Palestinian state alongside the Jewish state." The speech, however, was made only under intense pressure from the Obama administration, and the change of policy it announced was more apparent than real. A month after the speech, Benzion Netanyahu, the prime minister's octogenarian father, told a Channel 2 TV interviewer: "Binyamin does not support a Palestinian state, except on conditions that the Arabs will never ever accept. I heard this from him."

Throughout his time in power, Benjamin Netanyahu remained firmly wedded to the status quo: limited Palestinian autonomy under Israeli rule; in other words, an apartheid regime with Israel as the all-powerful colonial overlord. In his Bar-Ilan speech, Netanyahu called for negotiations without preconditions. But in the same breath, he posed a series of preconditions to the Palestinians. First, he dissociated himself from the understandings that his predecessor, Olmert, had reached with Abbas a year earlier. Second, he rejected Abbas's demand for a freeze on settlement expansion during the negotiations. In other words, while pretending to negotiate over the division of the cake, Netanyahu proposed to keep eating it. Third, there could be absolutely no return of the Palestinian refugees to their homes, not even in symbolic numbers. Fourth, he insisted that Jerusalem would remain Israel's united capital. Moreover, Netanyahu introduced a completely new condition: The Palestinians had to recognize Israel as the nation-state of the Jewish people. The reason Netanyahu stipulated this last condition was because he knew that no Palestinian leader, however moderate, could possibly accept it. It was an absurd condition, not least because it ignored the Palestinian citizens who make up a fifth of Israel's population. In short, Netanyahu never accepted a two state solution in good faith. In the run-up to the 2015 elections, he himself declared: "If I am elected, no Palestinian state will emerge on my watch." He was re-elected, and he was true to his word.

— THE BENNETT GOVERNMENT — — AND THE STATUS QUO —

After four inconclusive elections, Netanyahu's Likud was ousted from power in March 2021 and replaced by a very strange coalition government that includes the dovish Meretz, the Labor Party, several centrist parties, and a small Islamic party of Israeli Arabs. This marked the first time in Israel's history that an Arab party joined the government. The prime minister is Naftali Bennett, leader of the ultranationalist Yemina (Rightwards) party which has only six seats in the 120-member Knesset. Bennett is a religious nationalist and a former head of the settlers' council. He shares Netanyahu's strong opposition to Palestinian independence, but he used to go much further in advocating outright annexation of Area C, which consists of 60% of the West Bank where the great majority of the Jewish settlers live. Bennett's government can only survive in power by clinging to the status quo – colonial rule over the West Bank – and refraining from any major policy shift in either a dovish or a hawkish direction.

— THE TWO-STATE SOLUTION —
— WAS NEVER BORN —

In recent years, it has become fashionable to say that the two-state solution is dead. If not stone dead, this solution is surely "OBE – Overtaken By Events". Many different reasons combined to make this solution obsolete, but the most important is Israeli settlement expansion in the West Bank and the ethnic cleansing of East Jerusalem. Another cause of the death of the two-state solution is the security barrier that Israel has been constructing in the West Bank since 2003. Between them, the settlements and the wall de facto annex to Israel around 10% of the West Bank. The settlements represent the aggressive expansion of the Zionist colonial project beyond the Green Line. The wall is not just illegal but a brutal instrument of landgrabbing. What is left to the Palestinians is a collection of enclaves that cannot form a viable, territorially contiguous state.

It is therefore no exaggeration, or only a slight exaggeration, to say that the two-state solution is dead. I would go further and argue that the two-state solution was never born. The reason for this assertion is that no Israeli Government since 1967, with the possible exception of the Olmert government, has been willing to accept an independent Palestinian state over the whole of Gaza and the West Bank with a capital city in East Jerusalem.

Nor has Israel had to face any international sanction for its diplomatic intransigence, for its oppression of the Palestinians, or for its flagrant violations of international law. True, the UN has passed a raft of resolutions condemning Israel's annexation of Jerusalem, creeping annexation of the West Bank, systematic violations of Palestinian human rights, and successive assaults on the civilian population of Gaza. But Israel shakes off these resolutions like water off a duck's back.

That Israel has become an apartheid state is now beyond doubt. The claim is hotly disputed by Israel's supporters, but it is nevertheless a fact. That was the conclusion reached by B'Tselem, the highly respected Israeli human rights organization. Until recently, B'Tselem's reports used to focus on Israeli human rights violations in the occupied Palestinian territory. A point was reached, however, when Israeli practices and policies in the occupied territories could no longer be considered separately from the regime in Israel proper. In January 2021, B'Tselem issued a closely argued position paper entitled "A regime of Jewish supremacy from the Jordan River to the Mediterranean Sea: This is apartheid". According to the report: "The entire area Israel controls between the Jordan River and the Mediterranean Sea is governed by a single regime working to advance and perpetuate the supremacy of one group over another. By geographically, demographically and physically engineering space, the regime enables Jews to live in a contiguous area with full rights, including self-determination, while Palestinians live in separate units and enjoy fewer rights."[260]

Israel's principal Western backers, the United States and the European Union, know that apartheid is the reality on the ground and that this reality is incompatible with a two-state solution in any meaningful sense of the term. So why do they continue to parrot their support for the two-state solution at every opportunity? The answer is that they are afraid to admit that the root of the problem is the racist and colonial character of Israeli rule over the Palestinian territories. An open rift with Israel would be costly for the Western powers in political terms. It is therefore convenient for them to continue to pretend that Israel is a democratic state and that its conflict with the Palestinians can only be resolved by direct negotiations leading to the partition of the land between the river and the sea. They know full well that Israel will not mend its ways unless sanctions are imposed, but they are unwilling or unable to impose sanctions. In the meantime, in the absence of any Israeli Palestinian peace process, they are free to persist in the policy posture of useless hand-wringing and pious platitudes.

— ISRAEL MUST BE DECOLONIZED —

What emerges from this brief historical survey is that no Israeli Government, with one dubious exception, has been willing to accept Palestinian self-determination over the entire territory it captured in the June 1967 War. Rhetorical Western support for the elusive two-state solution makes them complicit in Israel's continuing crimes against the Palestinian people. Fundamentally, however, it is Israel's own opposition to Palestinian independence and statehood that make the much-vaunted two-state solution an illusion rather than a realistic possibility.

If one recognizes, as I do, that the root of the problem is the Jewish supremacist character of the state of Israel, it follows that ending the occupation is not enough; Israel, too, needs to be decolonized. The Palestinian citizens of Israel are second-class citizens.

True, they have the vote, but there is a whole raft of laws and practices that discriminate against them. A two-state solution would not address their problem. On the contrary, it would distance them further from the other branch of the Palestinian family. The best hope for resolving the century-old conflict between Jews and Palestinians lies not in the partition of Palestine but in building one democratic state from the river to the sea with equal rights for all its citizens, regardless of religion or ethnicity.

This piece was originally published under the same title in Palestine-Israel Journal of Politics, Economics and Culture, *26 (2), No. 3&4, 2021.*

— 2024 —

EPILOGUE

On Friday, 27 September 2024, as I sat down to write this epilogue, I learnt that Israel had assassinated Sayyed Hassan Nasrallah, Hizbullah's secretary-general, in a massive airstrike on his underground headquarters in the southern Beirut suburb of Dahiyeh. This marked a dangerous escalation from the inconclusive war in Gaza to a military offensive against Hizbullah on Israel's northern front. In Lebanon, as in Gaza, Israel embarked on a maximum pressure strategy, hoping to achieve a surrender of the resistance on the northern front that had eluded it in the south. The "new model" of brutal warfare against Hamas, what I regard as state terrorism, was now being replicated in the campaign against Hızbullah.

Hizbullah and Hamas both belong to the Iran-led "Axis of Resistance" to Israel. Hizbullah is the linchpin of this loose network of pro-Iranian groups across the

Middle East that includes Hamas, the Houthis in Yemen, and small militias in Iraq and Syria. On 8 October, the day after Israel had started pulverising Gaza in response to the Hamas attack, Hizbullah opened a secondary front against Israel. It did not launch a major offensive but began firing rockets and missiles into Israel in a show of solidarity with the Palestinian resistance. In his last speech Nasrallah pledged that "we'll never abandon Palestine".

Hizbullah, a predominantly Shia Muslim social movement, emerged in the wake of Israel's invasion of Lebanon in 1982 and gradually developed into a formidable antagonist. It has a fair claim to being the most effective Arab fighting force that Israel has had to confront since its foundation in 1948. In 1992, Israel assassinated Hizbullah's leader, Shaikh Abbas Mousavi, but was unable to bring the militia to its knees. Hassan Nasrallah, Mousavi's successor, was more radical, more capable, and more determined to confront Israel. Trained in Islamic theology in Iran, he was inspired by the new Islamic ideologies that were spreading through the Middle East at the time. In the years after 1992, Nasrallah transformed Hizbullah into a major political party and built up its military wing to unprecedented strength. He himself became a symbol of Arab resistance to Israel, which he dubbed "the usurping entity", and to American imperialism.

In 2000, under Nasrallah's leadership, Hizbullah was able to force an ignominious end to Israel's eighteen-year-old occupation and reign of terror in south Lebanon. The IDF retreated from Lebanon in haste and in chaos, and with its much-vaunted deterrence capability in tatters. Hizbullah held a victory parade in the town of Bint Jbeil. The key speaker was Hassan Nasrallah, and his words were directed at the entire Arab world: "My dear brothers, I say this to you: with all its atomic weapons, Israel is weaker than cobwebs".

In July 2006, following a Hizbullah raid into Israel and the capture of two Israeli soldiers, Prime Minister Ehud Olmert eschewed diplomacy and ordered a massive assault, including a ground invasion of south Lebanon. The principal war aim was to destroy or at least to forcibly disarm Hizbullah. This aim was unrealistic in the first place, and it was certainly not achieved. The operation, which involved the deliberate targeting of civilians in flagrant violation of the laws of war, was a manifest failure. Due to unprecedented Iranian military support to Hizbullah before and during the war, some commentators even consider it to have been the first round in an Iran–Israel proxy war, rather than a continuation of the Arab-Israeli conflict.

The assassination of Hassan Nasrallah was accomplished by eight F-15I fighter jets dropping dozens of bunker busting bombs on and around Hizbullah's underground headquarters. Six apartment blocks were reduced to rubble in the attack. The 2,000lb US-supplied bombs exploded five metres underground, caused massive destruction, and killed everyone in a radius of thirty-three metres. The use of these bombs in urban areas is proscribed by the laws of war but it is a central element in the IDF's military doctrine. The "Dahiyeh Doctrine" was formulated by IDF chief of staff Gadi Eisenkot during the 2006 Lebanon War, when this suburb, a Hizbullah stronghold, came under heavy bombardment. The doctrine calls for large-scale destruction of civilian infrastructure and the use of overwhelming force against the civilian population. The logic is to harm the civilian population so much that they turn against the militants and put pressure on them to sue for peace, or in other words, to surrender. Deliberate inflicting of suffering on non-combatants is of course an inherently criminal strategy. In Lebanon, however, as in Gaza, the ferocious application of this criminal doctrine completely failed to turn the civilian population against the resistance.

The assassination of Nasrallah was preceded by a new form of warfare against his organisation. On 17 and 18 September, thousands of handheld pagers and hundreds of walkie-talkies, recently supplied by Mossad-connected companies to members of Hizbullah, exploded simultaneously across Lebanon and Syria in an Israeli-instigated attack. Forty-two people were killed and over 3,400 were injured, some of them permanently. These explosions were war crimes. They were terrorist attacks by a state that consistently condemned terrorist attacks on its own citizens. They were deployed to degrade and demoralise Hizbullah and to sow panic and confusion in the country at large. Following the gruesome pager attack, the Israeli Air Force (IAF) followed up with a series of air raids in south Lebanon, the southern part of Beirut, and the Bekaa valley. These were the worst attacks Lebanon experienced in almost two decades. In one day alone 558 people were killed. Over the course of the week, more than 700 people were killed and nearly 6,000 injured. Some of the strikes were targeted assassinations of a string of Hizbullah's top commanders. But, true to form, the IDF offensive wreaked havoc on civilians. A million residents, one-fifth of Lebanon's population, were forced to flee from their homes. Schools were turned into shelters for refugees, roads were clogged up as people fled in panic, food was in short supply, and hospitals were overwhelmed by a constant inflow of the injured. Israelis were giddy with excitement at the assassination of Nasrallah and strongly supported the carnage their government was inflicting.

This dangerous, multi-pronged escalation was viewed with mounting consternation by the UN and

Israel came under growing international pressure to agree to a ceasefire. France and America took the lead in formulating a plan for a twenty-one-day ceasefire, which they had been given to understand that Benjamin Netanyahu, Israel's prime minister, would back. But as soon as they announced the ceasefire proposal, Netanyahu rejected it in what amounted as a slap in the face to his allies and to the UN. In a belligerent speech at the annual meeting of the General Assembly, just before the assassination of Nasrallah, Netanyahu denounced the UN as "a house of darkness" and a "swamp of antisemitic bile".

A ceasefire in Lebanon was closely linked to a ceasefire in Gaza. Hizbullah had consistently said that it would stop firing its rockets as soon as Israel accepted a ceasefire in Gaza. Israel, however, seemed intent on spreading the war and intensifying the violence. Having rejected successive proposals for a ceasefire in Gaza, it now sabotaged even the modest plan for a temporary ceasefire in Lebanon. Netanyahu claimed that Israel needed to create the conditions that would enable the sixty thousand Israelis who had been displaced from the north by the year-old border war to return to their homes. He proposed to create these conditions by applying military pressure. But if that was the objective, diplomacy was a much more likely route to achieving it than military force. Not only did

Israel refuse a lull in the fighting, but it also extended its operations to attack sites of the Popular Front for the Liberation of Palestine and the Popular Democratic Front for the Liberation of Palestine in central Beirut and other parts of the country.

At the same time, Israeli fighter jets bombarded the Yemeni port city of Hodeida in retaliation for the Houthi harassment of Israel-related shipping in the Red Sea and drone attacks on Tel Aviv. The IAF also pounded Iranian-related targets in Syria while continuing its relentless onslaught on Gaza and the West Bank. Israel was now waging war on four fronts. If this is a formula for security, it is hard to imagine what insecurity would look like. And it is difficult to avoid the impression that its real aim is not to escalate for the purpose of deescalating on the northern front but instead to exploit the moment to bring about a regional war that would draw in a reluctant America to confront Iran and its proxies. What is beyond doubt is that for a whole year, Israel practiced with complete impunity the Dahiyeh Doctrine in both Gaza and Lebanon, ignoring the tepid calls restraint from its American ally and armourer.

On 1 October, Israel made the highly significant move of introducing ground forces into south Lebanon in what it called Operation Northern Arrow. Israel presented this as a limited operation to destroy the infrastructure of Hizbullah and said it would withdraw as soon as this objective was achieved. Such adventures, however, are easy to launch but difficult to end or even to contain, as Israel discovered to its cost after the invasion of Lebanon in 1982. When one launches a land war, one knows how it will start, one does not know how it will end. This ground offensive was undertaken in defiance of American advice. The US was trying to stop the crisis in Gaza from spinning out of control into a regional war. Israel was doing the opposite.

The assault on Hizbullah, and the targeted assassination of its commanders, was a deliberate provocation of Iran. For nearly two decades, Netanyahu had been unsuccessfully demanding a joint American-Israeli military strike against Iran's nuclear facilities, to prevent the latter from acquiring nuclear weapons. Hizbullah, located on Israel's northern border, with an arsenal of about 150,000 sophisticated rockets and missiles, is Iran's strongest deterrent against an Israeli attack. Indirect provocation was followed by direct provocation. On 1 April 2024, the IAF struck the Iranian consulate in Damascus, killing sixteen people, including seven officers of the Islamic Revolutionary Guard Corps (IRGC). Having exercised restraint for months, in line with its long-standing doctrine of "strategic patience", Iran retaliated with a limited missile strike and said that as far as it was concerned, this was the end of the matter. But it was not the end of the matter for Israel.

On 31 July, Ismail Haniyeh, the Hamas leader, was assassinated by Israeli collaborators in Tehran, where he was attending the inauguration of newly elected Iranian President, Masoud Pezeshkian. Pezeshkian is a moderate and a reformist who seeks a rapprochement with the West. He later claimed that American and European leaders promised him a ceasefire in exchange for Iran not responding to the assassination of Haniyeh. Iran did not retaliate but no ceasefire materialised. Israel proceeded to assassinate Nasrallah and other top commanders of Hizbullah and the IRGC. This was a direct challenge to Tehran and to its credibility as the leader of the Axis of Resistance. To roll over and not retaliate would have been an admission of weakness. On 1 October, Iran retaliated by launching a barrage of 181 ballistic missiles against Israel, targeting military and intelligence assets. Israel vowed severe retaliation for the action it had provoked. This fed the long-harboured suspicions that Netanyahu was trying to manipulate tensions over Lebanon to eventually secure direct US strikes against Iran's nuclear facilities. He himself declared that his aim was to bring about regime change in Tehran and to change the overall military balance in the Middle East in Israel's favour.

This brief review of Israeli conduct in the year that followed the Hamas attack of 7 October reveals a consistent pattern of shunning diplomacy and relying on raw military force in dealing with its Palestinian, Arab, and Iranian opponents. The picture that emerges is of a country that lives by the sword, a country addicted to military force, a pugnacious, trigger-happy, ethno-nationalist, racially supremacist state, totally oblivious to international law. What are the sources of this preference for military force and coercion even when alternative diplomatic routes are available? One answer is that, like a man holding a hammer in his hand, Israel sees every issue as a nail.

A deeper explanation is that Israel is a settler-colonial project, and the logic of settler-colonialism is the displacement of the natives and the taking over of their land. This objective cannot be achieved by diplomacy and negotiations; it can only be achieved unilaterally and by military force. Violence, according to this analysis, is in the DNA of Israel as a colonial power. Israel claims that violence is not initiated by it but imposed on it, that all its wars have been defensive not offensive, that they are not wars of choice but rather wars of no-choice. Golda Meir personified this self-righteous position when she stated, "all the wars against us have nothing to do with us". This view, however, completely ignores the part that Israel has played, especially by its occupation of Arab and Palestinian lands, in spawning Arab-Israeli wars. All of Israel's wars since June 1967 have been about defending and expanding the Zionist colonial project beyond the Green Line.

Israel's unilateral disengagement from Gaza in 2005 did not mark the abandonment of the Zionist colonial project but its more aggressive pursuit on the West Bank. The ethnic cleansing of Palestine continued after the withdrawal from Gaza. In 1948, three quarters of a million Palestinians either fled their homes or were driven out. That was the Nakba, the catastrophe. The Nakba is not a one-off event but a continuous process. Following the withdrawal from Gaza, ethnic cleansing continued in the West Bank. In Gaza, Israel remained the occupying power under international law because it continued to control access to the territory by land, sea, and air. Israel offered the people of Gaza no political horizon but only blockade and the periodic application of brute military force. Every few years Israel would launch a military offensive in a never-ending cycle of violence that Israeli generals chillingly described as "mowing the lawn".

The Hamas attack of 7 October, brutal and murderous as it was, did not happen in a vacuum. It happened against this grim backdrop. In a very real sense, it was a response to half a century of brutal occupation and cruel oppression. But it was also unprecedented in its ferocity, its scale, and its success in breaking down the fence around the strip and attacking with ground forces Israeli settlements in the south. Israel's response to the surprise attack was also unprecedented in its ferocity. By my count, this was the eighth Israeli military offensive against Gaza since the disengagement of 2005. I therefore expected some, inevitably more brutal action, but still within the template of "mowing the lawn". I did not anticipate an all-out war to eradicate Hamas and to destroy much of Gaza. Nor did I expect the ethnic cleansing of Gaza, yet this turned out to be one of the government's objectives which has only been thwarted so far by firm Egyptian opposition. Still less did I expect that this military offensive would culminate in genocide.

Over the years I have written extensively and critically about Israel and its approach to the Palestinians. One suite of essays, published in *Irish Pages* in 2021, appeared under the heading "Israel and the Arrogance of Power". In other places I wrote about Israel's abuse of power. I compiled a long litany of complaints against the state of Israel, but genocide was not one of them. In my 2023 autobiography, *Three Worlds: Memoirs of an Arab-Jew*, I wrote:

> The Holocaust has frequently been used by Israel's friends to explain its obsession with

security and to justify its harsh treatment of the Palestinians. Israel's more extreme critics, on the other hand, have occasionally denounced Israel's treatment of the Palestinians as no better than Nazi Germany's treatment of the Jews. Such comparisons are far-fetched: for all its sins, Israel has not engaged in genocide. But nor is it justified to use the Holocaust as moral blackmail to silence legitimate criticisms of Israel's treatment of the Palestinians. Dehumanising "the other" is bound to have terrible consequences whoever "the other" may be. Israel's systematic dehumanising of the Palestinian people certainly has had dire consequences; it prepared the ground for their oppression and brutalisation.

The Holocaust stands out as the archetype of a crime against humanity. For me as a Jew and an Israeli therefore the Holocaust teaches us to resist the dehumanising of any people, including the Palestinian "victims of victims" [as Edward Said called them], because dehumanising a people can easily result, as it did in Europe in the 1940s, in crimes against humanity. (pp. 46-47).

In Gaza, in response to the attack of 7 October, Israel crossed the red line that separates common, all-too-common war crimes from genocide. Nations that commit genocide rarely admit it, let alone advertise it openly. They hide their genocidal actions behind a thick veil of secrecy. Israel's political and military leaders, by contrast, have made no attempt to conceal their genocidal intentions, as copiously documented in this book. Some of their rhetoric is truly spine-chilling. Moreover, the genocidal rhetoric was not just empty words; it was enacted through a vicious, sadistic onslaught against the people of Gaza, the slaughter of innocent civilians on an industrial scale, the methodical targeting of civilian infrastructure, the use of starvation as a weapon of warfare, the bombing of hospitals and health centres, and the subjugation of the people of Gaza to conditions of life calculated to bring about their death. For the first time in history, we can now see genocide livestreamed day in and day out on our TV screens.

The logic of this hideously cruel method of treating "the other" is intimately connected with Israel's very essence as a colonial settler-state. Underlying what Israel is doing is a nineteenth century, racist, settler-colonial ideology. Francesca Albanese, the UN Special Rapporteur on the Situation of Human Rights in the Palestinian Territories, articulated the connection with luminous clarity. In her 25 March 2024 report to the UN Human Rights Council, she wrote: "Israel's actions have been driven by a genocidal logic integral to its settler-colonial project in Palestine, signalling a tragedy foretold". The title of the report is "Anatomy of a Genocide".

Throughout the first year of the war, Israel committed war crimes on an almost-daily basis. It acted with complete impunity and in flagrant disregard of international humanitarian law. The reputational damage to the country was enormous. Following its birth in 1948, Israel enjoyed a huge amount of international sympathy and support on account of being a democracy. After 1967, this sympathy began to diminish while sympathy for the Palestinian cause steadily increased. The 2023 war in Gaza was a major landmark in Israel's slide to the status of international pariah.

The wheels of international justice move slowly but they have started to turn. The chief prosecutor at the International Criminal Court has applied for arrest warrants for Netanyahu, his defence minister, and the IDF chief-of-staff for committing war crimes and crimes against humanity. The chief prosecutor also applied for arrest warrants for the top three leaders of Hamas which is proscribed in the West as a terrorist organisation. The International Court of Justice has ruled that Israel's occupation of Palestinian territories is illegal and called for immediate withdrawal and reparations. In a separate ruling, in January 2024, the Court stated that there was a plausible risk of genocide in Gaza and ordered Israel to desist from genocidal rhetoric and actions. The United Nations General Assembly, on 18 September 2024, voted overwhelmingly to adopt a resolution that demands Israel "brings to an end without delay its unlawful presence" in the Occupied Palestinian Territory.

Israel's conduct in the year-long war in Gaza did not only damage its own reputation but also accelerated the decline of the US-led liberal international order that was put in place in the aftermath of the Second World War. Central to this order is the notion that all states are equal before the law and that all states without exception must be held to account for their actions. Israel, however, was treated as an exception and the US veto on the Security Council ensured that Israel was never sanctioned for its ostentatious rejection of UN resolutions or its egregious violations of international law. Western double standards are nothing new, of course, but they were highlighted by the striking contrast between the West's righteous indignation over Russia's invasion of Ukraine and its lockstep support for Israel's invasion of Gaza. The US is no stranger to double standards. The real change is not one of substance but rather the unapologetic brazenness and flagrancy with which it now enables the gravest transgressions. This compelled the rest of the world to recognise what the Global South had always known, namely, that international law is enforced only against the weak.

Another victim of Israel's lawlessness is world Jewry. Israel has always presented itself as not just a Jewish State but also as the state of all Jews wherever they may be, even as it has no democratic mandate to speak on behalf of Jews outside its territory. Another standard claim is that Israel offers a safe haven to Jews facing persecution in other parts of the world. Indeed, Israel is often said to be the only safe place in the world for Jews. The war in Gaza provided further proof, if this was needed, that Israel is in fact the least safe place for Jews in the entire world. Israel's conduct in Gaza has been the direct cause of a spike in antisemitic episodes in Britain and elsewhere.

Once a source of pride, Israel has become a source of embarrassment and a liability to liberal and progressive Jews round the world, and especially to the younger generation. More and more Jews in the Diaspora distance themselves from Israel's actions by declaring, "not in my name". I belong to several such groups in Britain, including Independent Jewish Voices, Jewish Voice for Labour, Free Speech on Israel, Jews for Justice for Palestinians, Israeli Academics in the UK, and UK Jewish Academic Network. The latter's Values

Statement refutes the notion that "the safety of the Jews rests upon oppression of Palestinians". In the US, Jewish Voice for Peace and If Not Now are the leading organisations of non-Zionist or anti-Zionist Jews.

It cannot be stated often enough that Zionism and Judaism are two different things. Zionism is a secular political ideology; Judaism is a religion. Zionist leaders, however, tried to co-opt Judaism in their struggle for a Jewish state. Although the Zionists did not believe in God, they invoked his authority as a land agent in claiming that he promised the whole Land of Israel to the Jewish people. Yet the two groups adhere to fundamentally different values. The core values of Judaism are altruism, truth, justice, and peace. The government headed by Benjamin Netanyahu, which authentically represents the centre of Israel's political gravity, is the antithesis of these core Jewish values. The essence of Judaism is non-violence. Netanyahu's government is the most aggressively nationalistic, ethnocentric, messianic, and violent government in Israel's history. Its aim is not peaceful coexistence with the Palestinians but hegemony and domination.

Benjamin Netanyahu, Itamar Ben-Gvir, and Bezalel Smotrich, the dominant figures in this government, are true believers in the doctrine that violence can mould the world to fit their racist, Jewish-supremacist vision. The fascist notion that might is right underlies much of their domestic as well as foreign policy. Placing the nation above the individual, discriminating against non-Jews, undermining the rule of law at home, and relying on naked military force abroad are all fascist tropes. Their rhetoric and their policy on the ground in Gaza exposes this triumvirate not just as fascists but as genocidal fascists.

Just as I was initially cautious in use of the term genocide, so I have hesitated to use the word fascist. As a scholar I am committed to weighing words carefully. Netanyahu's government does not display all the features of classical fascism but arguably enough of them, and especially militarism, to merit the label "fascist". True, this government was democratically elected. But so were the Nazi party in Germany, the Fascist party in Italy and, in our time, Viktor Orbán's right-wing populist party in Hungary.

As a Jew, I feel that I have a moral duty stand up and be counted, to speak truth to power, to denounce the Netanyahu government in the strongest possible terms, and to stand by the Palestinians in their hour of need. This collection of essays is my modest personal contribution to the fight against Zionist fascism and to the struggle for justice for the long-suffering Palestinian people. It is grounded in a conviction that the only democratic solution to the Israeli-Palestinian conflict is one state from the Jordan River to the Mediterranean

Sea with equal rights for all its citizens, regardless of religion or ethnicity.

Oxford
7 October 2024

A BLOODY WAR AGAINST CHILDREN

Although much of this volume has centred on genocide in terms of the political processes building up to it and of those enabling its continuance, it is absolutely essential to keep the humanity of its victims at the forefront as we surpass fifteen months of relentless destruction and slaughter. We are fortunate to be able to include in this volume a remarkable photographic record of Gaza's youngest citizens; their lives amid this genocide of over fifteen months, the loss of their families, homes and schools, their intense suffering and that of their families, as well as their creativity, strength and defiance. Regrettably in a settler-colonial society, indigenous children are not intended to have a future on their own land. Their growth must be stunted both physically and psychologically or they must be subjected to the colonial logic of elimination. All of Gaza's citizens resist and refuse this deadly logic.

A testimony to this refusal is to found in *Gaza I Spy*, a book of photographs compiled by Feda Shtia, documenting the lives of Gaza's children amidst the ongoing onslaught. The title is inspired by the familiar children's game "I spy with my little eye". It is published by Sunono books, Scotland, from which the following images have been selected.

Gaza I Spy is a testament to the indomitable spirit of Gaza's children, created in collaboration with highly talented Gaza based photographers, Anas Ayyad, Sabreen Al-Baz and Hammam Younis AlZyatuniya. The book features three hundred images from which we have selected sixteen. They depict the struggle for survival amid cataclysmic destruction, the desire to extract moments of liveability from amidst the horror and the determined continuance of human bonds, dignity and love despite deprivations and humiliations of every kind.

Anas and Hammam, the publisher makes clear, are not just photographers; they are courageous young journalists and witness bearers, risking their lives daily to document the truth and devastation in Gaza. These talented individuals often borrow equipment from friends or rent it as they don't have their own cameras. One day they told Feda Shtia that their press tent was bombed by an Israeli drone. Hammam messages her: "Last night I gave my spot in the tent to someone else, then the strike came." He narrowly escaped death.

ABOUT THE PUBLISHER OF *GAZA I SPY*

Feda Shtia is an author, educator, and the founder of Sunono Publishing. With a passion for children's literature and a deep commitment to advocating for young voices, Feda has dedicated her career to crafting stories that highlight resilience, empathy, and the untold experiences of children, particularly those affected by conflict. As an educator with strong roots in the Middle East, Feda's personal and professional experiences have fuelled her mission to bring attention to the struggles and strength of children living in war zones. *Gaza I Spy* offers a profound look into the lives of Gaza's children during the Israel war, using photography and storytelling to bridge the gap between their reality and the world that too often overlooks them. Through her writing and publishing efforts, Feda aims to foster understanding, awareness, and change, ensuring that the stories of the most vulnerable are not forgotten.

The author, Avi Shlaim, and the publisher, Chris Agee, are deeply honoured to be able to reprint these powerful images in *Genocide in Gaza*.

www.sunono.scot

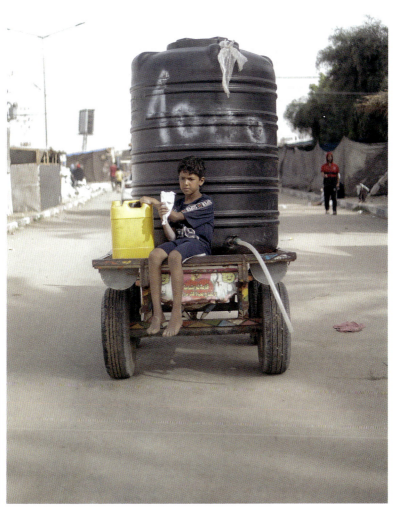

HAMMAM YOUNIS ALZYATUNIYA

HAMMAM YOUNIS ALZYATUNIYA

HAMMAM YOUNIS ALZYATUNIYA

HAMMAM YOUNIS ALZYATUNIYA

ANAS AYYAD

XIII

HAMMAM YOUNIS ALZYATUNIYA

XIV

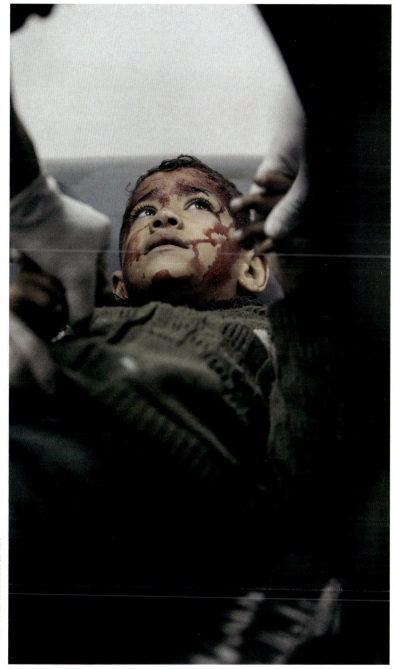

HAMMAM YOUNIS ALZYATUNIYA

XVI

— 2024 —

CODA: THE CASE BEFORE THE INTERNATIONAL COURT OF JUSTICE

APPLICATION OF THE CONVENTION ON
THE PREVENTION AND PUNISHMENT
OF THE CRIME OF GENOCIDE
IN THE GAZA STRIP
(SOUTH AFRICA V. ISRAEL)

*Statement by Ms Blinne Ní Ghrálaigh, KC,
Counsel and Advocate for the Republic of South Africa
to the International Court of Justice, The Hague
(11 January 2024)*

RISK OF FURTHER GENOCIDAL ACTS, RISKS OF IRREPARABLE PREJUDICE AND URGENCY

INTRODUCTION AND APOLOGY

Madame la présidente, Mesdames et Messieurs les juges, c'est un grand honneur pour moi que de paraître devant la Cour de nouveau. C'est également à la fois un privilège et une lourde responsabilité que de représenter l'Afrique du Sud dans cette affaire d'une si grande gravité.

Il me revient d'examiner l'urgence et le risque de préjudice irréparable aux droits revendiqués les deux dernières conditions auxquelles est subordonné l'exercice du pouvoir de la Cour d'indiquer des mesures conservatoires.

Je souhaiterais avant cela adresser aux Membres francophones de la Cour les excuses sincères de l'Afrique du Sud du fait qu'elle ne présente aucune de ses soumissions en langue française. L'Afrique du Sud vous prie de n'y voir aucun manque de courtoisie de sa part.

Je vais, si vous me le permettez, poursuivre ma plaidoirie en langue anglaise.

OVERVIEW

Madam President, Members of the Court, there is an urgent need for provisional measures to protect Palestinians in Gaza from the irreparable prejudice caused by Israel's violations of the Genocide Convention.

The United Nations Secretary-General and its Chiefs describe the situation in Gaza variously as "a crisis of humanity", a "living hell", a "blood bath", a situation of "utter, deepening" and unmatched "horror", where "an entire population" is "besieged and under attack, denied access to the essentials for survival", "on a massive scale". As the United Nation's Under Secretary-General for Humanitarian Affairs stated last Friday:

> "Gaza has become a place of death and despair ... Families are sleeping in the open as temperatures plummet. Areas where civilians were told to relocate for their safety have come under bombardment. Medical facilities are under relentless attack. The few hospitals that are partially functional are overwhelmed with trauma cases, critically short of all supplies, and inundated by desperate people seeking safety. A public health disaster is unfolding. Infectious diseases are spreading in overcrowded shelters as sewers spill over.

> Some 180 Palestinian women are giving birth daily amidst this chaos. People are facing the highest levels of food insecurity ever recorded. Famine is around the corner. For children in particular, the past 12 weeks have been traumatic: No food. No water. No school. Nothing but the terrifying sounds of war, day in and day out. Gaza has simply become uninhabitable. Its people are witnessing daily threats to their very existence – while the world watches on."

The Court has heard of the horrific death toll, and of the more than 7,000 Palestinian men, women and children reported missing, presumed dead or dying slow, excruciating deaths trapped under the rubble. Reports of field executions, and torture and ill-treatment are mounting, as are images of decomposing bodies of men, women and children, left unburied where they were killed – some being picked on by animals. It is becoming ever clearer that huge swathes of Gaza – entire towns, villages, refugee camps – are being wiped from the map. According to the World Food Programme, "[f]our out of five people … in the world …, in famine or a catastrophic type of hunger, are in Gaza right now". Indeed, experts warn that deaths from starvation and disease risk significantly outstripping deaths from bombings.

The daily statistics stand as clear evidence of the urgency and the risk of irreparable prejudice: on the basis of current figures, on average 247 Palestinians are being killed and are at risk of being killed each day, many of them blown to pieces. They include 48 mothers each day – two every hour; and over 117 children each day, leading UNICEF to call Israel's actions a "war on children". On current rates, which show no sign of abating, each day, over three medics, two teachers, more than one United Nations employee and one journalist will be killed – many while at work, or in what appear to be targeted attacks on their family homes or where they are sheltering. The risk of famine will increase each day. Each day, 629 people will be wounded, some multiple times over as they move from place to place, desperately seeking sanctuary. Each day, over 10 Palestinian children will have one or both legs amputated, many without anaesthetic. Each day, on current rates, an average of 3,900 Palestinian homes will be damaged or destroyed. More mass graves will be dug. More cemeteries will be bulldozed and bombed and corpses violently exhumed, denying even the dead any dignity or peace. Each day, ambulances, hospitals and medics will continue to be attacked and killed. The first responders who have spent three months – without international assistance – trying to dig families out of the rubble with their bare hands will continue to be targeted; on current figures one will be killed almost every second day, sometimes in attacks, launched against those attending the scene to rescue the wounded. Each day yet more desperate people will be forced to relocate from where they are sheltering, or will be bombed in places they had been told to evacuate to. Entire multi-generational families will be obliterated; and yet more Palestinian children will become "WCNSF": "Wounded Child No Surviving Family" – the terrible new acronym borne out of Israel's genocidal assault on the Palestinian population in Gaza.

There is an urgent need for provisional measures to prevent imminent, irreparable prejudice to the rights in issue in this case. There could not be a clearer or more compelling case. In the words of the Commissioner-General of the United Nations Relief and Works Agency, there must be "an end to the decimation of Gaza and of its people".

THE COURT'S CASE LAW

CRITERION OF URGENCY

Turning to the Court's case law, as the Court has recently reaffirmed, "[t]he condition of urgency is met when acts susceptible of causing irreparable prejudice can 'occur at any moment' before the Court makes a final decision on the case". That is precisely the situation here. Any of those matters to which I have referred can and are occurring at any moment. United Nations Security Council resolutions demanding "the immediate, safe, unhindered delivery of humanitarian assistance, at scale" throughout Gaza and "full, rapid, safe, and unhindered humanitarian access" remain unimplemented. United Nations General Assembly resolutions calling for a humanitarian ceasefire have been ignored. The situation could not be more urgent. Since these proceedings were initiated on 29 December 2023 alone, over 1,703 Palestinians have been killed in Gaza, and over 3,252 injured.

IRREPARABLE PREJUDICE: SERIOUS RISKS TO HUMAN LIFE AND OTHER FUNDAMENTAL RIGHTS

As to the criterion of irreparable prejudice, for decades now, the Court has repeatedly found it to be satisfied in situations where serious risks arise to human life or to other fundamental human rights.

In the cases of Georgia v. Russia, and Armenia v. Azerbaijan, the Court ordered provisional measures having found a serious risk of irreparable prejudice where hundreds of thousands of people had been forced from their homes.

In ordering provisional measures in the latter case, the Court noted the context of the "long-standing exposure of the population . . . to a situation of vulnerability" including "hindrances to the importation . . . of essential goods, causing shortages of food, medicine, and other life-saving medical supplies".

In Gaza, nearly two million people – over 85 per cent of the population – have been repeatedly forced to flee their homes and shelters – not just once or twice but some three, four or more times over – into ever-shrinking slivers of land, where they continue to be bombed and killed. This is a population that Israel had already made vulnerable through 16 years of military blockade and crippling "de-development".

Today, Israel's "hindrances" to the import of food and essential items have brought Gaza "to the brink of famine", with adults – mothers, fathers, grandparents – regularly foregoing food so that children can eat at least something every day. Medicine shortages and the lack of medical treatment, clean water and electricity, are so great that large numbers of Palestinians are dying and are at imminent risk of dying preventable deaths; cancer and other services have long shut down, women are undergoing caesarean sections without anaesthetic, in barely functioning hospitals described as scenes from a "horror movie", with many undergoing otherwise unnecessary hysterectomies in an attempt to save their lives.

In Canada and the Netherlands v. Syria, the Court made clear that "individuals subject to torture and other acts of cruel, inhuman or degrading treatment or punishment . . . are at serious risk of irreparable prejudice". Palestinians in Gaza are also at risk of such irreparable prejudice, with videos of Palestinian boys and men, rounded up and stripped and degraded, broadcast to the world, alongside footage of serious bodily harm, and accounts of serious mental harm and humiliation.

In Qatar v. United Arab Emirates, the Court considered provisional measures to be justified having regard to the risk of irreparable prejudice deriving from factors such as people being forced to leave their places of residence without the possibility of return; the "psychological distress" of "temporary or potentially ongoing separation from their families", and the harm associated with students being "prevented from taking their exams". If provisional measures were justified there, how could they not be in Gaza, where countless families have been separated – with some family members evacuating under Israeli military orders, and others staying behind at extreme risk to care for the wounded, infirm and the elderly; where husbands, fathers and sons are being rounded up and separated from their families, taken to unknown locations for indeterminate periods of time.

In the Qatar v. United Arab Emirates case, the Court issued a provisional order where harm to approximately 150 students was in issue. In Gaza, 625,000 schoolchildren have not attended school for three months, with the United Nations Security Council "[e]xpressing deep concern that the disruption of access to education has a dramatic impact on children, and that conflict has lifelong effects on their physical and mental health". Almost 90,000 Palestinian university students cannot attend university in Gaza. Over 60 per cent of schools, almost all universities, and countless bookshops and libraries, have been damaged or destroyed, and hundreds of teachers and academics have been killed, including deans of universities, and leading Palestinian scholars, obliterating the very prospects for the future education of Gaza's children and young people.

PROVISIONAL MEASURES AND GENOCIDE

Notably, the Court has found provisional measures to be justified in all three cases where they were previously sought in relation to violations of the Genocide Convention. It did so in Bosnia v. Serbia in 1993, finding – on the basis of evidence that was certainly no more compelling than that presently before the Court – that it was sufficient to determine that there was "a grave risk of acts of genocide being committed". The Court found provisional measures to be justified in The Gambia v. Myanmar case, on the basis of a risk of irreparable prejudice to the Rohingya, "subjected to ... mass killings ... as well as beatings, the destruction of villages and homes, denial of access to food, shelter and other essentials of life".

More recently, in indicating provisional measures in Ukraine v. Russia, the Court considered that Russia's military activities had "resulted in numerous civilian deaths and injuries" and "caused significant material damage, including the destruction of buildings and infrastructure", giving rise to a risk of irreparable prejudice. The Court had regard to the fact that the "[a]ttacks are ongoing and are creating increasingly difficult living conditions for the civilian population", which it considered to be "extremely vulnerable". The Court also considered the fact that "[m]any persons have no access to the most basic foodstuffs, potable water, electricity, essential medicines or heating", and that many were attempting to flee "under extremely insecure conditions". This is occurring in Gaza on a much more intensive scale, to a besieged, trapped, terrified population that has nowhere safe to go.

PROVISIONAL MEASURES IN SITUATIONS OF ARMED CONFLICT

Lest the contrary be suggested, it is clear from Ukraine v. Russia that the fact that the urgent risk of irreparable harm arises in a situation of armed conflict does not undermine much less preclude a request for provisional measures. That is also clear from the Court's other judgments.

In the case of Armed Activities on the Territory of the Congo (Democratic Republic of the Congo v. Uganda), for example, the Court ordered provisional measures based on its finding "that persons, assets and resources present on the territory of the Congo, particularly in the area of conflict, remain extremely vulnerable", and that there was "a serious risk that the rights at issue in this case . . . may suffer irreparable prejudice". Similarly, in Costa Rica v. Nicaragua, the Court indicated provisional measures in part on the basis that the presence of troops in the disputed territory gave "rise to a real and present risk of incidents liable to cause irremediable harm in the form of bodily injury or death".

In relation to the Genocide Convention in particular, the Court recalled in Gambia v. Myanmar, that "States parties expressly confirmed their willingness to consider genocide as a crime under international law which they must prevent and punish independently of the context 'of peace' or 'of war' in which it takes place".

More recently, in the Guyana v. Venezuela case, the Court considered that the serious risk of Venezuela "acquiring and exercising control and administration of the territory in dispute" gave rise to a risk of irreparable prejudice to the rights asserted in the case. Similar factors are in issue here, having regard to the territorial ambitions and settlement plans for Gaza being raised by members of the Israeli government, and the relationship of those factors to the very survival of Palestinians in Gaza as such.

PROVISIONAL MEASURES AND MITIGATION OF RISK

Similarly, any scaling up by Israel of access of humanitarian relief to Gaza in response to these proceedings or otherwise would be no answer to South Africa's request for provisional measures. In the case of Iran v. United States, the Court found a risk of irreparable harm from the exposure of individuals to "danger to health and life" caused by restrictions placed on "medicines and medical devices", "foodstuffs" and other "goods required for humanitarian needs". That was notwithstanding the assurances offered by the United States for it to expedite the consideration of humanitarian issues; and notwithstanding the fact that essentials were in any event exempt from United States sanctions. The Court considered that the assurances were "not adequate to address fully the humanitarian and safety concerns raised" and that "there remain[ed] a risk that measures adopted" by the United States "may entail irreparable consequences".

In Armenia v. Azerbaijan, unilateral undertakings to alleviate restrictions alongside the full resumption of humanitarian and commercial deliveries did not defeat a request for the indication of provisional measures. The Court was clear that while contributing "towards mitigating the imminent risk of irreparable prejudice resulting from" the military operation, those developments did "not remove the risk entirely". Indeed, in Georgia v. Russia, the Court made clear that it considers a "serious risk" to subsist where "the situation . . . is unstable and could rapidly change". The Court considered that "given the ongoing tension and the absence of an overall settlement to the conflict in this region . . . populations also remain vulnerable".

Israel continues to deny that it is responsible for the humanitarian crisis it has created, even as Gaza starves. The aid it has belatedly begun to allow in is wholly inadequate, and does not come anywhere close to the average 500 trucks being permitted daily before October 2023. Any unilateral undertakings Israel might seek to give about future aid would not remove the risk of irreparable prejudice, not least considering Israel's past and current conduct towards the Palestinian people, including the 16 years of brutal siege on Gaza.

In any event, as the United Nations Secretary-General has made clear, it is "a mistake" to measure "the effectiveness of the humanitarian operation in Gaza based on the number of trucks" allowed in. As he has stressed, "[t]he real problem is that the way Israel is conducting this offensive" means that "the conditions for the effective delivery of humanitarian aid no longer exist". That would require "security, staff who can work in safety, logistical capacity, and the resumption of commercial activity. It requires electricity and steady communications. All of these remain absent". Indeed, only shortly after Israel opened the Kerem Shalom crossing to goods in late December 2023, it was struck in a drone attack, killing five Palestinians, and leading to another temporary closure.

Nowhere and nobody is safe. As the United Nations Secretary-General and all its Chiefs have made clear, without a halt to Israel's military operations, crossings, aid convoys, and humanitarian workers – like everyone and everything else in Gaza – remain at imminent risk of further irreparable prejudice. An unprecedented 148 United Nations staff have been killed to date. Without a halt to Israel's military activity in Gaza, there will be no end to the extreme situation facing Palestinian civilians.

PROVISIONAL MEASURES AND GAZA

Madam President, Members of the Court, if the indication of provisional measures was justified on the facts in those cases I have cited, how could it not be here, in a situation of much greater severity, where the imminent risk of irreparable harm is so much greater? How could they not be justified in a situation that humanitarian veterans from crises spanning as far back as the killing fields of Cambodia – "people who" (in the words of the United Nations Secretary-General) "have seen everything" – if they say is so utterly "unprecedented" that they are "out of words to describe" it.

It would be a complete departure from the long and distinguished line of jurisprudence that this Court has firmly established – and recently reconfirmed – for the Court not to order provisional measures in this case. The imminent risk of death, harm and destruction that Palestinians in Gaza face today, and that they risk every day during the pendency of these proceedings, on any view justifies – indeed compels – the indication of provisional measures. Some might say that the very reputation of international law – its ability and willingness to bind and to protect all peoples equally – hangs in the balance.

ELEMENTARY PRINCIPLES OF MORALITY

But the Genocide Convention is about more than legal precedent. It is also, – fundamentally – about the "confirm[ation] and endorse[ment of] elementary principles of morality". The Court recalled the 1946 General Assembly Resolution on the crime of genocide which made clear that:

> "Genocide is a denial of the right of existence of entire human groups, as homicide is the denial of the right to live of individual human beings; such denial of the right of existence shocks the conscience of mankind, results in great losses to humanity in the form of cultural and other contributions represented by these human groups, and is contrary to moral law and to the spirit and aims of the United Nations."

Notwithstanding the Genocide Convention's recognition of the need to rid the world of the "odious scourge" of genocide, the international community has repeatedly failed. It "failed" the people of Rwanda. It had failed the Bosnian people, and the Rohingya, prompting this Court to take action. It failed again by ignoring the early warnings of the "grave risk of genocide to the Palestinian people" sounded by international experts since 19 October of last year.

The international community continues to fail the Palestinian people, despite the overt dehumanising genocidal rhetoric by Israeli governmental and military officials, matched by the Israeli military's actions on the ground; despite the horror of the genocide against the Palestinian population being livestreamed from Gaza to our mobile phones, computers and televisions screens – the first genocide in history where its victims are broadcasting their own destruction in real time in the desperate – so far vain – hope that the world might do something. Gaza represents nothing short of a "moral failure", as described by the usually circumspect International Committee of the Red Cross. As underscored by United Nations Chiefs, that failure has "repercussions not just for the people of Gaza . . . but for the generations to come who will never forget these [over] 90 days of hell and of assaults on the most basic precepts of humanity".

As stated by a United Nations spokesperson in Gaza last week, at the site of a hospital clearly marked with the symbol of the Red Crescent, where five Palestinians – including a five-day old baby – had just been killed: "The world should be absolutely horrified. The world should be absolutely outraged . . . There is no safe space in Gaza and the world should be ashamed".

CONCLUSION

Madam President, Members of the Court, in conclusion I share with you two photographs. The first is of a white board at a hospital – in Northern Gaza – one of the many Palestinian hospitals targeted, besieged, bombed by Israel over the course of the past three

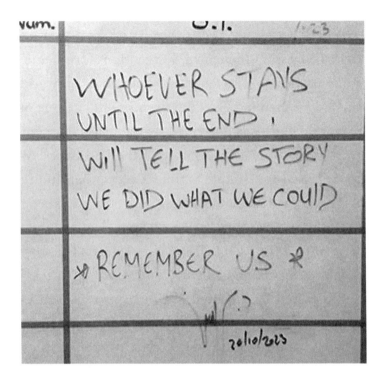

brutal months. The white board is wiped clean of no longer possible surgical cases, leaving only a hand-written message by a Médecins Sans Frontières doctor which reads: "We did what we could. Remember us".

The second is of the same whiteboard, after an Israeli strike on the hospital on 21 November 2023 that killed the author of the message, Dr Mahmoud Abu Nujaila, along with two of his colleagues.

Just over a month later, in a powerful Christmas Day sermon, delivered from a church in Bethlehem — on the same day Israel had killed 250 Palestinians, including at least 86 people, many from the same

family, massacred in a single strike on Maghazi Refugee Camp – Palestinian Pastor Munther Isaac addressed his congregation and the world. He said:

> "Gaza as we know it no longer exists. This is an annihilation. This is a genocide. We will rise. We will stand up again from the midst of destruction, as we have always done as Palestinians, although this is by far maybe the biggest blow we have received." But he said: "No apologies will be accepted after the genocide . . . What has been done has been

done. I want you to look at the mirror and ask, 'where was I when Gaza was going through a genocide.'"

South Africa is here before this Court, in the Peace Palace. It has done what it could. It is doing what it can, by initiating these proceedings, by seeking interim measures against itself as well as against Israel.

South Africa now respectfully and humbly calls on this honourable Court to do what is in its power to do, to indicate the provisional measures that are so urgently required to prevent further irreparable harm to the Palestinian people in Gaza, whose hopes – including for their very survival – are now vested in the Court.

ENDNOTES

THE DIPLOMACY OF THE ISRAELI-PALESTINIAN CONFLICT, 1967-2023 (REPORT FOR THE ICJ)

1. Avi Shlaim, *Lion of Jordan: King Hussein's Life in War and Peace* (London: Penguin Books, 2007).
2. Raja Shehadeh, *We Could Have Been Friends, My Father and I: A Palestinian Memoir* (London: Profile, 2022).
3. Quoted in Avi Shlaim, *The Iron Wall: Israel and the Arab World* (London: Penguin Books, 2014), p. 261.
4. Avi Raz, *The Bride and the Dowry: Israel, Jordan, and the Palestinians in the Aftermath of the June 1967 War* (New Haven: Yale University Press, 2012).
5. Avi Shlaim's interview with King Hussein: "His Royal Shyness: King Hussein and Israel", *The New York Review of Books*, 15 July 1999.
6. Gershon Gorenberg, *The Accidental Empire: Israel and the Birth of the Settlements, 1967-1977* (New York: Times Books, 2006), pp. 99-101.
7. Golda Meir, *My Life* (London: Weidenfeld and Nicolson, 1975), p. 312.
8. Walter Laqueur and Barry Rubin, eds., *The Israel-Arab Reader: A Documentary History of the Middle East Conflict*, seventh edition (London: Penguin Books, 2008), pp. 162-63.
9. Seth Anziska, *Preventing Palestine: A Political history from Camp David to Oslo* (Princeton: Princeton University Press, 2018).
10. Yitzhak Shamir, *Summing Up: An Autobiography* (London: Weidenfeld and Nicolson, 1994), pp. 174-75.
11. During the Cold War, American policymakers did their best to exclude the Soviet Union from the diplomacy surrounding the Arab-Israeli conflict. But Mikhail Gorbachev's rise to power in Moscow opened the door to cooperation in many fields, including the Middle East.
12. For the text of the speech see Laqueur and Rubin, *The Arab-Israeli Reader*, pp. 394-400.
13. Afif Safieh, *The Peace Process: From Breakthrough to Breakdown* (London: Saqi, 2010), p. 158.
14. Interview with Yosef Harif, *Ma'ariv*, 26 June 1992.

15. Shamir, *Summing Up*, p. 257.
16. Hamas is the Arabic acronym for the Islamic Resistance Movement. It is a Palestinian Sunni fundamentalist and nationalist organization. It was founded in Gaza in 1988 during the First Intifada. It has a social service wing, Dawah, a political bureau and a military wing, the Izz ad-Din al-Qassam Brigades.
17. Benjamin Netanyahu, *A Place Among the Nations: Israel and the World* (London: Bantam, 1993).
18. "Israel's Response to the Roadmap", Appendix 7 in Jimmy Carter, *Palestine: Peace Not Apartheid* (New York: Simon and Schuster, 2006), pp. 243-47.
19. Remarks by President Barack Obama at Cairo University, 6 June 2009, *available at* https://obamawhitehouse.archives.gov/the-press-office/remarks-president-cairo-university-6-04-09.
20. Avi Shlaim, "Israel Needs to Learn Some Manners", *New York Times*, 30 January 2014.
21. Baruch Kimmerling, *Politicide: Ariel Sharon's War against the Palestinians* (London: Verso Books, 2006), pp. 3-4.
22. If the UN wishes to educate itself on the subject and explore genuine pathways to peace, there is no better place to start than by reading the reports of Francesca Albanese, the current "UN Special Rapporteur on the Situation of Human Rights in the Palestinian Territories Occupied Since 1967".

BENJAMIN NETANYAHU'S WAR AGAINST PALESTINIAN STATEHOOD

23. David Brennan, "The Weak Are Slaughtered, the Strong Prevail: Netanyahu Says Israel Will Not Shy Away from Conflict", *Newsweek*, 31 August 2018.
24. Benjamin Netanyahu, *A Place Among the Nations: Israel and the World* (London: Bantam Press, 1993), pp. 102-3.
25. *Ibid.*, p. 121.
26. *Ibid.*, p. 232.
27. *Ibid.*, p. 287.
28. David Bar-Illan and Victor Cygielman, "Palestinian Self-Rule, Israeli Security – An Interview", *Palestine-Israel Journal*, vol. 3, no. 3, 1996.

29. Israel Ministry of Foreign Affairs, "PM Netanyahu Addresses Students in Eli", *gov.il* (30 January 2024).

30. Israel Ministry of Foreign Affairs, "PM Netanyahu in French in TF1 Interview", *gov.il* (30 May 2024).

31. Gantz withdrew from the governing coalition in June 2024.

32. Raoul Wootliff, "'Parts of Gaza Sent Back to Stone Age': Gantz Videos Laud His IDF Bona Fides", *Times of Israel*, 20 January 2019.

ISRAEL, HAMAS AND THE CONFLICT IN GAZA: AN OVERVIEW (REPORT TO THE ICC)

33. Avi Shlaim, "Zionism, the founding fathers, and the Palestine Arabs", in Na'eem Jeenah, ed., *Pretending Democracy: Israel, An Ethnocratic State* (Johannesburg: Afro-Middle East Centre, 2012), pp. 53-70.

34. Avi Shlaim, *The Iron Wall: Israel and the Arab World* (New York: W. W. Norton, 2000).

35. Ibid., 2nd ed. (New York: W.W. Norton; London: Penguin Books, 2014).

36. http://www.jabotinsky.org/multimedia/upl_doc/doc_191207_49117.pdf

37. David Makovsky, *Making Peace with the PLO: The Rabin Government's Road to Oslo* (Boulder, Colorado: Westview Press, 1996).

38. For text of Oslo Accord 1993, "Declaration of Principles on Interim Self-Government Arrangements" see: http://news.bbc.co.uk/1/hi/in_depth/middle_east/israel_and_the_palestinians/key_documents/1682727.stm.

39. Yoram Meital, *Peace in Tatters: Israel, Palestine, and the Middle East* (Boulder, Colorado: Lynne Rienner, 2006), pp. 43-46; and Avi Shlaim, "The Rise and Fall of the Oslo Peace Process" in Louise Fawcett, ed., *International Relations of the Middle East* (Oxford: Oxford University Press, 2005), pp. 241-61.

40. Benjamin Netanyahu, *A Place among the Nations: Israel and the World* (London: Bantam Press, 1993).

41. *Likud Party Charter*, 1999: "The Jewish communities in Judea, Samaria and Gaza are the realization of Zionist values. Settlement of the land is a clear expression of the unassailable right of the Jewish people to the Land of Israel and constitutes an important asset in the defense of the vital interests of the State of Israel. The Likud will

continue to strengthen and develop these communities and will prevent their uprooting." See http://mondoweiss.net/2011/11/netanyahu%E2%80%99s-party-platform-flatly-rejects-establishment-of-palestinian-state#sthash.lUWvvMLM.dpuf.

42. Avi Shlaim, "Prelude to the Accord: Likud, Labour and the Palestinians", *Journal of Palestine Studies*, 23: 2, Winter 1994, pp. 5-19.

43. Avi Shlaim, *Lion of Jordan: King Hussein of Jordan: A Life in War and Peace* (London: Allen Lane/Penguin Books, 2007), pp. 570-76.

44. Meron Benvenisti, *Intimate Enemies: Jews and Arabs in a Shared Land* (Berkeley: University of California Press, 1995), pp. 58-67.

45. Raja Shehadeh, *Palestinian Walks: Notes on a Vanishing Landscape* (London: Profile Books, 2007), p. 33.

46. Ibid., p. 62.

47. See *Peace Now* 2009 report on "Settlements & the Netanyahu Government: A Deliberate Policy of Undermining the Two-State Solution": (*Peace Now* is the leading voice of Israeli public pressure for peace: http://peacenow.org.il/eng/).

48. Ari Shavit, "Dov Weissglas interview with Ha'aretz – The Big Freeze", *Ha'aretz*, 8 October 2004: http://www.jmcc.org/Documentsandmaps.aspx?id=698.

49. Ibid.

50. Avi Shlaim, "How Israel brought Gaza to the brink of humanitarian catastrophe", *The Guardian*, 7 January 2009: http://www.theguardian.com/world/2009/jan/07/gaza-israel-palestine.

51. See, for example, Avi Shlaim, *Collusion across the Jordan: King Abdullah, the Zionist Movement, and the Partition of Palestine* (Oxford: Clarendon Press; New York: University of Columbia Press, 1988).

52. "Palestinian Elections: Trip Report by Former US President Jimmy Carter", *Carter Center*, 30 January 2006: http://www.cartercenter.org/news/documents/doc2287.html.

53. Paul Morro, "International reaction to the Palestinian Unity Government", *CRS Report for Congress*, 9 May 2007: http://fas.org/sgp/crs/mideast/RS22659.pdf.

54. Dan Murphy and Joshua Mitnick, "Israel, US, and Egypt back Fatah's fight against Hamas", *The Christian Science Monitor*, 23 May 2007: http://www.csmonitor.com/2007/0525/p07s02-wome.html; see also Ali Abunimah, The Electronic Intifada, "The Palestine Papers

and the 'Gaza coup'", 27 January 2011, http://electronicintifada.net/content/palestine-papers-and-gaza-coup/9200.

55. David Rose, "The Gaza Bombshell", *Vanity Fair*, April 2008: http://www.vanityfair.com/politics/features/2008/04/gaza200804.

56. Palestine Papers obtained by Al Jazeera, and released between 23-26 January 2011: http://www.aljazeera.com/palestinepapers/2011/01/201112214310263628.html.

57. "The whole of Gaza's civilian population is being punished for acts for which they bear no responsibility. The closure therefore constitutes a collective punishment imposed in clear violation of Israel's obligations under international humanitarian law." Excerpt from *International Committee of the Red Cross* (ICRC), news release 10/103, 14 June 2010: http://www.icrc.org/eng/resources/documents/update/palestine-update-140610.htm.

58. Edward Said and Christopher Hitchens, eds., *Blaming the Victims: Spurious Scholarship and the Palestinian Question* (London: Verso Books, 1988).

59. Khaled Hroub, *Hamas: A Beginner's Guide* (London: Pluto Press, 2006).

60. Shlomi Eldar, *Lehakir et Hamas* [Introducing Hamas] (Jerusalem: Keter, 2012) [Hebrew].

61. Israel's basic policy was summed up by senior Israeli advisor Dov Weissglas: "The idea is to put the Palestinians on a diet, but not to make them die of hunger." Source: Conal Urquhar, "Gaza on brink of implosion as aid cut-off starts to bite", *The Guardian*, 16 April 2006: http://www.theguardian.com/world/2006/apr/16/israel.

62. "IDF Operation in Gaza: Cast Lead", *Israel Ministry of Foreign Affairs*, 21 January 2009: http://www.mfa.gov.il/mfa/foreignpolicy/terrorism/palestinian/pages/aerial_strike_weapon_development_center%20_gaza_28-dec-2008.aspx.

63. The IDF asserted that responsibility for civilian casualties lies primarily with Hamas: "Terrorist organizations that hide behind civilians bear the primary responsibility for civilian casualties" (from slide 10 from unclassified powerpoint presentation by the Military-Strategic Information Section of the Israeli Ministry of Foreign Affairs, entitled "Operation Cast Lead IDF: Limiting Harm to Civilians", 14 January 2009).

64. The Dahiya Doctrine emerged during the second Lebanon War in 2006. It involved the disproportionate use of force against civilians.

Major General Gadi Eisenkot, the Israeli Northern Command Chief explained the doctrine: "What happened in the Dahiya quarter of Beirut in 2006 will happen in every village from which Israel is fired on. [...] We will apply disproportionate force on it and cause great damage and destruction there. From our standpoint, these are not civilian villages, they are military bases. [...] This is not a recommendation. This is a plan. And it has been approved." Quote in Richard Goldstone "Human Rights in Palestine and Other Occupied Territories", Report of the United Nations Fact-finding Mission on the Gaza Conflict, A/HRC/12/48, 25 September 2009, ¶ 1194-95, p. 254: http://www2.ohchr.org/english/bodies/hrcouncil/docs/12session/A-HRC-12-48.pdf.

65. Ibid., ¶ 43, p. 20; ¶ 705, p. 159; ¶ 711, p. 161; ¶ 750, p. 169.
66. Ibid., ¶ 32, p. 17.
67. Ibid., ¶ 1883, p. 406.
68. Ibid., ¶ 1893, p. 408.
69. *Ha'aretz* journalist Amira Hass spoke of Israel's "moral implosion" and "ethical defeat" – a defeat that "will haunt us for many years to come". Leader: "Israel's moral defeat in Gaza", *New Statesman*, 7 August 2014.
70. Harriet Sherwood, "Israel proposes Jewish state loyalty oath for new citizens", *The Guardian*, 10 October 2010: http://www.theguardian.com/world/2010/oct/10/israel-jewish-oath-new-citizens.
71. According to Baskin, the assassination of Ahmed Jabari "killed the possibility of achieving a truce". See Nir Hasson, "Israeli peace activist: Hamas leader Jabari killed amid talks on long-term truce", *Ha'aretz*, 15 November 2012: http://www.haaretz.com/news/diplomacy-defense/israeli-peace-activist-hamas-leader-jabari-killed-amid-talks-on-long-term-truce.premium-1.478085.
72. Nathan Thrall, "Hamas's Chances", *London Review of Books*, 21 August 2014: http://www.lrb.co.uk/v36/n16/nathan-thrall/hamass-chances.
73. Abbas said that Israel had threatened to boycott the government the moment it was announced: "Israel wants to punish us for agreeing with Hamas on this government", he said. "Israel PM warns against Hamas-Fatah 'terror' cabinet", *BBC*, 1 June 2014: http://www.bbc.co.uk/news/world-middle-east-27656300. See also "Netanyahu urges Abbas to dismantle Hamas-Fatah unity pact", *Al-Bawaba News*, 27 June 2014: http://www.albawaba.com/news/netanyahu-abbas-hamas-fatah-pact-586474.

74. Joel Greenberg, "Netanyahu calls on world to reject unity government", *The Financial Times*, 1 June 2014: http://www.ft.com/cms/s/0/3c2dfafa-e99f-11e3-bbc1-00144feabdc0.html#axzz3IOg6AfRo.
75. Jim Zanotti, "US Foreign Aid to the Palestinians", *Congressional Research Service*, 3 July 2014: http://fas.org/sgp/crs/mideast/RS22967.pdf.
76. Robert Tait, "Hamas kidnapping: Islamist group to blame for youths' 'kidnapping', Benjamin Netanyahu says – The Israeli leader says the Islamist militant group was behind the disappearance of three teenagers in the West Bank and links the event to its recent pact with Mahmoud Abbas", *The Telegraph*, 15 June 2014: http://www.telegraph.co.uk/news/worldnews/middleeast/israel/10901225/Hamas-kidnapping-Islamist-group-to-blame-for-youths-kidnapping-Benjamin-Netanyahu-says.html.
77. Editorial: "Gaza: A war that should never have been fought", *The Guardian*, 25 September 2014.
78. The first two goals were the officially stated "Operation Goals" of Protective Edge on the IDF Blog: http://www.idfblog.com/operationgaza2014/downloads/convert-jpg-to-pdf.net_2014-08-27_14-20-38.pdf. See also "Operation Protective Edge by the Numbers": http://www.idfblog.com/blog/2014/08/05/operation-protective-edge-numbers/.
79. David Shulman, "Gaza: The Murderous Melodrama", *The New York Review of Books*, 20 November 2014.
80. Baruch Kimmerling, *Politicide: Ariel Sharon's War against the Palestinians* (London: Verso Books, 2006), pp. 3-4.
81. The original Hebrew name for this operation was Miv'tza Tzuk Eitan, meaning Operation "Mighty Cliff" or "Solid Rock"; the choice of translation is considered as a softening of the original Israeli term, masking the aggressive aims of the IDF mission to the international public. See Shoshana Kordova, "Word of the Day / Tzuk: Cast Lead II – Why is the English name of Operation Protective Edge so different from the Hebrew version? And what does Tzuk Eitan really mean anyway?" *Ha'aretz*, 19 July 2014: http://www.haaretz.com/news/features/word-of-the-day/.premium-1.605936.
82. Mouin Rabbani, "Israel mows the lawn", *London Review of Books*, 13 July 2014: http://www.lrb.co.uk/v36/n15/mouin-rabbani/israel-mows-the-lawn.
83. Goldstone Report 2009.

84. This ranking is based on the 2014 Global Firepower Index, taking into consideration 50 different factors: http://www.globes.co.il/en/article-idf-ranked-as-worlds-11th-most-powerful-army-1000954101; and the Business Insider UK measure of the most powerful militaries in the Middle East 2014: http://uk.businessinsider.com/most-powerful-militaries-in-the-middle-east-2014-8?op=1?r=US.

85. Patrick Cockburn, "Israel-Gaza conflict: What has Israel achieved in 26 bloody days?" *The Independent*, 3 August 2014: http://www.independent.co.uk/voices/comment/israelgaza-conflict-what-has-israel-achieved-in-26-bloody-days-9644508.html.

86. Giora Eiland, "In Gaza, there is no such a thing as 'innocent civilians'", Ynet News, 8 May 2014: http://www.ynetnews.com/articles/0,7340,L-4554583,00.html; "Israeli General: No Civilians in Gaza", *The Daily Beast*, 4 August 2014: http://www.thedailybeast.com/cheats/2014/08/04/israeli-general-no-civilians-in-gaza.html. As another instance of dehumanisation of Palestinians, an op-ed article by blogger Yochanan Gordon entitled "When Genocide is Permissible" published in *The Times of Israel* on 1 August 2014, was removed due to its inappropriate content; see http://www.thedailybeast.com/articles/2014/08/01/the-blogger-who-offered-an-argument-for-palestinian-genocide.html.

87. "Support for Netanyahu plummets in new poll", *The Times of Israel*, 28 August 2014: http://www.timesofisrael.com support-for-netanyahu-plummets-further-in-new-poll/.

88. "Gaza: Ban condemns latest deadly attack near UN school as 'moral outrage and criminal act'", *UN News Centre*, 3 August 2014: http://www.un.org/apps/news/story.asp?NewsID=48396#.VF0Pk1541zQ.

ISRAEL'S ROAD TO GENOCIDE

89. Francesca Albanese, *Anatomy of a Genocide: Report of the Special Rapporteur on the Situation of Human Rights in the Palestinian Territories Occupied Since 1967*, UN Human Rights Council A/HRC/55/73 (25 March 2024), para. 7.

90. Norman G. Finkelstein, *Image and Reality of the Israel-Palestine Conflict*, second ed. (London: Verso, 2003), pp. 7–11.

91. Avi Shlaim, *The Iron Wall: Israel and the Arab World*, updated ed. (London: Penguin, 2014), p. 10.

92. Ze'ev Jabotinsky, "The Iron Wall", en.jabotinsky.org (4 November 1923).
93. Fayez A. Sayegh, *Zionist Colonialism in Palestine* (Beirut: Palestine Liberation Organization Research Centre, 1965), pp. 24–25.
94. Patrick Wolfe, *Settler Colonialism and the Transformation of Anthropology: The Politics and Poetics of an Ethnographic Event* (London and New York: Cassell, 1999), pp. 1–2.
95. Benny Morris, *The Birth of the Palestinian Refugee Problem Revisited* (Cambridge: Cambridge University Press, 2004), p. 60.
96. UN General Assembly Official Records, A/PV.2400 (10 November 1975), para. 248.
97. Gershon Shafir, *Land, Labor and the Origins of the Israeli-Palestinian Conflict, 1882–1914*, updated ed. (Berkeley: University of California Press, 1996), p. 198.
98. Morris, *Birth*, pp. 42, 588.
99. Morris, *Birth*, pp. 47–48.
100. Shlomo Ben-Ami, *Scars of War, Wounds of Peace: The Israeli-Arab Tragedy* (Oxford: Oxford University Press, 2006), p. 45.
101. Avi Shlaim, "The Debate About 1948", *International Journal of Middle East Studies* 27.3 (1995), pp. 287–304; *Iron Wall*, pp. 32–33.
102. Benny Morris, *Israel's Border Wars, 1949–1956: Arab Infiltration, Israeli Retaliation, and the Countdown to the Suez War* (Oxford: Clarendon Press, 1993), pp. 137, 416.
103. Sabri Jiryis, *The Arabs in Israel* (New York and London: Monthly Review Press, 1976), pp. 81–82.
104. Oren Yiftachel, *Ethnocracy: Land and Identity Politics in Israel/Palestine* (Pennsylvania: University of Pennsylvania Press, 2006), pp. 108, 110, 137–140, 143, 199.
105. Avi Raz, *The Bride and the Dowry: Israel, Jordan, and the Palestinians in the Aftermath of the June 1967 War* (New Haven and London: Yale University Press, 2012), p. 3.
106. Shlaim, *Iron Wall*, p. 258.
107. Raz, *Bride*, pp. 103–115, 125–134, 270.
108. Human Rights Watch (HRW), *A Threshold Crossed: Israeli Authorities and the Crimes of Apartheid and Persecution* (April 2021), p. 16.
109. Sara Roy, *The Gaza Strip: The Political Economy of De-development*, third ed. (Washington, DC: Institute for Palestine Studies, 2016), pp. 175–176.

110. B'Tselem, *A Regime of Jewish Supremacy from the Jordan River to the Mediterranean Sea: This Is Apartheid* (January 2021), p. 5.

111. *Legal Consequences Arising from the Policies and Practices of Israel in the Occupied Palestinian Territory, Including East Jerusalem*, Advisory Opinion, ICJ Reports 2024, pp. 64–65, paras. 224–229 (quotes at 225, 227). Emphasis in original.

112. HRW, *Threshold*, p. 10.

113. Benny Morris, *Righteous Victims: A History of the Zionist-Arab Conflict, 1881–2001* (New York: Vintage, 2001), p. 253 ("consensus"). B'Tselem, *Land Grab: Israel's Settlement Policy in the West Bank* (May 2002), p. 11 (governments). Amnesty International, *Israel's Apartheid Against Palestinians: Cruel System of Domination and a Crime Against Humanity* (2022), p. 12 ("all").

114. Shira Robinson, *Citizen Strangers: Palestinians and the Birth of Israel's Liberal Settler State* (California: Stanford University Press, 2013), pp. 35–36, 39, 41–42, 48. Yotam Berger, "Declassified: Israel Made Sure Arabs Couldn't Return to Their Villages", *Ha'aretz* (27 May 2019).

115. Amnesty International, *Apartheid*, pp. 107–108, 245.

116. Musa Abuhashhash, "The Quiet Front: Reflections from the West Bank", in Jamie Stern-Weiner ed., *Deluge: Gaza and Israel from Crisis to Cataclysm* (New York and London: OR Books, 2024), pp. 149–151.

117. Quoted in US Ambassador to Israel, Daniel C. Kurtzer, "Israeli Officials Brief Djerejian on Improved Regional Security Situation; Unilateral Disengagement Plans", 04TELAVIV1952_a (31 March 2004), Wikileaks.

118. Sara Roy, "'A Dubai on the Mediterranean'", *London Review of Books* 27.21 (3 November 2005) ("depression"). United Nations Special Rapporteur John Dugard, *Situation of Human Rights in the Palestinian Territories Occupied Since 1967* (27 September 2006), para. 70 ("sanctions").

119. Sara Roy, "Econocide in Gaza", in Stern-Weiner, *Deluge*.

120. Dov Weisglass quoted in Conal Urquhart, "Gaza on Brink of Implosion as Aid Cut-Off Starts to Bite", *Observer* (16 April 2006).

121. International Crisis Group, *After Gaza* (2 August 2007), p. 24, footnote 210.

122. Karen Koning AbuZayd, "This Brutal Siege of Gaza Can Only Breed Violence", *Guardian* (23 January 2008).

123. UN Conference on Trade and Development, *Report on UNCTAD Assistance to the Palestinian People: Developments in the Economy of the Occupied Palestinian Territory* (6 July 2015), p. 12 ("unlivable"). "IDF

Intel Chief Warns Despair in Gaza Could Explode Toward Israel", timesofisrael.com (24 February 2016) (agreed). UN Country Team in the Occupied Palestinian Territory (UNOPT), *Gaza Ten Years Later* (July 2017), pp. 2–3, 28 (optimistic).

124. Tom Miles, "U.N. Sets Up Human Rights Probe into Gaza Killings, to Israel's Fury", reuters.com (18 May 2018).

125. "Gaza Children Living in 'Hell on Earth' Secretary-General Tells General Assembly, as Calls for End to Violence Crescendo, News of Israel-Hamas Ceasefire Breaks", GA/12325, press.un.org (20 May 2021).

126. Norman G. Finkelstein, *Gaza: An Inquest into Its Martyrdom* (Berkeley: University of California Press, 2018), pp. 17–38, 212–214.

127. B'Tselem, *Apartheid*, p. 1.

128. "IDF Intel Chief".

129. Yaakov Amidror, "Finding a Humanitarian Solution to the Gaza Problem", jiss.org.il (8 July 2018) ("operations") [Hebrew]. Yaakov Amidror, "Yaakov Amidror: 'Whoever Proposes to Occupy Gaza Is Talking Nonsense'", *Ma'ariv* (15 August 2018) ("rise") [Hebrew].

130 Independent Commission of Inquiry, *Detailed Findings on Attacks Carried Out On and After 7 October 2023 in Israel*, A/HRC/56/CRP.3 (10 June 2024).

131. Yoel Guzansky quoted in Ronen Bergman and Patrick Kingsley, "How Israel's Feared Security Services Failed to Stop Hamas's Attack", *New York Times* (10 October 2023).

132. Mouin Rabbani, "Gaza Apocalypse", securityincontext.com (26 January 2024).

133. UN OCHA, "Gaza Strip: Reported Impact Snapshot, Day 278", ochaopt.org (10 July 2024).

134. Based on Save the Children, "Gaza: 3,195 Children Killed in Three Weeks Surpasses Annual Number of Children Killed in Conflict Zones Since 2019", savethechildren.org.uk (29 October 2023).

135. Kate Nicholson, "Doctor Reveals New Medical Acronym 'Unique to Gaza' to Describe Particular War Victim", huffingtonpost.co.uk (6 November 2023). Mai Khaled et al., "How the Loss of Entire Families Is Ravaging the Social Fabric of Gaza", *Financial Times* (13 December 2023).

136. Save the Children, "12,000 Children a Day Forcibly Displaced in Gaza, as New 'Evacuation Orders' Issued to Civilians", savethechildren.org.uk

(22 December 2023) (children). UNRWA, "Situation Report 106 on the Situation in the Gaza Strip and the West Bank, Including East Jerusalem", unrwa.org (7 May 2024) (multiple). Andrea De Domenico, head of UN OCHA in the OPT, quoted in AFP, "About 90% of People in Gaza Displaced Since War Began, Says UN Agency", theguardian.com (July 3, 2024) (ten).

137. US Vetoes Resolution on Gaza Which Called For "Immediate Humanitarian Ceasefire", news.un.org (8 December 2023).

138. Hoda Osman et al., "Israel's War on Gaza Is the Deadliest Conflict on Record for Journalists", theintercept.com (25 June 2024) (journalists). Medical Aid for Palestinians, "500 Healthcare Workers Killed During Israel's Military Assault on Gaza", map.org.uk (26 June 2024) (health). UN Secretary-General António Guterres, "As Civilians in Gaza Are Pushed into 'Ever Deeper Circles of Hell', Donors Must Act Now to Protect UN Palestine Refugee Agency, Secretary-General Urges Pledging Conference", press.un.org (12 July 2024) (UN).

139. Charles Birch (United Nations Mine Action Service) interviewed by Isaac Chotiner, "Gaza's Unexploded-Bomb Crisis", *New Yorker* (8 May 2024).

140. "UN Official Deems Kill Rates in Gaza Highest in the World Since Rwandan Genocide", middleastmonitor.com (21 February 2024).

141. UNICEF, "Gaza: The World's Most Dangerous Place to Be a Child", unicef.org (19 December 2023). International Rescue Committee, "Gaza: Continuous Israeli Attacks on Aid Workers Are Severely Hampering Life-Saving Aid Efforts, Warns the IRC", rescue.org (4 April 2024). International Crisis Group, "Israel Has Made Gaza the Deadliest Place for Aid Workers", crisisgroup.org (7 May 2024). ACLED, "Palestine Is Now the Most Dangeorus Place in the World", acleddata.com (31 July 2024).

142. Amnesty International, *Israel/Gaza: Operation "Cast Lead": 22 Days of Death and Destruction* (July 2009). *Report of the United Nations Fact-Finding Mission on the Gaza Conflict*, A/HRC/12/48 (25 September 2009), para. 1893.

143. Breaking the Silence, *This Is How We Fought in Gaza: Soldiers' Testimonies and Photographs from Operation "Protective Edge" 2014* (May 2015), pp. 66, 101, 166.

144. *Report of the Detailed Findings of the UN Commission of Inquiry on the Protests in the Occupied Palestinian Territory*, A/HRC/40/CRP.2 (18 March 2019), paras. 518–519, 526, 536–537.

145. Yaniv Cogan, "Targeting Civilians: Its Logic in Gaza and Israel", in Stern-Weiner, *Deluge*, pp. 100–105.
146. Philip Webber and Stuart Parkinson, "Gaza: One of the Most Intense Bombardments in History?" sgr.org.uk (13 March 2024), using Israeli military data.
147. Independent International Commission of Inquiry on the Occupied Palestinian Territory, including East Jerusalem, and Israel [International Commission of Inquiry], *Detailed Findings on the Military Operations and Attacks Carried Out in the Occupied Palestinian Territory from 7 October to 31 December 2023*, A/HRC/56/CRP.4 (10 June 2024), para. 58.
148. UN Environment Program, *Environmental Impact of the Conflict in Gaza: Preliminary Assessment of Environmental Impacts* (June 2024), p. 23.
149. Julia Frankel, "Israel's Military Campaign in Gaza Seen as Among the Most Destructive in Recent History, Experts Say", apnews.com (11 January 2024).
150. Finkelstein, *Gaza*, pp. 35–36.
151. Ruben Durante and Ekaterina Zhuravskaya, "Attack When the World Is Not Watching? US News and the Israeli-Palestinian Conflict", *Journal of Political Economy* 126.3 (2018), pp. 1085–1133.
152. Benjamin Netanyahu on HBO's Real Time with Bill Maher (8 September 2006).
153. Menachem Shalev, "'Use Political Opportunities'. Netanyahu Recommends Large-Scale Expulsions", *Jerusalem Post* (19 November 1989).
154. Finkelstein, *Gaza*, p. 215.
155. Israel Prime Minister Benjamin Netanyahu, post by @IsraeliPM on X (formerly Twitter), 9 October 2023 ("change"). Emergency War Cabinet Member Benny Gantz quoted in James Shotter et al., "Israel's New Unity Government Pledges to Change 'Strategic Reality' in Gaza", *Financial Times* (11 October 2023) ("reality").
156. Meir Ben Shabbat, "Israel Must Make It Clear: The Era of Surgical Strikes Is Over", *Israel Hayom* (8 October 2023).
157. Tamir Hayman, "Israel at War: An Unprecedented Event and a Strategic Change of Direction", inss.org.il (8 October 2023)
158. Ben Caspit, "Israel's Cruel Dilemma as It Embarks on Ground Operation in Gaza", al-monitor.com (13 October 2023).
159. Ofer Shelah, "Where Do We Go from Here?" inss.org.il (11 October 2023).

160. Quoted in David Landau, "Rabin Expresses His Frustration with Palestinian Stance in Talks", *JTA Daily News Bulletin* 70.171 (4 September 1992), p. 2.

161. Israel Defence Minister Yoav Gallant quoted in Yoav Zitun, "Gallant: 'We Will Change Reality in Gaza for the Next 50 Years'", ynet.co.il (7 October 2023) [Hebrew].

162. *Application of the Convention on the Prevention and Punishment of the Crime of Genocide in the Gaza Strip (South Africa v. Israel)*, Public Sitting Verbatim Record of 12 January 2024, ICJ Reports 2024, paras. 40, 49.

163. A compendium of incriminating statements by Israeli political and military leaders, as well as rank-and-file soldiers, has been compiled by Yaniv Cogan, with assistance from Jamie Stern-Weiner. As of July 2024, it ran to hundreds of entries. This section draws on that unpublished database. Cogan also contributed or verified most of the Hebrew translations that follow.

164. Likud MK Revital "Tally" Gotliv (10 October 2023) quoted in Al-Haq, "Statements by Israeli Officials, Soldiers and Civil Society on Genocide", alhaq.org, p. 9 ("flattening"). Israel Energy Minister (from 1 January 2024, Foreign Minister) Israel Katz, post on X (formerly Twitter), 13 October 2023 ("leave"). Likud MK Eliyahu Revivo (1 November 2023) quoted in Al-Haq, "Statements", p. 13 ("crushing"). Otzma Yehudit MK and Judicial Selection Committee member Yitzhak Kroizer quoted in Editorial, "Fire Israel's Far Right", *Ha'aretz* (6 November 2023) ("death").

165. Israeli President Isaac Herzog (13 October 2023), quoted in Chris McGreal, "The Language Being Used to Describe Palestinians Is Genocidal", *Guardian* (16 October 2023) ("nation"). Israel National Security Minister Itamar Ben-Gvir, "At the Height of the Fighting: The IDF Tightened the Regulations for the Use of Fire in the Gaza Strip", now14.co.il (30 December 2023) ("innocents") [Hebrew].

166. Likud MK Galit Distel Atbaryan, post on X (formerly Twitter), 1 November 2023 ("monsters") [Hebrew]. Knesset Deputy Speaker and Likud MK Nissim Vaturi, post on X (formerly Twitter), 17 November 2023 ("Burn") [Hebrew].

167. Yesh Atid MK Meirav Ben Ari on 16 October 2023, quoted in Jonathan Ofir, "Israeli Politician: 'The Children of Gaza Have Bought This Upon Themselves'", mondoweiss.net (18 October 2023). Yisrael Beytenu leader and former Israel Defence Minister Avigdor Lieberman, post on X (formerly Twitter), 30 November 2023 ("innocents") [Hebrew].

168. *South Africa v. Israel*, Application Instituting Proceedings of 29 December 2023, ICJ Reports 2024, pp. 66–67, para. 106.
169. "Letter from the Permanent Representative of South Africa to the United Nations Addressed to the President of the Security Council", S/2024/419 (29 May 2024), Annex III, pp. 17–22, paras. 19–24.
170. Former Likud MK Moshe Feiglin interviewed on Channel 14, translated by @YehudaShaul on X (formerly Twitter), 11 November 2023 [Hebrew].
171. Jerusalem Deputy Mayor Arieh King (17 October 2023), recorded and translated by @YehudaShaul on X (formerly Twitter), 11 November 2023 [Hebrew]. 103FM, "Israel Should Make Gaza Look Like Auschwitz Museum – Council Head", jpost.com (19 December 2023).
172. Ali Abunimah, "Watch: Israeli Children Sing, 'We Will Annihilate Everyone' in Gaza", electronicintifada.net (19 November 2023). "Letter from South Africa", Annex III, pp. 25–26, paras. 32–33.
173. Yaniv Kubovich, "Graphic Videos and Incitement: How the IDF Is Misleading Israelis on Telegram", *Ha'aretz* (12 December 2023).
174. Likud MK Moshe Sa'ada on Channel 14, recorded and translated by @ireallyhateyou on X (formerly Twitter), 3 January 2024 [Hebrew].
175. Younis Tirawi and Eran Maoz, "Inside Israel's Insta-Genocide", zeteo.com (10 June 2024); "May Gaza Burn: The Flood of Genocidal Rhetoric from Israel's Soldiers", zeteo.com (13 June 2024).
176. Laura Silver and Maria Smerkovich, "Israeli Views of the Israel-Hamas War", pewresearch.org (30 May 2024). Author correspondence with Pew researchers (24 July 2024), on file.
177. Diana Buttu, "A Diary of a Palestinian Living in Israel", zeteo.com (7 May 2024).
178. Israel Ministry of Foreign Affairs, "Statement by PM Netanyahu", gov.il (20 October 2023). "PM in Missive to Troops: 'Our Dear Heroes, I Am Confident in Our Complete Victory'", timesofisrael.com (3 November 2023).
179. 1 Samuel 15:3.
180. B'Tselem, *Manufacturing Famine. Israel Is Committing the War Crime of Starvation in the Gaza Strip* (April 2024), p. 11.
181. Likud MK Revital "Tally" Gotliv, "Tally Gotliv: 'If I Were Prime Minister I Would Erase Gaza'", ice.co.il (12 October 2023) (nuclear) [Hebrew]. Likud MK Boaz Bismuth, "MK Boas Bismuth: 'There Is

No Space for Any Humanitarian Gesture – The Memory of Amalek Must Be Obliterated'", inn.co.il (16 October 2023) ("humanitarian") [Hebrew]. Finance Minister Bezalel Smotrich quoted in "Letter from South Africa", Annex I, pp. 20–21, para. 12.

182. *South Africa v. Israel*, Order of 26 January 2024, ICJ Reports 2024, p. 17, paras. 50–52 (censured). Divrei HaKnesset, 25th Knesset, Session No. 191 (10 July 2024), pp. 9 ("Amalek"), 35 (demolition) [Hebrew].

183. "Letter from South Africa", Annex II, p. 21, paras. 14–15.

184. Raz, *Bride*, pp. 268–270. Omri Shafer Raviv, "Israeli Emigration Policies in the Gaza Strip: Crafting Demography and Forming Control in the Aftermath of the 1967 War", *Middle Eastern Studies* 57.2 (2021), pp. 342–356.

185. See, e.g., Oren Yiftachel, "The Shrinking Space of Citizenship", in Joel Benin and Rebecca L. Stein eds., *The Struggle for Sovereignty: Palestine and Israel, 1993–2005* (California: Stanford University Press, 2006), pp. 169–171.

186. Bezalel Smotrich, post on Facebook, 14 November 2023 [Hebrew]. Gila Gamliel, "Victory Is an Opportunity for Israel in the Midst of Crisis", jpost.com (19 November 2023). Itamar Ben Gvir, post on X (formerly Twitter), 1 January 2024 [Hebrew]. Amichai Eliyahu quoted in 103FM, "After Attacking Gallant: Minister Eliyahu's Plan Regarding the Future of the Gaza Strip", *Ma'ariv* (5 January 2024) [Hebrew].

187. Israel Prime Minister Benjamin Netanyahu, "Statement by Prime Minister Benjamin Netanyahu", gov.il (7 October 2023) ("Leave"). Mati Tuchfeld, "The Prime Minister's Plan for the Citizens of the Gaza Strip: The Direction – Out", *Israel Hayom* (30 November 2023) ("minimum") [Hebrew]. Ma'ariv Online, "Confrontation Between Danon and Netanyahu: 'It Is Unacceptable That the Head of the National Security Council Should Contradict the Government's Position'", *Ma'ariv* (25 December 2023) (absorb) [Hebrew].

188. Likud MK Ariel Kallner, post on X (formerly Twitter), 7 October 2023 ("Nakba") [Hebrew]. Likud MK Amit Halevy, "This Is How We Will Return to Gaza", olam-katan.co.il (11 October 2023) ("responsibility") [Hebrew]. Yisrael Beytenu MK and former Israel Defence Minister Avigdor Lieberman quoted in Moran Azulay, "Liberman: Let the Gazans Establish a Refuge City in the Sinai", ynetnews.com (17 October 2023) ("refuge"). Yesh Atid MK, former deputy head of the Mossad, and former head of the Knesset National Security Commission Ram Ben Barak speaking on Channel 12, posted by @ItamarCohen100 on

X (formerly Twitter), 1 November 2023 ("scatter") [Hebrew]. Likud MK Danny Danon (appointed ambassador of Israel to the UN in June 2024), "What Does the Day After the War Look Like in Gaza? A Likud Party Official's Perspective", *Newsweek* (15 December 2023) ("relocation"). Religious Zionism MK Zvi Sukkot, chairman of the Subcommittee on Judea and Samara to the Knesset Foreign Affairs and Defence Committee in video posted by @KnessetT on X (formerly Twitter), 3 January 2024 ("Tel Aviv") [Hebrew].

189. Yuval Abraham, "Expel All Palestinians from Gaza, Recommends Israeli Gov't Ministry", 972mag.com (30 October 2023). Abraham notes that the Intelligence Ministry is not very influential.

190. Quoted in Gideon Rachman, "Western Diplomats Are Walking an Impossible Tightrope with Israel", *Financial Times* (13 October 2023).

191. Mordechai Bar-On, *The Gates of Gaza: Israel's Road to Suez and Back, 1955–1957* (New York: St. Martin's Press, 1995), pp. 80, 217.

192. Finkelstein, *Gaza*, p. 66.

193. IDF officer quoted in Yossi Yehoshua, "No Time to Waste: Hamas Must Feel Israeli Wrath Immediately", ynetnews.com (9 October 2023) ("obliterate"). Giora Eiland, "The Military, Moral and Political Challenge", ynet.co.il (28 October 2023) ("chaos") [Hebrew]. IDF Company Commander Major Yair Ben David in video posted by @YinonMagal on X (formerly Twitter), 19 December 2023 ("Beit Hanoun") [Hebrew].

194. Netanyahu, "Statement" ("avenge"). Sara Netanyahu quoted by @Israel-Galey on X (formerly Twitter), 10 October 2023 ("hope") [Hebrew]. IDF soldier quoted in Dion Nissenbaum et al., "Scene of Massacre Becomes Staging Ground for Israel's Invasion of Gaza. 'I Am Looking for Revenge'", *Wall Street Journal* (11 October 2023) ("straight"). IDF Colonel Erez Eshel featured in "'Revenge Is an Important Value': Our Reporter Joined Our Forces on Manoeuvres in the Heart of Gaza", now14.co.il (4 November 2023) ("value") [Hebrew].

195. B'Tselem, "Revenge Policy in Motion: Israel Committing War Crimes in Gaza", btselem.org (10 October 2023). "Former Shin Bet Chief. The IDF Only Remains in Gaza Because of the Hostages", israelnationalnews.com (1 February 2024).

196. Yaniv Kubovich, "Israeli Army Occupies Gaza Homes – Then Burns Them Down", *Ha'aretz* (31 January 2024). Yagil Levy, "Israeli Soldiers' Looting in Gaza Is Part of the Revenge", *Ha'aretz* (19 February 2024).

Secunder Kermani, "Israeli Soldier Speaks Out on War in Gaza", channel4.com (24 April 2024). Oren Ziv, "'I'm Bored, So I Shoot': The Israeli Army's Approval of Free-For-All Violence in Gaza", 972mag.com (8 July 2024).

197. Tovah Lazaroff, "'Resettling Gaza Was Never in the Cards', PM Netanyahu Says in a CNN Interview", jpost.com (22 May 2024) (Netanyahu). Tirawi and Maoz, "Insta-Genocide" (soldiers). Yarden Michaeli and Avi Scharf, "Road to Redemption: How Israel's War Against Hamas Turned Into a Springboard for Jewish Settlement in Gaza", *Ha'aretz* (8 July 2024) (one-third).

198. Stacey Eldridge, "'City of Tents': Israeli Defence Official Vows Every Building in Gaza Will Be Destroyed in 'Ground Manoeuvre'", skynews.com.au (12 October 2023) ("tents"). IDF Spokesperson Daniel Hagari, "Watch the IDF Spokesperson's Statement", idf.il (31 October 2023) ("massacre") [Hebrew]. Emanuel Fabian, "Gallant Warns 'Mistake' by Hezbollah Chief 'Will Seal the Fate of Lebanon'", timesofisrael.com (4 November 2023) ("fate"). Deputy Head of the Civil Administration and Deputy Defence Establishment Comptroller Brigadier General Yogev Bar Sheshet featured in "'Revenge Is an Important Value': Our Reporter Joined Our Forces on Manoeuvres in the Heart of Gaza", now14.co.il (4 November 2023) ("scorched") [Hebrew]. Former Acting Head of Israel's Civil Administration Yigal Carmon quoted in Dor Levinter, "'Southern Gaza Will Become a Huge Refugee Camp. The Rest Will Become a Memorial Site, Like Normandy. It Will Be a Closed Military Area and the Fighting Will Not Stop'", epoch.org.il (7 November 2023) ("ruins") [Hebrew]. Michael Hauser Tov, "'We're Rolling Out Nakba 2023', Israeli Minister Says on Northern Gaza Strip Evacuation", *Ha'aretz* (12 November 2023) ("Nakba").

199. Giora Eiland, "This Is Not Revenge. It's Either Us or Them", ynet.co.il (10 October 2023) ("unfit") [Hebrew]; "It's Time to Rip Off the Hamas Band-Aid", ynetnews.com (12 October 2023) ("crisis", "entire", "exist"); "'A New Turning Point in the History of the State of Israel. Most People Don't Understand That'", fathomjournal.org (October 2023) ("siege", "starve").

200. Robert Pape, "Israel's Failed Bombing Campaign in Gaza", *Foreign Affairs* (6 December 2023) ("intense"). B'Tselem, "Humanitarian Catastrophe as Policy", btselem.org (7 December 2023).

201. Marc Garlasco, post on X (formerly Twitter), 12 October 2023.

202. Robert Pape, "Hamas Is Winning", *Foreign Affairs* (21 June 2024).

203. Jean-Philippe Rémy, "Inside Gaza with the Israeli Army as It Hunts for Hamas Tunnels", *Le Monde Diplomatique* (19 November 2023). Isabel Debre, "Gaza Has Become a Moonscape in War. When the Battles Stop, Many Fear It Will Remain Uninhabitable", apnews.com (23 November 2023).

204. Nagham Mohanna, "Israeli Forces Withdraw After 20-day Operation Destroys 70 Per Cent of Gaza's Jabalia Camp", thenationalnews.com (31 May 2024).

205. Mehul Srivastava and Alan Smith, "Visual Analysis: The Wastelands in Gaza's Two Biggest Cities", *Financial Times* (21 December 2023) ("wasteland"). Samuel Forey and Louis Imbert, "Gaza City Has Been Reduced to Hunger and Chaos", *Le Monde Diplomatique* (7 March 2024) ("hunger", "ravaged"). Visual Journalism Team, "Gaza Strip in Maps: How Life Has Changed", bbc.co.uk (22 March 2024) ("razed").

206. Mai Khaled et al., "How Israeli Air Strikes Destroyed a Busy Neighbourhood in Gaza", *Financial Times* (25 October 2023) (Rimal). "'We Have Nothing': Palestinians Return to Utter Destruction in Gaza City After Israeli Withdrawal", apnews.com (11 July 2024) (Shuja'iya). UN World Food Programme, "WFP Palestine Emergency Response: Situation Report 27", reliefweb.int (18 July 2024), p. 2 ("disaster").

207. Sebastian Usher, "Gazans Return to Scenes of Devastation in Khan Younis", bbc.co.uk (8 April 2024) ("devastated"). Anas Baba and Daniel Estrin, "A First Glimpse of Khan Younis, A Gaza City Now Lying in Ruins", npr.org (10 April 2024) ("destroyed"). UN OCHA, "Gaza – Khan Younis Destruction", unocha.org (23 May 2024) ("flattened" – quoting UN OCHA Humanitarian Affairs Officer Yasmina Guerda). Jason Burke, "Clearing Gaza of Almost 40m Tonnes of War Rubble Will Take Years, Says UN", *Guardian* (15 July 2024) ("insane").

208. Adam Goldman, "In Rafah, We Saw Destruction and the Limits of Israel's Gaza Strategy", *New York Times* (7 July 2024) ("shredded"). Jeremy Diamond, "Israel Says Its Operation in Rafah Is 'Limited'. Fighting There Has Left Parts of It Unrecognizable", edition.cnn.com (7 July 2024) ("unrecognizable"). Dov Lieber, "On the Ground in Rafah: Flattened Buildings and a Shattered Gateway", *Wall Street Journal* (7 July 2024) ("wasteland"). Matt Bradley and Chantal Da Silva, "Devastated Rafah a Ghost Town as Cease-Fire and Hostage Release Talks Go On", nbcnews.com (8 July 2024) ("husk").

209. Based on UN Satellite Centre (UNOSAT), "Gaza Strip 7th Comprehensive Damage Assessment", unosat.org (31 May 2024) (40 percent).

Decentralized Damage Mapping Group, conflict-damage.org, update on 3 July 2024 (60 percent).

210. World Bank, European Union, and United Nations, *Gaza Strip Interim Damage Assessment* (29 March 2024), pp. 1 (health), 13 (cultural), 15 (roads, electricity, water), 16 (waste). "UN Experts Deeply Concerned over 'Scholasticide' in Gaza", ohchr.org (18 April 2024) (university). UN OCHA, "Day 278" (homes, school, commercial).

211. Decentralized Damage Mapping Group, conflict-damage.org, update on 3 July 2024 (three-quarters). Oxfam, *Water War Crimes: How Israel Has Weaponised Water in Its Military Campaign in Gaza* (July 2024), p. 6 (wells).

212. Yinon Magal (16 November 2023), quoted in Cogan, "Targeting Civilians", p. 99 ("over"). Lieutenant Colonel Oren Schindler, serving as commander of IDF battalion 74 in Gaza, quoted in Hagai Segal, "'They Won't Be Able to Return Here for At Least a Hundred Years': An In-Depth Tour of Shujai'ya", *Makor Rishon* (16 December 2023) ("sand") [Hebrew]. Deputy Commander of IDF battalion 749 in video posted by @yonibmen on X (formerly Twitter), 20 December 2023 ("beautiful") [Hebrew]. Lieutenant Colonel Israel Rosenfried interviewed by Kan Digital, "'This Whole Valley Is Full of Launchers': Docutime in the Heart of Gaza", youtube.com (uploaded 26 December 2023) ("enemy") [Hebrew]. IDF soldier Hay Deree in video posted by @ytirawi on X (formerly Twitter), 13 February 2024 ("wonderful") [Hebrew].

213. Ziv, "Bored".

214. Religious Zionism Party CEO Yehoda Vald, post on X (formerly Twitter), 1 February 2024 ("proud") [Hebrew].

215. "Gaza: UN Expert Condemns 'Unrelenting War' on Health System Amid Airstrikes on Hospitals and Health Workers", ohchr.org (7 December 2023) ("obliterated"). Frances Vinall and Mohamad El Chamaa, "Mapping the Damage to Gaza's Hospitals: Battered, Abandoned and Raided", *Washington Post* (21 May 2024) (targeted).

216. Katie Polgalse et al., "How Gaza's Hospitals Became Battlegrounds", edition.cnn.com (12 January 2024).

217. Geneva Abdul, "'They're Targeting Healthcare Workers': Airstrikes a Constant Fear for UK Doctors in Gaza", *Guardian* (7 April 2024 – quoting British surgeon Professor Nick Maynard).

218. International Committee of the Red Cross, "Gaza: Repeated Mass Casualty Events Put Hospitals Under Severe Strain", icrc.org (18 July 2024). Javid Abdelmoneim, "A Day in the Life at the Last Remaining Hospital in Southern Gaza", msf.org (22 July 2024).

219. Chris McGreal, "Israeli Weapons Packed with Shrapnel Causing Devastating Injuries to Children in Gaza, Doctors Say", *Guardian* (11 July 2024).

220. Amber Harouda et al., "As Gaza Hospitals Collapse, Medical Workers Face the Hardest Choices", *New York Times* (6 November 2023). Netta Ahituv, "The Chilling Testimony of a US Neurosurgeon Who Went to Gaza to Save Lives", *Ha'aretz* (9 May 2024).

221. Quoted in Cogan, "Targeting Civilians", p. 98.

222. Save the Children, "Gaza: More Than 10 Children a Day Lose a Limb in Three Months of Brutal Conflict", savethechildren.net (7 January 2024).

223. "Gaza City: Babies Dying in Hospital Amid Scenes of Devastation", news.un.org (13 November 2023). Cogan, "Targeting Civilians", p. 107.

224. Likud MK Amit Halevy in video posted by @ytirawi on X (formerly Twitter), 8 July 2024.

225. World Health Organisation quoted in AFP, "WHO Says 9,000 Patients Need Emergency Evacuation from Gaza", france24.com (30 March 2024).

226. MSF, "Five Facts About the War in Gaza", doctorswithoutborders.org (24 July 2024).

227. No Comment TV, " 'We Are Fighting Human Animals' Said Israeli Defence Minister Yoav Gallant", youtube.com (10 October 2023).

228. COGAT Major General Ghassan Alian, post by @cogatonline on X (formerly Twitter), 10 October 2023.

229. Airwars Staff, "Two Weeks Under Scrutiny: Patterns of Harm Reported in Gaza Following ICJ Ruling", airwars.org (26 February 2024). UN Human Rights Office in Occupied Palestinian Territory, "UN Human Rights Office Strongly Deplores Killing of at least 112 Palestinians During Food Aid Distribution in Gaza City", un.org (1 March 2024).

230. Roy, *De-development*. Independent Commission of Inquiry, *Detailed Findings*, A/HRC/56/CRP.4, paras. 282, 300.

231. Oxfam, *Water*, p. 5.

232. Integrated Food Security Phase Classification (IPC), "Gaza Strip: IPC Acute Food Insecurity | November 2023–February 2024", ipcinfo.org (21 December 2023), p. 1 ("highest"). IPC, "The Gaza Strip: IPC Acute Food Insecurity Analysis 15 February–15 July 2024", ipcinfo.org (18 March 2024), p. 1 ("imminent").

233. In March and April, the ICJ, USAID, and chief prosecutor of the International Criminal Court had publicly asserted that famine was present in Gaza. Israeli leaders later explained that supply of humanitarian essentials to Gaza was increased to maintain "international legitimacy" for the "war". Israel Defence Minister Yoav Gallant, Divrei HaKnesset, 25th Knesset, Session No. 191 (10 July 2024), p. 16 [Hebrew].

234. IPC, *Famine Review Committee: Gaza Strip, June 2024: Conclusions and Recommendations* (25 June 2024), pp. 1–3.

235. Independent Commission of Inquiry, *Detailed Findings*, A/HRC/56/CRP.4, para. 479 ("overcrowded"). Daniel Johnson, "Polio Stalks Gazans as 'Anarchy' Spreads, Humanitarians Warn", news.un.org (19 July 2024) ("perfect").

236. "Letter from South Africa", Annex I, pp. 18–19, para. 12.

237. WHO Director-General Tedros Adhanom Ghebreyesus, post on X (formerly Twitter), 19 July 2024 (poliovirus). WHO, *Public Health Situation Analysis* (22 July 2024), p. 16 (cases).

238. Henry Mance, "UN Aid Chief Martin Griffiths: 'The War in Gaza Isn't Halfway Through'", *Financial Times* (18 December 2023).

239. Raz Segal, "A Textbook Case of Genocide", *Jewish Currents* (13 October 2023). "Gaza: UN Experts Decry Bombing of Hospitals and Schools as Crimes Against Humanity, Call for Prevention of Genocide", un.org (19 October 2023).

240. *South Africa v. Israel*, Application Institution Proceedings, ICJ Reports 2024, p. 1, para. 1.

241. *South Africa v. Israel*, Order of 26 January 2024, ICJ Reports 2024, pp. 24–25, para. 86.

242. Martin Shaw, *What Is Genocide?* second ed. (Cambridge: Polity Press, 2015), chap. 3.

243. *Application of the Convention on the Prevention and Punishment of the Crime of Genocide (Croatia v. Serbia)*, Judgment of 3 February 2015, ICJ Reports 2015, p. 67, para. 148. Emphasis added.

244. Oxford English Dictionary, s.v. "genocide (n.)", July 2023, https://doi.org/10.1093/OED/1052801400.

245. International Commission of Inquiry, *Detailed Findings*, A/HRC/56/CRP.4, paras. 420, 422, 427, 434, 437–438, 450, 451, 458, 464, 468. According to Commission Chair Navi Pillay, the scope of its mandate meant it was not open for the Commission to accuse Israel of genocide. Juan Cole, "UN Human Rights Commission: Israel's Is Among Most Criminal Armies in the World, Clear Intention of Forcible Dislocation", juancole.com (20 June 2024).

246. AFP, "About 90% of People in Gaza Displaced Since War Began, Says UN Agency", *Guardian* (3 July 2024). "Optimistic Plans for Post-War Gaza Have Little Basis in Reality", *Economist* (18 July 2024).

247. Rasha Khatib et al., "(Correspondence) Counting the Dead in Gaza: Difficult but Essential", *The Lancet* 404.10449 (20 July 2024), pp. 237–238.

248. International Commission of Inquiry, *Detailed Findings*, A/HRC/56/CRP.4, para. 136.

249. McGreal, "Clearing".

250. AP, "UN Warns Gaza Is Now 'Uninhabitable' as War Continues", *Guardian* (6 January 2024).

251. Patrick Wolfe, "Settler Colonialism and the Elimination of the Native", *Journal of Genocide Research* 8.4 (2006), p. 387.

252. William A. Schabas, *Genocide in International Law: The Crime of Crimes*, second ed. (Cambridge: Cambridge University Press, 2009), p. 234.

253. Ian S. Lustick, "The Red Thread of Israel's 'Demographic Problem'", *Middle East Policy* 26.1 (2019), pp. 142–143, 146–147.

254. Peace Now, *While We Were At War: The Israeli Government's Annexation Revolution in the West Bank Since October 7th*, peacenow.org.il (July 2024) (settlement). Noa Shpigel, "With Gantz's Backing, Israel's Parliament Passes Resolution Opposing Palestinian Statehood", *Ha'aretz* (18 July 2024) ("threat"). B'Tselem, "Forcible Transfer of Isolated Palestinian Communities and Families in Area C Under Cover of Gaza Fighting", btselem.org (19 October 2023; updated 17 April 2024).

THE TWO-STATE SOLUTION: ILLUSION AND REALITY

255. Avi Shlaim, *Collusion across the Jordan: King Abdullah, the Zionist Movement, and the Partition of Palestine* (Oxford: Clarendon Press, 1988).

256. Avi Shlaim, *Lion of Jordan: The Life of King Hussein in War and Peace* (London: Allen Lane/Penguin Books, 2007).

257. Avi Raz, *The Bride and the Dowry: Israel, Jordan and the Palestinians in the Aftermath of the June 1967 War* (New Haven: Yale University Press, 2012).

258. Edward Said, *Peace and its Discontents: Gaza-Jericho, 1993-1995* (London: Vintage, 1995), p. 2.

259. On the impact of domestic politics on foreign policy see Amnon Aran, *Israeli Foreign Policy since the End of the Cold War* (Cambridge: Cambridge University Press: 2020).

260. https://www.btselem.org/publications/fulltext/202101_this_is_apartheid.

GENERAL NOTE

The Publisher and the Editors apologize if any material has been included without permission or without appropriate clearance, and would be glad to be told of anyone who has not been consulted.

ACKNOWLEDGEMENTS

In preparing this book for publication I received help from a number of people which it is my pleasure to acknowledge. The first thing to say is that this is not an entirely new book but a collection of essays many of which were published previously. As the sub-title makes clear, not all the articles deal with the conflict in Gaza. Some of them deal with related aspects of the Israeli-Palestinian conflict such as "Britan and the Nakba" and "The Two-State Solution: Illusion and Reality". "Israel, Hamas, and the Conflict in Gaza" is a report on war crimes I originally submitted to the International Criminal Court in 2019. "The Diplomacy of the Israeli-Palestinian Conflict, 1967-2023" was a report I prepared for the Qatari government for its submission to the International Court of Justice last year when it was considering the legal status of Israel's occupation of the Palestinian territories. Three articles I wrote especially for this collection: "Benjamin Netanyahu's War Against Palestinian Statehood"; "Israel's Road to Genocide"; and "Green Light to Genocide: Joe Biden and Israel's War in Gaza".

These articles and reports were written between 2009 and 2024. They were intended for different audiences, and they were published in different places. Some are research-based scholarly articles with endnotes; some are expert reports for international courts; some are opinion pieces. Inevitably, there is some repetition and overlap between the different articles, especially the ones that deal with the history of the conflict in Gaza. I had the option of removing repetitions and of editing the articles with what is usually called the benefit of hindsight. But hindsight is not necessarily or invariably a benefit. Having considered the matter, I decided to reprint each article exactly as it appeared originally. Each article is based on the information that was available to me at the time of writing. When new information became available, I reassessed my position and sometimes changed my mind. Some of my judgements may appear questionable in the light of subsequent developments. But I thought that reprinting the articles in their original form would be more honest and more authentic.

This was certainly the advice I received from my publisher and friend, Chris Agee. Indeed, the entire project of a collection of essays on Gaza was his idea. Chris is a writer, a poet, and the Editor of *Irish Pages*, a literary journal, and of The Irish Pages Press. Chris is the most interventionist, the most conversational, and the most imaginative editor that I have come across in my fifty years as a publishing author. I am grateful to him not just for suggesting this book but also for all the advice, support, and encouragement he gave me in the process of bringing it to fruition.

Chris's son, Jacob Agee, is the Managing Editor of The Irish Pages Press. He is a brilliant young scholar, a specialist in Holocaust studies, and a first-rate editor. I am grateful to him for the commitment, hard work, and meticulous attention to detail he devoted to all aspects in the production of this book, including the design, the maps, and illustrations.

The illustrations are the work of the artist Peter Rhoades, my Oxford colleague and friend. These drawings were originally made as a response to media coverage of the first Israeli military offensive in Gaza in 2008-2009, code-named "Operation Cast Lead". They formed a tribute to the suffering and deprivations that the Palestinians endured during Israel's merciless bombardment of Gaza. A selection of these drawings was reproduced in 2016 in a book titled *Gaza – An Artist's Response* for which I wrote the Foreword. Peter had not only produced a set of haunting and stunningly eloquent images of man's cruelty to man, but he also rendered a valuable public service in remembering, recording, and bearing witness to the martyrdom of Gaza. As he says in his introductory remarks, these drawings are intended as "a protest against unjustified and illegal brutality". This is precisely why they fit so well in this book. I am deeply grateful to Peter for allowing me to reproduce some of his drawings in this volume.

My thanks also go to my former student and friend, Jamie Stern-Weiner for doing all the research and co-authoring with me the article on "Israel's Road to Genocide". Jamie is the editor of the 2024 volume of essays *Deluge: Gaza and Israel from Crisis to Cataclysm*. Chapter One in this volume is my essay on "Israel's War on Gaza". I am grateful to Jamie for giving me permission to reprint this essay here. But I owe him a much more profound debt for his constructive editing and proof-reading of all the new material in this book.

My thanks also go to a number of highly able former graduate students who helped me in various ways with the research, the writing, and the editing of several of the articles in this collection. They are Célestine Fünfgeld, Frederike Onland, Francesca Vawdrey, Shahd Dibas, and Doaa Hammoudeh. I greatly enjoyed working with these young scholars because of their technical skills, their intellectual input, their high moral standards, and their commitment to the Palestinian cause.

I owe a special debt of gratitude to the Irish barrister Blinne Ní Ghrálaigh, KC, for giving me permission to include the text of her speech to the International

Court of Justice in The Hague as the Coda to this collection of essays. Ní Ghrálaigh was a member of South African legal team which brought the case that Israel is committing the crime of genocide in Gaza. Her rigorous, powerful, and moving speech of 11 January 2024 made a deep impact on the world court and on the vast international audience that watched it on social media. Ní Ghrálaigh is a leading expert on genocide whereas I am not. It is therefore an honour and a privilege for me to be able to include her iconic speech as the Coda to *Genocide in Gaza*.

Last but not least, I would like to thank my wife Gwyn Daniel and our daughter Tamar Shlaim for their informed contribution, for many stimulating debates, for their critical comments on my work over many years, and for marching with me in national demonstrations against the genocide in Gaza. It is to Gwyn and Tamar that this book is dedicated.

Avi Shlaim
Oxford
13 October 2024

On *Genocide In Gaza:*
Israel's Long War On Palestine

Clear, forthright and cogent, Genocide in Gaza *is essential reading for both those who understand little of Palestine-Israel and those who have followed the unfolding horrors for decades. As a historian, Shlaim is meticulous, thoughtful and robust. As a person who has lived in three worlds – Iraqi, Israeli and British, with a Jewish religion and an Arab ethnicity – few understand it as well on a personal level. His political vision is clear-sighted, his ideal humane.*

Selma Dabbagh

In these bold and courageous essays, Avi Shlaim picks up a bullhorn to shout truth to power. An outspoken advocate for Palestinian rights, he holds everyone from Whitehall to the White House responsible for their failings to stop the Netanyahu government's genocidal war. These are the arguments driving prosecutors in the International Criminal Court and the International Court of Justice. We should all pay heed.

Eugene Rogan

Each of Avi Shlaim's essays since October 2023 by themselves provide an incisive and bold insight on the situation in Palestine you will not find in the mainstream media. Reading all of them in one place, however, offers much more than that: we are served with a comprehensive historiographical context that exposes the origins of the violence that has rattled Israel and Palestine since October 2023.

This is a must-read for policy makers as well the wider public that will help to see through the fabrication, distortions and denial that characterizes most of our sources of information in the West.

Ilan Pappé

Avi Shlaim writes about the Israeli-Palestinian conflict with exceptional erudition, insight, and humanity. For those troubled by the suffering in Gaza, Shlaim's long held and clearly explained account of Israel's trajectory as an aggressive, violent, overtly racist, and genocidal state, as set out in this collection of essays, is a perfect place to start. They deserve the widest possible readership, especially among Israel's uncritical supporters in the West.

Sir Geoffrey Nice, KC